# A boy from Samsonvale
## By Ken Gold

An autobiographical account of the
life and times of the community of
Samsonvale from 1932 to 1980 as seen
through the eyes of one of its citizens.

© Copyright 2013 Ken Gold. Brisbane, Australia.

National Library of Australia Cataloguing-in-Publication Data:

Author: Gold, Ken

Title: A boy from Samsonvale : an autobiographic account of the life and times of the community of Samsonvale / Ken Gold.

ISBN: 9780646594897 (pbk.)

Notes: Includes index.

Subjects: Country life ---Queensland---Samsonvale---History.

Samsonvale (Qld) --- History

Dewey Number: 994.31

Printed by Watson Ferguson & Company, 1/655 Toohey Rd., Salisbury, Qld 4107

# Foreword

In his later years my father, Andrew James Gold, set himself the task of recording many of the details of life in Samsonvale from its first settlement in 1843 until 1960. He had a sense of history and a great appreciation of the heritage that our pioneers passed on to his generation, the children of the first settlers. His father and he were keen photographers and we are fortunate that many of their photos taken onward from the late 1800s were safely preserved to tell their story to later generations.

Andrew was born on 19<sup>th</sup> September 1890 and died on 14th October 1964. He lived all of his 74 years in Samsonvale on the land selected and freeholded by his father. He felt that someone should record the stories he had heard from the pioneers and also the life and times that he lived through. The result was a rather bulky set of three photo albums into which were inserted typed accounts of his memories concerning a variety of subjects of historical significance.

Some years after his death the Mt Samson State School P & C Association produced a printed version of these writings along with a few of the original photos. The production run of 500 copies entitled *Samsonvale* was sold out in a few weeks and there were frequent requests for more copies over the years. The Pine Rivers Shire Library filled a need when it produced a slightly edited run in 1996 and sold these through its library service.

In the process of assisting with this later production it became clear to me that there was a need to continue the record. I determined, as a kind of sequel, to set down an account of the times that I have lived through. My aim, like my father's, was not to write a personal autobiography as such, but to produce a picture of the changing times in the district in which we lived and worked as farmers and active citizens.

As I assembled material and organised my memories I began to comprehend the great degree of change that has taken place in Samsonvale since European settlement of the area. While the clearing of forest and introduction of agricultural endeavour brought such unimaginable change in landscape and living conditions in the first 80years or so, the acceleration of technology and mechanisation of all aspects of life over the latter 80 years has been no less breathtaking. Some attempt to record these changes seems necessary if modern citizens are to fully appreciate their heritage.

The life and times of Samsonvale are not particularly special. Similar observations regarding the changing times can be made concerning every district in the Shire and indeed right across Australia. I trust that following generations will gain through such humble works as this, some insight into the times and experiences that helped shape our character and ethos as Australians.

*William Joyner, the first settler in the upper reaches of the North Pine River, named his cattle station SAMSON VALE. That is the form of address officially used well into the 1950s. The post office address was in the two-word format and the subsequent railway station took that format. I have not been able to discover when and for what reason the one-word form was adopted.*

# Acknowledgements

I must acknowledge that the events and observations recorded in this volume would not have been possible without the upbringing that was rendered to me by two caring parents, Andrew and Dorothy Gold. In my childhood they allowed me great freedom to explore my rural surroundings and to develop a sense of independence and self-confidence. At the same time they set firm standards and expectations of compliance to their wishes. In my teen years, when relatively few country kids got the opportunity to gain a secondary school education, they sacrificed to send me to boarding school for four years. When I returned to the family farm they made every effort to treat me as an equal partner in the business and encouraged my every venture into new pursuits. They set an example to follow in relation to becoming a community-minded citizen. On the many paths that my later life took me I so often used to ask myself if my actions would meet with their high standards. They surely gave me a good start in life.

I must also acknowledge the part that my dear late wife, Glenda, played in our most agreeable 54year walk together. She, too, had the benefit of a similar upbringing to mine in the care of her parents, Sam and Lilly Stubbings at Mount Pleasant. Glenda was a most capable and resourceful woman in every respect as she set a high standard in her work as homemaker, mother, farmer's assistant and community worker. She was justly proud of her cooking, needlework, her gardens and of her children, Paul and Jennifer. She supported and joined me in many adventures and many times gave a valuable cautionary opinion on some of my less sensible ideas. Words cannot describe the feeling of loss that engulfed me when she lost her brave, uncomplaining, three-year struggle with cancer. Life has been lonely and lacking in much meaning without her. This volume is largely a tribute to her life, for in almost every chapter she is an important silent partner.

I must also thank many friends who from time to time encouraged me to press on with this work. Others supplied information when my memory was found wanting for details.

Finally, I want to thank Marian Brown, Rod Burton and Judith Burton for their considerable assistance in proof-reading, suggesting improvements and leading the way in relation to the many aspects of producing a book. It might not have come into being without her capable and generous assistance.

# Content

# Chapter 1.

## Childhood

I was born in Brisbane on 6th January 1932 to Dorothy Marie and Andrew James Gold, who lived at that time at "The Pines", Samsonvale. To establish the family setting it may be helpful to record some details concerning my parents and grandparents.

Dad was engaged in dairy farming on most of the property pioneered by his father, Henry Gold, who migrated from England in 1864 at the age of 19. He later selected the Samsonvale land known as "Sunnyside" in 1868.

Grandfather Henry's brother, William Gold, came to Australia alone in 1869, at the age of 16. He worked with his brothers, Henry and Charles, at Samsonvale before selecting land at Connondale. He later sold that selection to return to Samsonvale, where in about 1883 he took the opportunity to buy "Burnside", which adjoined "Sunnyside".

In his later life Grandfather Henry leased his farm to his third and fourth sons who were my Uncle William and my father. They worked in partnership until Willie died at 51 years of age, when Dad bought the farm from the family estate to continue farming in his own right. Dad's three unmarried sisters bought the adjoining farm, "Burnside". With the use of a section of "Sunnyside", including the large house and the original dairy building and yards, they carried on dairy farming. For most of the time they employed Percy Houghton and his various sons to do the manual work.

Dad's oldest brothers, Henry and John, had left the district to take up sugar-cane farming at North Arm on the Maroochy River and Ted, the youngest, had become employed as a movie-picture projectionist and later got involved in the infant science of radio. He eventually established 4GR, "Gold Radio" at Toowoomba.

By the time I was born my grandfather Henry had died and my grandmother, Janet Gold lived as an invalid with my maiden aunts,

1

Mary, Caroline and Georgina. She had suffered a stroke and was confined to a wheelchair. Janet was the oldest child of John and Janet McKenzie, who migrated from Scotland in 1855 and had established a timber-sawing business at Terrors Creek (Dayboro) in 1866.

My mother's father, John Robins, was foreman of the Campbell Brothers sawmill at Albion and lived at Roblane Street, Windsor with my grandmother, Kate. About 10 days after I was born grandfather Robins was killed in the mill.

Mum had come to the Samsonvale district as a companion and domestic helper to Mrs Tom Salisbury and she met Dad at social functions in the district. They were married in St George's Church of England, Windsor, Brisbane in April 1925. Dad built a large, new, high-set weatherboard house on the property with money he received from the estate of a maiden aunt in England. I seem to recall hearing that the basic structure cost about £250 ($500). It was built by his uncle and well known carpenter, Peter De Hayr. Their first child, Jill, was born on 25<sup>th</sup> April 1927.

*Our home 1932*

### Earliest Recollections

My earliest recollections are hazy, but one is of lying in a cot in my parents' bedroom with a view of sky and clouds. I remember hearing bird sounds somewhere outside. Another relates to being bowled over by a cow because I walked too close to her calf that was resting near the fowlhouse. I recall my chair-bound grandmother and the grave atmosphere which developed when she died. I was three and wanted to know what happened to people when they died. I was told that they went to Heaven and somehow that translated in my infant mind to her flying in an angel-like fashion upwards and to the south of the house.

I remember that I had an imaginary hero called Johnny Hardy who was wise and bound to help me with childhood projects and was the stated source of childhood fantasies. I think he was invented from listening to adult conversations and a combination of names that were mentioned. I was not sure if I had ever met him, but I had a fair idea that he was a very capable young man. This imaginary person seemed to cause my parents some amusement.

I can remember that at there was grave concern at Jill's health. She had contracted lead poisoning. It was supposed that she had collected her sickening dose of lead through handling or licking the lead paint on the top edge of the veranda railings when she was just the right age and height to do so, while peering over the top to sights beyond. Patchy recollections exist concerning an apparently serious bout of gastroenteritis that I caught. Such ailments are readily treated

*Our family 1937*

these days, but in times before antibiotics gastro could lead to death, so I was taken to Grandma Robins' house at Windsor to be treated by the family doctor who lived next-door.

Visits to Grandma Robins were fairly frequent. She acted as babysitter while Mum and Dad did shopping and business in the city. During one of these visits I was playing with my cousin, Vernon Larsen, when I broke his toy car. He was angry and said that I would have to buy him a new one. I knew that the shops were near the tall building (General Hospital) that could be seen far down the street (Lutwyche Road). It seems that I set off unnoticed and caused a proper panic when I was eventually missed. I seem to remember being apprehended down towards the place where the Ferny Grove railway line crosses Lutwyche Road. There was some scolding and some relief all round, including my relief about not having to replace the broken toy car.

In those pre-school days there were rides on the horse-drawn wagons and the slide; playing mud pies in the dirt under the high-set house; joining in games with Jill and the Clay and Houghton kids; accompanying adults to tennis parties, church, picnics, dances, fetes, etc. Percy Houghton, who worked the adjoining farm for my aunts, had seven children, including Bill, who was my age and constant playmate. Vic and Dot Clay rented the general store from Dad and we saw a lot of their three kids.

The old homestead in which my aunts lived was built by Grandfather Henry in 1900. It replaced the original house nearer to Kobble Creek and was about 200 yards (180 metres) from our house. I spent a lot of time there and

*The Old house and Post Office*

I think I was fairly spoilt by the benevolent middle-aged women, especially with cakes and cordial. It seems that Mum failed to produce pudding for the usual hot midday meal once and that this really upset me. I seized a toy suitcase belonging to Jill, packed a few clothes and cleared out to live with my aunts "who always had pudding with meals".

I recall finding a magazine that had advertisements for several bicycles in it. Every night I would get it out and discuss the various machines with Dad. When I turned six Dad bought an 18-inch fixed-wheel model for me. What delight! Attempts to ride it gave everyone a lot of laughs. Each night, to the amusement of all, I would struggle up the back stairs of the house with the bike and park it in the bathroom or my bedroom. I think all the kids living near our farm learnt to ride on it, even though it was too small for Jill and most of the Houghton kids.

In this remarkably free childhood I recall that we were allowed to make and use "shanghais" (known as gings or catapults to some). With great effort we would select a tree-branch with a near-perfect, Y-shaped fork and strip off the bark, then carve a groove in the upper arms into which rubber bands would be tightly bound with string ties. The bands would come from strips cut from old rubber motor tubes. The weapon was completed with a pouch made from an old leather shoe and bound to the other end of the rubber bands. This pouch was the repository for the small stone that acted as ammunition.

*My first bike*

Holding the fork with one fully extended arm and stretching the bands as far as possible, with the other hand gripping the stone inside the pouch, aim would be taken. Then by releasing the pouch the stone would be propelled at great speed towards the target. Accuracy was always fairly poor where I was concerned. Mostly we aimed at tins-cans on a post or such. Occasionally we would get the hunter instinct and go after birds. I can remember actually hitting a bird only once. I think it was a mickey bird (noisy miner) and I can still remember my sudden regret when picking up the limp bundle of feathers at having taken its life for no good reason.

There was an old disused rifle range on "Burnside" (my aunts' farm). The target butt was on the west side of Joyner's Hill. If we dug in the earth behind the target mound we could recover the old bullets fired by our fathers and grandfathers years earlier as members of the Samsonvale Rifle Club. These could be placed in an old jam tin over a fire to produce molten lead. If we made some pattern in some wet sand or clay the molten lead could be poured to make small trinkets or sinkers for fishing. Before we were 10 we were in the foundry business.

We were familiar with poultry as they ranged freely about the farm. Guinea fowls were always wild and untamed and very rowdy if anything upset them. Turkeys and ducks made good eating. Assisting in killing, plucking and dressing poultry was second nature to kids. I recall that we had a flock of ducks that always seemed to travel about in a line, like soldiers marching. I recall that if we got them out on some open land, away from the patch of natural hoop- pine scrub that was a central feature of the farm and its buildings, they could be made to travel in any desired direction by positioning ourselves appropriately. This grew into a game for Bill and me when we were about eight. I can remember the amusement of our elders as they discovered us drilling the ducks just like officers on a parade ground with shouted commands such as "Quick march", "Right turn" and "Company halt".

### Caloundra

Grandma Kate Robins moved to Shelly Beach, Caloundra in 1934. She bought a weatherboard house with verandas facing the sea, along with about an acre (0.4 ha) of land fronting the beach dunes. It was surrounded by bush; the nearest houses were about 150 metres away, including the old Francis Hotel in Albert Street. I recall wonderful summer holidays there, sometimes with the Fearnside or Larsen and Barke cousins, uncles and aunties, all members of Grandma's side of the family. Eating and sleeping conditions would be rather crowded at these times.

There would be swimming, fishing, exploring every inch of the beachfront for miles north and south. It was a time for getting to know "family" whom we seldom saw. Our Aunt Olive was not married at that time and was a good sport. All cousins remember with glee the singsongs around the piano, which she was very competent at playing. We were encouraged to make "paper combs" (stiff tissue paper stretched over a comb and held to the lips as we hummed the tunes). These caused a squeaky vibrating sound and tickled the lips at the same time. We were also invited to get pots and pans from the kitchen and use them as drums to count out the rhythm with wooden spoons or some other kind of drumstick. The racket was something to hear as everyone in high spirits joined the orchestra. Thank goodness there were no near neighbours. But, oh! What fun! I think that Aunt Olive rated these sessions much more fun than when she played for various dances and parties in the small community of Caloundra in those days.

Dad and Mum bought an acre (0.4 ha) of land between Banksia Street and Shelly Beach about 1937 for £200 and built a fibro cottage on it by Christmas 1938. The house next-door at that time was rented to an Aboriginal family, the Daltons, so the Dalton kids were our playmates during holidays for a few years. We got on well together and knew no reason to treat them differently because they were black. I do remember our parents showing some reserve regarding how much friendship should develop with the adults in the family.

That house was eventually purchased by Mr Jack Woodward, a pineapple and poultry farmer from Pullenvale, for his retirement. He demolished the old timber house with its detached kitchen and built a large brick stucco home on the block. The Daltons moved to a house on the corner of King and Albert streets. As development proceeded they gravitated to some second-class accommodation on the fringes of Golden Beach. Many years later the local Member of Parliament, Mike Ahern, told me that he had arranged for the last members of the Caloundra Aborigines to be accommodated in some nursing home. I believe that one of them was Barbara Dalton, one of those playmates of 1938.

In a shack to the west of our new house there resided a South Sea Islander who was a descendant of one of the labourers transported to Queensland for cane cutting in the 1850s and known in those days as Kanakas. His name was John MacAvoy. He was kept busy as a handyman and labourer around Caloundra for many years. Dad employed him for such work as painting and clearing the timber and weeds on our land.

We used to travel to Caloundra in Dad's 1932 Morris Cowley Tourer, all loaded up inside in the days before cars had boots for

7

luggage. The journey was a major event over considerable stretches of dirt road where often the boggy patches were made safer by laying ti-tree saplings across the track.

If Dad could not spare the time away from the farm, Mum, Jill and I would be taken to Petrie, where we would ride the steam train to Landsborough. There, we would take the co-ordinated bus to Caloundra and carry all our gear along the bush track to the house for the last half-mile or so.

These holidays ceased for two years during the war when the Army commandeered all houses in the area for the defence forces. Grandma came to Samsonvale to live with us for the duration of this crisis period. Just before this suspension of Caloundra holidays. When they resumed afterwards, I recall exploring the various defence works such as

*Our 1932 Morris Cowley tourer*

trenches, machine-gun emplacements, 25-pounder artillery establishments and the signal tower on Point Wickham. The latter interrogated all shipping passing in and out of the bay by means of a signal light and morse code or by radio situated in the underground bunker beneath the tower. The foreshore had been completely cleared and a maze of barbed-wire entanglement stood in place to slow down an invading army. There was real concern that the Japanese might land at Caloundra as they had done all the way south through Asia.

At one stage Grandma took in boarders from the local Army contingent and one of the soldiers staying at her house reported that while on sentry duty in the early hours he had seen a bright flash on the horizon south-east of Caloundra. It turned out to be the Japanese torpedoing of the hospital ship *Centaur* on 14th May 1943. A few days later Grandma wrote to say that a bed mattress marked *Centaur* had washed up on Shelly Beach in front of her house. She brought it home, dried it out and it was used by the family for many years. In subsequent days much more flotsam washed on to beaches.

When Grandma was forced to give up her house she came to Samsonvale and took over my bedroom. I was allocated a stretcher bed on the front veranda. It was fairly exposed to the wind. I can remember how I would be covered with a heap of blankets and curled up like a possum with my head under the blankets to sleep on cold or windy nights.

It was nicely cool in summer, although the mosquitoes used to visit in force. We all slept in mosquito nets, which were like a cotton-mesh tent suspended over the bed from a frame at the head of the bed. These kept the insects out quite well. The sound of the little devils flying around trying to get at the tasty meal that they could smell through the light cotton mesh was a pain as we dropped off to sleep.

### *The Post Office*

The Gold family kept the Samsonvale Post Office from about 1870 to 1949 and the manual telephone exchange from 1919 to 1949. I seem to recall that in all the Samsonvale district there were only 19 telephone subscribers. The switchboard was in the old home and attended to by one of the aunts. It was a manual exchange. Callers would turn a handle on their home phone, that would drop a numbered shutter and ring a bell on the switchboard. That was a signal for the operator to drop what they were doing around the house, rush to the switchboard in a small room set aside for the Post Office. They would poke a plug into a socket with the same number as the fallen shutter was displaying. A flick of a switch would allow a conversation to proceed. The caller would request connection to another phone. This was done by plugging a second paired plug into the appropriate numbered socket, turning a handle to ring the phone of the called party, establishing contact and throwing the switch to complete the connection. As I got older I was occasionally allowed to act as operator.

I would watch and ask many questions of the visiting telephone technician working on the old switchboard and I would seize any old parts that were replaced, including almost- spent batteries. I remember fitting the batteries, some wire, a switch and an old torch bulb together to produce electric light above my pillow. As Samsonvale had no electricity in those days I had the only electric bed-lamp in the district.

The mail bag from Brisbane arrived on the 6pm railmotor five days per week and was returned on the 8am railmotor each weekday morning. One of the Houghton family was paid pocket money to carry the large sealed, canvas bags from the train to the office on foot in all kinds of weather. I wonder if those who received mail ever appreciated that effort. Many residents would call at the post office for mail. Others would make arrangements for the milk carrier to carry it daily to their road stop.

Australia suffered the effects of the Great Depression all through the 1930s. Many people were out of work. Farm produce prices were low and there were few luxuries for most people. We were better off than most Australians because we lived on the land. We had free milk, eggs and poultry meat. It was a weekly chore for kids to turn the butter churn on Saturdays to make butter from the cream separated from the milk at home. We grew many of our own vegetables and some of our own fruit such as citrus, pawpaw, pineapples and bananas. All this involved manual work and had to be fitted into the daily grind of dairy farming by our parents.

The General Store

Grocery supplies from the local store were very basic compared to the vast selection available from modern supermarkets. Mum provided us with an interesting diet using relatively few grocery lines and a home-cooking recipe book. The grocery needs of a whole district of about 250 people were stored in two rooms approximately 20 feet

(6 metres) square at the local store, that was owned by my father. He had bought the business in 1919 when merchants who followed the Dayboro railway construction camp moved on to a new location. He had operated it himself for several years before his marriage, assisted from time to time by his sister, Caroline, as well as a cousin, Don MacKenzie.

The original store was located beside the level-crossing just south of the Samsonvale railway station. A few years later Dad had it relocated to the junction of Strathpine Road with the Dayboro to Samford road. This move posissioned the store next to the Samsonvale public hall at that time. The old store had yet another relocation to the junction of Basin Road with the Dayboro to Samford road where it occupied the land on which the old Samsonvale Dairy Comapny factory stood between 1892 and 1903 and was part of Henry Gold's original Portion 26 selection. A few years later the hall was relocated to that area and enlarged in the process. About 1930 Dad leased the business to Vic Clay, who with his wife Dot, continued for about 14 years, to be followed by a sequence of lessees until about 1960.

Shopping was something of a social occasion where, with good planning, one could be there when other residents were present for a yarn and exchange of news. Typically orders would be in list form, often sent in advance to allow the store-keeper to make it up from bulk supplies. Flour was in calico bags or in bulk sack bags to be measured out on the scales, into brown paper bags. Brown and white sugar, sago, rice, salt, biscuits and similar ingredients were also dispensed this way. Some preferred to buy supplies in bulk from city mail-order retailers such as Queensland Pastoral Supplies. Sugar was in 70 pound (31.75kg) bags, plain flour in 25 pound (11.34kg) calico bags, rolled oats in 5 pound (2.26kg) calico bags.

Bacon would come in flitches or sides wrapped in a cotton-mesh bag and would be cut by the storekeeper into slices with a knife or hand-turned rotary slicer. Cheese arrived in 10 or 20 (4.5kg or 9kg) loaf form, covered with cheesecloth. This would be cut by knife

*The Samsonvale general Store*

using experienced judgement into chunks weighing nearly that which was ordered. These commodities were originally invented to keep well without refrigeration, which the shop did not have until the 1940s.

Syrup came in two or seven-pound (907gms or 3.175kg) tins and a variety of jams and preserved fruits lent colour to the shelves row on row. As with most items there was little choice in flavour or variety.

The shop would also carry a small range of hardware such as files, rat traps, lamps, wicks, globes for kerosene lamps, bulk kerosene, axe handles, sandshoes and so on. It also had the districts' only petrol bowser. This device stood about eight-feet (2.4 metres) high. Petrol was pumped by the back and forth movement of a lever into a large, elevated, glass measuring cylinder. The amount was determined in advance by vertically sliding a handle into the desired slot. Only multiples of half gallons (2.27 litres), up to 6 gallons (27.25 litres), were available. When the required amount had been pumped and the surplus overflowed back into the underground tank, movement of a drain lever allowed the petrol to gravitate, at one of two selectable rates, into the vehicle or petrol can. Only one grade of petrol was available and I believe it would be rated at about 70 octane by current standards. That was sufficient for the low compression engines of the day.

Almost universally these supplies were noted in an account book and bills would be sent out monthly. In difficult times the storekeeper would often be supporting customers with credit and could have the embarrassing task of collecting overdue accounts

Our farm situation made life much easier when wartime food rationing limited the availability of food items such as meat, sugar, butter and tea. Each person was issued with a ration book containing a limited number of coupons. The grocer or butcher could sell quantities of food only if the customer had the equivalent number of ration coupons.

Clothing and petrol were similarly rationed. Our allocation of petrol was 4 gallons (just over 18 litres) per month. This allowed so little travel that our car battery was constantly flat; in the end Dad deregistered the car. We resorted to walking to church, the general store and the hall, since these were all located within our farm boundaries. Business in Brisbane was conducted by travelling there as required by railmotor, which stopped not only at stations but at various official sidings along the line. We used the "22 Mile Stop", a pair of huge gates used for crossing the railway by cattle or vehicles. Since the stop was in the middle of our farm it was convenent place to load milk and to board the railmotor.

It was very common for children to wear hand-me-down clothes in those days. Younger members of the family would have the clothes of older brothers or sisters handed down to them to wear. In my case I got a reasonable supply handed down from my cousin, Vernon, who was a few years older than me.

Since we never wore shoes around the farm or to school I had only one pair, which would be worn with much discomfort to Sunday School, church, dances and the rare trips to Brisbane. When I grew out of these shoes and other clothing they would usually be passed on to a younger cousin, Peter Fearnside, to wear.

Other formal wear would consist of shirt and junior size tie and a woollen serge suit. The trousers were lined with lawn stitched in place. We never wore underpants in those days. For younger boys the trousers did not have a button-up fly, but instead were designed with a small slit at the right place to allow access to the equipment needed to perform a pee. There was a little flap of material that was tucked inside to hide private parts. Another popular combination consisted of a shirt that had four or five buttons at waist height. These engaged with holes in the waistline of the trousers and were hidden by a loose belt. Elastic braces to hold trousers up were also common for both boys and men

*Dressed for Sunday School*

Boys always wore short pants and long socks held up by elastic garters. At least that was the intention. Long woollen socks had a bad habit of working down and looking rather untidy. It was unheard of for lads below teen age to wear long trousers. Leather belts were the order of the day for all pants until about 1944, when the extended waistband and adjusting straps at the sides became popular. For older boys and men the fly was always fitted with buttons. Zippers began to appear in the late 1950s.

It was the fashionable thing to wear some type of badge on the lapel. I recall my favourite being a set of wings about 2 inches (5 cm) wide declaring membership of the Kellogg's Flying Corps, of which I was a member. One became a member by posting four cardboard lids from cornflakes packets to headquarters. In return one got a badge and a book describing how to fly a plane and other items of air force interest. It would be another 40 years before I really learnt to fly a plane, but this pair of wings probably planted the seeds of the desire. During the war we had a variety of patriotic badges to wear, most of which remain in my collection of odds and ends to this day.

### Dressing Up and Going Out

The most regular outings were weekly Sunday School in the Presbyterian Church on land that my grandfather had gifted for the purpose out of part of the farm. He had originally been Church of England. Judging by the books in his library that I saw years after his death, he was a student of theological subjects. He had a hand in organising early church services in the district and is said to have provided music for hymns on a foot-pumped organ called a harmonium. It seems that it was the Presbyterians working from a base in Fortitude Valley, Brisbane, who were in a position to supply an itinerant minister. From that beginning most people in the district from a variety of denominational backgrounds became Presbyterian or supporters and attendees at services.

My father and his unmarried sisters were strong supporters of the church. Aunts Caroline and Georgina played the foot-pumped reed organ and taught Sunday School to about 25 children each week. I dutifully attended throughout my primary school days. This usually involved staying on to sit through the following church service, or at least part of it up to the point of the sermon, when some ministers released the children to the waiting open, spacious countryside.

At least once each year my Aunt Caroline would organise some kind of concert in the church, that would be lit by four large kerosene lamps. This would include several religious songs by members of the congregation, perhaps some recitations and usually some respectable songs of a lighter nature. There would be an entrance charge and always the night would conclude with supper and general conversation. This was before the advent of television and at a time when not everyone owned a wireless to bring music into the home. These entertainment nights were therefore well attended and filled a need in the lives of the community.

I recall a special night when we were treated to a "Magic Lantern" show. Mr Walter Herron from Closeburn had gone from the local congregation to be a missionary in Bolivia, South America. He was on leave from that posting and had a collection of photo slides to show to his former congregation. The projector was quite a large contraption made of brass, complete with chimney and a lens combination on front. It was a forerunner to the modern slide projector and in this case was powered by a couple of car batteries. The slides were 3 inch (75 mm) photo positive transparencies encased in two thin sheets of glass. The resulting images on a large white sheet were indeed magical to my way of thinking.

### *The Christmas Tree*

Another well-remembered event was the annual Sunday School Christmas Tree. This would be held in the district hall and attended by almost everyone irrespective of religious affiliation or denomination. The day would be spent in building a tree inside the hall, using branches from hoop-pine trees. Oh, what excitement as the hall filled with people and the arrival of Santa Claus was awaited by the kids. He would arrive with loud shouts and blowing of a trumpet and walk to the tree, under which there was waiting a present for every kid in the district. There would be some special prizes for Sunday School pupils in relation to excellent attendance record or lessons well done.

The simple toys were highly appreciated in a time when the world was staggering out of the Great Depression and such items as toys were very few. I sometimes feel sad for the children of the later part of the 20th century because they have so many toys of such sophistication. It would seem that each one enjoys a rather short time of appreciation. Modern kids appear to miss the huge thrill that we got from receiving this one simple, "valuable" gift to add to one that might come soon after in our Christmas stocking at home.

## Concerts

Aunt Caroline took much pleasure in organising social functions for the district and usually produced a concert each year, that featured acts by children and adults alike. There would be a theme for each, such as American cowboy songs and acts, songs of Stephen Foster with Negro themes, nursery rhymes and so on. I can recall training for the part of Little Jack Horner and getting dressed up in a fancy brown costume that she made. These concerts would attract a full hall and everyone was full of appreciation and applause for the efforts of local amateur artists.

## Sunday School Picnics

It had long been a tradition in Samsonvale for the Presbyterian Sunday School to hold an annual picnic in the very attractive surroundings of the flat area on our farm bounded by Kobble Creek and the Dayboro road. The practice was for everyone in the district, irrespective of religious following, to be invited to gather there at mid morning. Water from the creek would be boiled on a 4 gallon (20 litre) kerosene tin over an open fire. Tea, cordial drinks and cakes would be enjoyed during a good old fashioned yarn and exchange of news. It was not unusual for over 100 people to gather for this social event.

The kids would be led in a variety of games and competitions and let loose to explore the creek banks and adjacent forest.

Lunch would consist of pooled sandwiches and cakes brought by each family. Often the minister from Dayboro would make a speech and the superintendent of the Sunday School would say a few words.

Following lunch there was usually some sport and races for the kids and parents. Those not able to play would gather to cheer or sit in the shade of trees, enjoying convivial company until milking time, when each family returned to their farm.

### Tennis Parties

The old family home was about 2450 square feet (225 square metres) and set in a garden of about a third of and acre (1200 square metres). The aunts often held garden parties to raise funds for the

*The next generation and their mothers at a picnic in 1936*

church or some other charity. These events would include stalls for sale of donated cakes, needlework, jams, sweets, pickles or fruit and vegetables from the farms. There might be a competition for the best decorated bike or the silliest hat or best apron. There were usually competitions such as throwing a rolling pin, bowling at a wicket, guessing the distance between two pegs, quoits, written quiz questions. Of course plenty of conversation and swapping of gossip took place, also. Often there would be tennis going on as well. These functions seemed to generate a sense of enthusiasm, willingness to participate and show of enjoyment that I have seldom seen in later years. They were such simple pleasures for a time when life seemed to be in the slow lane by today's standard of rush and bustle.

Tennis was a regular Saturday afternoon event and my main recollection was the loads of eye-popping spread of homemade cakes and biscuits at afternoon tea time. Those farmers' wives knew how to produce the lightest sponge cakes and scones from their wood-burning stoves and the icing and cream fillings were a boy's dream come true.

At one stage we had two tennis courts going to cope with the number of families who wished to spend the afternoon "out" before returning home to milk their cows. Many of those who came did not even play. They just enjoyed the outing among friends. Kids more or less taught themselves to play. The idea was to have fun and enjoy each others' company as much as winning points.

## *Picture Shows*

Before television was even thought of, town kids enjoyed the pleasures of picture shows at theatres in every suburb. We country kids had no such thing near us and it was a highlight of the year if we were lucky enough to get to town and see the movies. A typical movie session would start with an onscreen picture of King George VI and playing of the National Anthem of that time, "God Save the King", to which all would stand in homage. The following program would consist of a cartoon for laughs; some newsreel that would visualise what had been going on in other parts of the world, weeks or months previously; a travelogue depicting some desirable tourist location and its people; and two full-length movies. The whole event might take three and a half hours and include an interval for drinks and eats. Typically these would be carried into the theatre by waiters who moved down the aisles carrying trays on their shoulders calling "Peanuts, lollies and chocolates." In the flasher theatres these people would be in smart uniforms.

In the Wintergarden Theatre in Queen Street the gathering audience would be treated to a theatre organ recital. The very large white Wurlitzer organ console would arise out of the pit in front of the stage, illuminated by a bright spotlight, as the organist played as it came up into view. This act was repeated during interval.

Back in Samsonvale our lack of movies in the late 1930s was remedied when a Mr Hyde established a travelling picture show. He had a large van set up to carry an engine to generate electricity (not available in Samsonvale until 1952) and two projectors. The van was parked well away from the hall to minimise distracting noise. Cables carried the power to the projectors, which were set up on the entrance veranda of the hall. I seem to remember that kids were charged sixpence (5c) for the show. We sat on the hard, old forms (wooden benches) rearranged from where they normally stood around the walls of the hall for dances. We thought it was the greatest thing to happen

18

in a long time.

I think the routine was scheduled for fortnightly or monthly visits and that Mr Hyde ranged through Samford, Dayboro, Mt Mee, Woodford, etc. All films were in black and white with sound (silent movies were a feature of earlier years). Only fleeting memories return in relation to the programs, but I can remember laughing untill my sides hurt at the antics of George Formby and being scared to silence by some of the scenes in the Cowboy and Indian movies.

The coming of the war killed this feature in our lives. Years later Wally O'Hara ran a weekly picture show in Dayboro that we occasionally attended. We were also able to travel to far away Kallangur or Strathpine or even to Chermside to see movies of particular interest. In the 1950s the drive-in picture show became popular and most of the old established theatres began to close. The advent of television in 1959 precipitated the final demise of the suburban theatre. Drive-in theatres persisted against the onslaught of TV mainly for other cultural reasons. The ability to take in a movie with the whole family packed into the family car was attractive. When the small kids fell asleep in the back seat they were no problem. For young courting couples there was a whole range of exciting possibilities while viewing movies from the privacy of a car or van.

So, these are some random memories of my earliest days at Samsonvale. Looking back, I cannot think of a better environment in which to grow up and form attitudes and standards to take into later life.

*The home of my boyhood*

19

*Mums garden*

*Learning to plough*

# Chapter 2.

## Mt Samson State Primary School

In 1938 at the age of six I began my education at Mount Samson State Primary School. I travelled to and from school by railmotor or steam train. The railway ran through the centre of our farm and we loaded our cans of milk, bound for Metro Milk Co-op in South Brisbane, six mornings per week, at the railway siding known as the "22 Mile Stop".

The afternoon train was a goods train and the guard had the unenviable task of unloading considerable quantities of freight such as bags of stock feed, boxes of groceries and farm supplies and household items at each station along the line. This caused the train to arrive at quite irregular times. The 10 to 15 kids waiting for this train at Mt Samson Station would play various games while we waited. Since our teacher lived in Dayboro, he also travelled by train and would be present in the station waiting room. We were under his strict, watchful eye at these times. Often a few boys would pluck up courage to beg the guard to ride in his guard's van with the mailbags and parcels. If we were successful our horizons of experience would be widened as we observed the duties and the lonely life of a guard.

In later years the goods-train service was reduced to three days per week and it became practical to walk home rather than wait for the 6pm railmotor. Some kids walked up to six miles (9.6 kms). I must add that the walk was not always too rushed and in a direct line. We usually tracked cross-country in two or three groups. For the older warriors there would usually be a "boys only" group that would visit the creeks along the way. If it was hot there would be a swim in the nude if we were sure we would not be discovered. There were eels and mullet to hunt in shallow, sandy-bottomed, Samson Creek. In season there were guava trees to be raided for a feed of fruit. There were swallows' nests under the bridges to be investigated. Perhaps we could trap a bee-eater bird in its nesting burrow in a creek bank or try to dam the creek when the flow was low. Occasionally there would be a snake to kill or throw stones at, or an iguana to chase up a tree.

Time could fly on such expeditions, but most kids had to keep an eye on the setting sun (no-one owned watches) because there were usually some mandatory jobs to do when we got home. This might be collecting kindling to start the kitchen wood-burning stove next morning; feeding the calves with separated milk; collecting eggs from the fowlhouse and locking the door against fox or dingo raids; watering the vegetable garden with water drawn from a gully in a bucket; husking or shelling corn from the cobs or driving the cows to the night paddock.

Other kids rode horses to school. Country schools of the day usually had enough land to include a horse paddock where the horses were released during school hours. It was not unusual for two kids to ride double on a horse to get to school. The artist Jolliffe

***Mount Samson State School***

often drew cartoons in which three or four kids rode on one horse, but I never saw more than two. Other kids rode bicycles. In fact, I used to ride my bike during the last few years at Mt Samson. The distance was 2.3 miles (3.69 kms). I remember this because during the period of wartime shortages it was necessary to get a permit to buy new tyres for a bike and this was not possible if the journey was less than 2 miles (3.21 kms). I qualified for a new tyre when the old one finally failed after several patches, sleeves and string stitches.

### Dress for School

Almost everyone went barefooted in those days. Shoes were such limiting things. Without shoes the skin on the soles of our feet became hard and as thick as leather. However, there were frequent thorns, skinned toes from accidentally kicking things, cuts and stone bruises to put up with. In winter the skin sometimes cracked between the toes and this was a painful complaint. In spite of these problems no-one would be sissy enough to wear shoes.

Hats were worn by everyone in those days. They were mostly straw or battered old felt models. Primary school kids would never be seen in long trousers. I think I was about 16 before I had long trousers. Since these were the years of slow recovery from the Great Depression, patched trousers and shirts were not uncommon nor looked on as particularly significant.

Our teacher was Harold Spencer Smith, a short, fat man in his 50s. He had a ruddy complexion and close-cropped, balding hair. He always arrived at school in a suit with a small, narrow, ironed cotton tie. I understand that he had spent his early working life driving a bullock team and as an itinerant teacher in western Queensland. He would travel from property to property teaching resident children. He married a country girl before settling into the task of teaching up to six classes in one-teacher schools. I think that he had been educated at Rockhampton Grammar, but I do not think that he had any formal

*My first day to school*

teacher training as we know it today. It seems that aspiring teachers served a kind of apprenticeship under an approved experienced teacher. Smith had served in the First AIF overseas and told stories of Gallipoli. He told many stories of the bush and included bushcraft lessons as a normal part of a day's program. He was fond of reading aloud, in serial form, such stories as *Robinson Crusoe* and *Huckleberry Finn*. He was very fond of the accounts of exploration of Australia which formed a major part of the Australian history curriculum at the time.

The equipment in schools of the time was very basic. Long

blackboards were attached to the walls and at the appropriate time large roll-up maps would be hung for geography lessons. Most of our writing and figuring was done on slates. These consisted of a thin shingle of imported slate stone in a wooden frame much like a picture frame about A4 size. The pencil was a soft slate composition about 4 mm thick and usually held in a tin tube when the composition became worn down to short length. To attain neat results the pencil would be sharpened with a pocket knife or worn down on a flat stone. When the work was no longer needed it was wiped out with a wet sponge or damp rag. Each kid had a small tin or jar for this purpose.

State primary schools were built to a standard timber design consisting of one large room with many windows at each end to provide effective ventilation. There were verandas to the long sides. Floors were untreated hardwood and standing off the ground on wooden stumps. Water was collected from the roof into tanks for drinking purposes and each kid had a cup or enamel mug that stood on the corner of the tank stand, ready for use. Smelly earth-closet toilets were well removed across the paddock from the schoolroom.

We sat at wooden desks for four or five kids, side by side. Seating was a wooden form of equal length with no back rest. A slot in the front of the desk held the slate vertically when not in use and a groove held pen, pencil and ruler. Our pen consisted of a steel nib attached to a wooden shaft. Ink was kept in a china inkwell which dropped into a recessed hole to the right of the pupil. Left-handed writing was definitely frowned upon and even forbidden. We would cut a flat tab on the wooden end of a pencil or pen with a knife and write our initials on the flat section for proof of ownership.

Ink was made at the school by adding water to a packet of powder supplied by the Department of Education. Writing progressed by dipping the steel nib into the ink to wet a small slotted reservoir in the split-ended nib. One dip would last perhaps six or eight words and then the nib had to be dipped in ink again. The ink could take a few minutes to dry and any touch would cause an ugly smudge. To prevent this blotting paper was pressed on the new work to soak up surplus ink. A dreaded problem with using pens and inkwells was that too much ink on a nib could lead to a drop falling from the nib to the work page. This would spoil the whole page and we certainly knew the origin of the saying "to blot one's copybook".

Writing skills were achieved by reproducing the script printed on the top of each page of a copybook. In early years lead pencils were permitted and later we graduated to ink, where blots and mistakes were permanent evidence of our carelessness.

Many adults, particularly those who had a lot of writing to do, had "fountain pens". These had gold nibs fed with a continuous supply of ink stored in a refillable bladder in the stem of the pen. They had a screw-on cover to protect the nib when not in use and a clip that secured it conveniently, nib uppermost, in a coat pocket. They often came with a propelling pencil in a matching set. Loose shafts of lead were stored in the body of the pencil and as the point wore down a twist of the shaft screwed out a new supply of lead. Such luxuries were never seen in our school, although I did acquire a set when I reached high school.

The ballpoint pen was not on the market until late in the 1940s. The first model I saw was a "Biro" brand. It quickly gained popularity because there was less trouble with messy ink. After patents expired there was a multiplicity of brands of ballpoint pens on the market, but the generic name "biro" persists for pens, even 50 years later. At first the ballpoint pen was discouraged or even banned from many schools.

Reading was taught from standard reading books for each grade. Reading was often practised aloud in unison or with individuals taking turns. The whole schoolroom would resort to scorn and cause embarrassment if we made any mistakes.

A feature of learning arithmetic was the reciting aloud, parrot fashion, each of the "Times Tables." *"Five ones are five, five twos are ten, five threes are fifteen"* and so on up to twelve. Twelves were important for there were 12 pence to the shilling and most things were sold in dozens. This method of teaching may appear unbelievable by today's standards but I am often thankful that such commonly used facts are printed in my brain as clearly as my name. Easy recall makes life much easier than reaching for a calculator to achieve simple computations.

We were given little homework and did very little reading outside school hours. The big event of the week was the weekend "Exercise" or essay on some subject. This was done in one of the few notebooks we received. Marks went towards the half-yearly Report Card, so it was advisable to do one's best with fancy printing, some drawings and neat writing.

The big event of the year would be the visit by the School Inspector. The purpose of these official visits was to check the general conduct of the school and in particular the efficiency of teachers in achieving desirable standards. Questions would probe the abilities of each class. Manners and tidiness would be observed and the general condition of the buildings and equipment would be noted. No doubt teacher promotions and transfers depended upon the reports of the Inspector.

Smith could be quite short-tempered and hand out "the cuts" with a cane at short notice for such offences as misbehaviour or even being slow to learn something that he thought was simple. Boys got it on the backside or hand and girls, as I recall it, only on the extended hand. His perceived moods sometimes caused him to be controversial among parents. Smithy was a shortish, fat man with a ruddy complexion and I suspect that he may have been a victim of high blood pressure which, in those days, was rarely detected and almost untreatable. There may well have been a good reason for his bad temper on many occasions.

When I began school in January 1938 there were four in my class. Smithy had to cope with teaching up to seven classes at once and I think the difficulties of the teachers in one-teacher schools of the time were largely not understood by most parents. There were long periods when pupils had to cope unassisted in progressing through the work that had been set for them before moving on to the next class for its period of concentrated attention.

The visiting inspector considered these difficulties when he visited during my Grade Two year. He proposed that our grade be merged into Grade Three. I am not sure that this advancement was in our best interests in matters such as reading and spelling skills were concerned. Somehow we managed and life for Mr. Smith was made easier.

Small country schools did not enjoy such subjects as Manual Arts, although the girls received Needlework instruction one day a week when Smith's wife attended to coach the girls. She also took a singing session for the whole school on such days. As a concession to one-teacher schools we were not required to study English History.

Religious instruction was presented through use of a standard book approved by the government for multi-denominational use. Very occasionally a minister of religion might visit for one period of instruction. On such occasions we would be segregated according to the denomination nominated in the enrolment register by our parents. The "other kids" would go out to play or do lessons outside the one large schoolroom.

*Our lower age classes*

It may seem strange in these modern times but if some rare happening such as an aeroplane flying overhead or some unusual vehicle passed by the school the whole school room would be released to run outside to see the spectacle.

A monthly or quarterly School Paper used to arrive by mail from somewhere and sold for one penny. It had stories, puzzles and instructions on things to make, which were in a lighter vein than class lessons.

In later years there was a travelling library, which arrived by train. It consisted of a shallow wooden chest with carry handles at each end and a screwed on lid. This chest would be present at the school for a few months and then all the books would be repacked and the lid screwed down prior to forwarding by rail to another school. I cannot recall reading many of these books. I was a rather slow reader and there seemed to be so much of more interest to claim my attention.

## Outside The Classroom

Long before barbecues became popular Harold Smith taught us how to cook meat on an open fire. About once per fortnight he would arrange for the Samford butcher to supply grilling steaks as ordered and paid for by each pupil. A healthy chunk of beef would cost sixpence (5 cents). A large fire was prepared and lit at "little lunch" using dry wood from the nearby paddocks. Smithy taught us to recognise that forest oak made the best coals. At "big lunch" the coals would be just right to place the steak on. We each made a wriggly shaped meat-holder from fence wire. With this we could place our meat in a chosen area of hot coals and pick it up for turning or applying salt and pepper with ease. Occasionally a damper would be made in the coals. There were some distinct advantages in attending a country school with a teacher like "Smithy".

There was no electricity supply to the district in those days so one of the pupils would be delegated to boil the billy for Smith's tea at dinner hour. This was my task for some time. I would have to watch the clock on the wall to ensure that I left class in time to make a fire in the open fireplace, boil about one pint of water (about half a litre) and throw in a spoonful of tea-leaves by the time 12.30pm break started.

In balance I can only say that he carried out his duties with a sense of great responsibility. Teaching five to seven separate classes of three to eight kids each would be almost beyond the abilities of many modern, highly trained teachers, yet he struggled away year after year at the task.

One solution to the staffing problem was to select one of the brightest Grade 7 kids and send them across the room to teach the lower grades in such fundamentals as arithmetic or spelling.

A measure to reduce the number of classes was to assess the number of children reaching the age of five in the coming year. If the number was only two or three the parents of these children would be asked to delay commencement for a year in order to make up a reasonable number of starters the following year. In those days of co-operation and down-to-earth realism parents seem to have been content with the arrangement.

28

Smithy seemed to realise that a full length school day was a big ask for beginners. I recall that in mid-afternoon soon after I started he asked each beginner if they would like to sit next to a big brother or sister and play at drawing. When my turn came I was asked if I would like to sit next to my sister, Jill. My reply is reported to have been *"No! I hate her"*. This seems to have caused a bit of laughter in which I am sure Harold Smith would have joined.

He was insistent on a code of ethical behaviour in class as well as play and extended this to the conduct of pupils as they travelled to and from school. He invariably supervised games at lunch hour. He would be the pitcher for both sides in "rounders" and the umpire of cricket or football games in which boys and girls played as equals. Games were changed fairly often and lunch would be gobbled down to maximise play time. I recall games such as "Red Rover", "French Cricket" and "Bedlam" (which was rather rough and I suspect was an invention of Mt Samson kids).

There were other games played under the school on wet days such as "beam". This consisted of throwing a tennis ball at the four inch by three inch beam that supported the floor joists under the high-set school. Each team had a sequence of throwers who had to precisely hit the beam and catch the ball on its return. Missing the beam or letting the ball touch the ground gave the ball to the other team. I do not know if this game was unique to Mt Samson school, but it certainly ate up the minutes of lunch hour.

Another wet-weather game was Hopscotch. The space under the high-set school was dirt. A special shaped court of circles and squares would be drawn in the dirt with a stick and both girls and boys would compete in the "taw" (small stone) throwing and retrieval, following a special sequence of hops on one or two feet. Any infringement of feet over the lines of the court would be plainly revealed by the footprints in the dirt and lead to retirement as the next competitor tried for a perfect performance.

In summer Smithy would get permission from Sam Wagner, who owned the farm next to the school, to dam Samson Creek below a small waterhole about half a mile(0.8 km) from the school. The boys would take shovels and bags and block the creek in order to raise the water level enough to create a swimming hole. At lunch hour there would be a beeline for the creek and hi-jinks would follow, supervised by our teacher. Few kids owned swimming togs so costumes consisted of old short trousers for the boys and blouses and bloomers for the girls. We got changed behind designated clumps of bushes and no-one realised that we were deprived by city standards. We surely could not have had less fun than our city cousins.

Another game was called "Huts" and consisted of building grass huts from the long kangaroo grass that grew in the school grounds. Hours were spent cutting grass with reaping hooks, building a frame with dry gum-tree branches and laying the grass on the frame to form an igloo or tepee-shaped hut. Each hut was the work of a group formed spontaneously with classmates of the same year or some other grouping based on undefined empathy. Always the group was exclusively boys or exclusively girls and visiting each others' huts was very rare. There was an air of secrecy and exclusiveness about each hut with its narrow child-sized doorway that was entered on hands and knees. Inside there were secret hiding places for "valuable" possessions. The interior was very dark and there were partitions and tunnels between rooms that were most exciting. The huts grew with time until, for some reason, expectations would change and the huts would be wrecked with great pleasure and spectacle. Next week might see "Rounders" or "Red Rover" back in favour for lunchtime play.

One external influence was known as the Project Club. The Department of Public Instruction had a section that employed itinerant organisers to encourage specific projects such as the Calf Club, the Beekeepers' Club or the Vegetable Club. These would hold meetings just like adults in which motions would be debated and voted on and the members would participate in some specific project, making observations and keeping records in a project book. On the big day, when the visiting organiser came, prizes would be awarded for the work done. Our project was always about vegetable growing and we dug up plots to make our first attempts at raising crops from seed.

Another big event was the visit by a travelling magician, who seems to have been approved to make a living by visiting schools to give his little show for a fee of one shilling (10c) per pupil.

School photos seem to have been part of our school life from way back in history. Many photos of school days exist today to remind us of old pals and those long past experiences that shaped our lives.

*Mt Samson v Strathpine schools cricket in a cow paddock*

End of year was very special. For a few days before the school holidays all the book cupboards would be cleaned out. There would be a stocktake and an order for materials was sent to the Department for replenishment of slates, pencils, exercise books, chalk, handwriting copy-books and such. Desks would be taken out on to the verandas and thoroughly scrubbed with hot water and sand-soap untill they gleamed fresh and bright. The floors were similarly scrubbed and everything was replaced in readiness for the next year.

Then came the "breakup" picnic. First, via the milk truck, would come the two large, green insulated canvas containers that held dozens of small buckets of ice cream with wooden spoons to assist in eating the treat. This would be the only time in the year that many of the children would see ice cream. It was kept cold by chunks of dry ice.

Then parents and citizens in general would begin to arrive in their picnic clothes. It was a big thing to play games in which our parents took part. We could mostly outrun them and their participation and foolery and good-natured breaking of the rules had us all in the highest spirits. There would be foot races and novelty races such as three-legged, wheelbarrow and egg and spoon races. There were prizes for winners in the one shilling range, but every participant got at least sixpence (5c).

The participation of our childhood heroes, mostly those who had graduated in the previous 10 years, was especially appreciated. The older women formed their own circle and talked no doubt about their children, budding romances and any other gossip. They also had the important responsibility of supervising sandwiches and cakes.

When dinner was called everyone gathered under the school to take a seat on forms and to be waited on with soft drinks, tea, sandwiches and home-made cake. We celebrated the end of year with some true gluttony. To further mark the occasion there would be another issue of ice cream as well as a handout of stone fruit and boiled lollies.

This was also a time for someone to thank the teacher and for him to respond with comments about the school and the committee that assisted his endeavours.

As is usual in a dairying district the crowd began to dwindle about 3pm when milking time took precedence over social activity.

The above celebrations were the responsibility of the School Committee. This was a loyal band of parents who met as required to assist the head teacher provide extras for the school such as swings, sporting materials, water supply for the gardens, etc. My father was Chairman for several years and our neighbour, Ernie Bennett, was Secretary for perhaps 12 years or more. It was an unexpected surprise in later years for these men to receive a letter from the Executors of H.S. Smith's estate, advising that Smithy had left them some money in appreciation of their help and friendship during his many years at

### Mt Samson school.

Primary school ended with the State Scholarship exam in December. Those who passed this standard state-wide external exam were rewarded with free tuition at State secondary schools. Those going to private schools received about £2/10/0 ($5) a term subsidy. Those who failed were required to pay full fees to further their education.

In our case we had to travel to Dayboro to sit the Scholarship exam in Maths, Geography, English and History, spread over two days. Pupils from one-teacher schools started the race at quite some disadvantage and the record of passes from Mount Samson was not great. I was rather poorly prepared for the big hurdle because I had been in bed for four days with some raging diarrhoea complaint. I maintained the school's reputation by failing overall. I passed only in one subject, Australian History.

A few years later, while on secondary school holidays, I visited Smithy at Mount Samson school and over a cup of tea he apologised for not being a good enough teacher to get more of his pupils through the Scholarship exam. I felt sorry that he thought this of himself. I think that his record had more to do with trying to cope with too many classes in a school of about 25 kids and his place in the evolution of our education system in Queensland. Perhaps he had the misfortune to have to teach a succession of dull kids or young people who had so many other more exciting things to do than knuckle down to serious study.

Well, as I turned 14 life began in a very new arena. The rather carefree days of a one-teacher country school were at an end and great changes lay ahead as I grew nearer to adulthood.

# Chapter 3

## Outside School Hours

For country kids there is little chance of becoming bored at weekends or during school holidays. We could join our elders in some of the farm activities or run wild in exploring the bush or the creeks. In retrospect our parents seem to have been rather relaxed about allowing us almost unlimited freedom. No doubt we got into some potentially dangerous situations. In one instance I climbed an old hoop-pine tree almost to its top. I guess that the successive layers of branches allowed me to climb up to more than 120 feet (36.57 metres). I was surprised how much I could see from that height.

With the Houghton kids we built a tree house, perhaps 20 feet (about 6 metres) above the ground, in a large Moreton Bay fig tree. No doubt modern architects would not approve the safety of the design or the people loads it bore without incident. We made canoes from flattened-out sheets of corrugated iron and took to Kobble Creek in its various seasonal conditions. Mostly a capsize would not have been serious, but I sometimes wonder how we avoided bad cuts from the sharp edges of the craft during play.

*We built a dug-out air raid shelter*

We dug caves in soft earth banks, which luckily did not fall in. We played Slippery Slides down a very steep bank of about50 yards (45 metres) length, riding sheets of tin, wide boards or the seed cases of the cocos palm at high speed and finally passing under a barbed wire fence at the bottom in a laid-back position. A later version of the downhill run was played on the frame of an ancient motorbike with its engine removed. It took ages to push this heavy contraption up the hill towards the house, then in turns we would take off down the steep hill towards the creek at break-neck speed. At one particular hump we could leave the ground and fly for a few feet if we were going fast enough.

This game ended in an ultimate version when it was found to be fun to charge over the six foot high (1.82 metre) bank of the creek into the deep water. We would dive for the machine, drag it out and someone else would go over the edge at high speed. I think the frame eventually broke its back and was left to rust away. How I wish that I had that ancient motorbike today. It was a mistake for my father to allow me to wreck something that would have become such a valuable collectors' item in later years.

The creek was the centre of entertainment when it had enough water to swim in. I am not sure how I learnt to swim. I did not have lessons. I think I just copied the bigger kids and got braver and braver at the pranks. The favourite swimming hole had been set up with a trapeze and

*Kobble Creek - our playground*

launching platform. It was our version of Tarzan flying through the air to eventually drop into the middle of the stream from the T-bar. Soon we could all do dives and somersaults from the bar.

There were several waterholes in Kobble Creek as it meandered along the northern boundary of our farm. The size of the swimming party could be from two to twenty depending on the occasion. A typical Saturday adventure might include only the school boys from the Bennetts, Houghtons and Golds. If it was a boys only group and out of sight of the road and houses we would usually strip off and swim in the nude. If girls were present we would simply swim in our short pants and the girls would wear lawn bloomers. If they were old enough to have anything to hide they would wear a blouse as well. Most bush kids did not own the luxury of a swimming costume.

I recall an occasion when four of us were a bit foolhardy and stripped off in the bushes down near the road crossing to have a bare-skin swim and fun on the trapeze. Alas! A passing car full of townies stopped to admire the scenery! All of us went for the deep water and showed only our heads while these curious visitors hung around staring. They just would not move on. We had a quiet conference as the time dragged on and on. In the end we swam about 100 yards upstream where a bend in the creek blocked their view of us. We crept out and under cover of the bushes got back to our clothes, dressed in silence and melted away.

These swimming parties were often accompanied by a bunya nut cook-up. The nuts usually fall in February. We would light a fire, impale nuts on lengths of fencing wire and hold them in the fire until they burst open with a bang which signalled that they were cooked. They made a great feast, especially if someone remembered to bring some salt.

*Who needs swimming baths?*

These were the years of recovery from the Great Depression when money was scarce and amenities such as a piped water supply were unknown. Water for drinking, washing and bathing came from one or two galvanised 1000 gallon (4546 litre) tanks, which caught rainwater from the roof. In times of drought water for the house and the dairy was obtained by digging in the bed of the creek and inserting a barrel or an old cream can to form a kind of well. From this the water was drawn by bucket and carried to the houses in cans placed in the horse-drawn cart or slide. As kids we often played our part in bailing water or carting it in company with one of our elders.

Kobble Creek would often shrink to a series of waterholes in dry seasons. Mullet and catfish would retreat to a few deeper pools. We would sometimes find some wire netting and drag a mesh barrier across the pool to harvest some enjoyable fish meals

Catfish were not always easy to catch by line, even though their circular nests of brushed stones were plainly visible in the normally clear water. In time of flood or fresh when the water was muddy, however, they would bite well on worms from the garden. Unfortunately there often seemed to be more turtles and eels than tasty catfish. At these flood times the creek banks would be alive with mosquitoes and sitting quietly waiting for a catch would be most painful. It was common to light a smoky fire of twigs and cow manure and take refuge in the smoke. The mozzies were too sensible to put up with that kind of smoke.

The swimming season coincided with the ripening of guavas, wild raspberries and a wild cherry from a variety of lilly-pilly trees. There were also certain mango and macadamia- nut trees to be attended to in the course of wanderings in the bush. It must be almost impossible for modern children, especially those who grow up in cities, to imagine the freedom and adventure that we enjoyed in the 1935 to 1945 era.

### *Farm Chores*

All was not play of course. Most farm kids grew up with certain jobs to do each day. Since cooking was done on wood stoves the fire had to be lit each morning. This involved crumpling up a page of newspaper and placing it through the small door on the front of the stove on to the grille of the fire box of the stove. The light kindling wood or fine twigs would be laid on top of the paper. A match would be used to set the paper alight. As the flame from the paper increased and the kindling wood caught alight larger chips or twigs would be added until eventually larger wood would catch fire and produce enough heat for cooking to begin. In these days of so-convenient gas or electric stoves we seldom pause to remember the skilled and tedious process involved in cooking on a wood fired stove. Another childhood chore could be the disposal of the ashes that these stoves produced by carrying the ash tray to some distant disposal area. Ashes were often used as covering material in earth toilets.

In the days prior to milking machines most also had a few cows that they were expected to milk by hand each morning and evening. Many were delegated the task of bucket feeding some calves, collecting the eggs from the fowlhouse and feeding the hens. I recall having to tear the husk from cobs of corn and turn the handle of the corn sheller to remove the grain from the cob to produce chook feed. This was a task that I did not like much - it was boring and cranking the large handle was physically demanding.

My father often planted cash crops of peas or cucumbers or potatoes and we kids were expected to do our share of harvesting. I hated the task of picking rows of peas by hand. It was backbreaking, seemed to go on for ever and there seemed to be so many better things for kids to do. In this later enlightened age some might accuse our parents of child slavery, for there was no pay attached to this family labour. That was the way it was in the later stages of the Great Depression. Indeed the history of Australian farming must be sprinkled with the fact that children have always played a part in helping out with farmwork. It was probably character building, educational and important in building generations of people who hopped in and pulled their weight with any project that they were associated with.

### The War Years

In the dark days of the Pacific War we shared the concerns of our parents as each day's news brought further accounts of the seemingly unstoppable advance of the Japanese invasion forces. We would see the pictures and headlines in the *Courier-Mail* and hear the nightly news broadcasts on the wireless. Battery power would be carefully saved in order to hear the 7pm evening news. I can particularly remember the anguish at the news that the hospital ship *Centaur* had been torpedoed as near to us as Cape Moreton.

The stark reality of war was brought home to us quite early in a very personal way when Stewart Houghton, serving with the AIF in Palestine, was notified as dead from pneumonia, never to return to

Samsonvale again. There was great sadness and a dawning realisation that war was cruel and dangerous and a serious matter of life and death for us at Samsonvale. These feelings were intensified as the Japanese invasion of most of Asia brought their presence to Australia's doorstep and further casualties were reported. I remember the distric's pride when a local lad, John Nolan, was awarded the Military Cross for bravery in New Guinea.

There was news also of the failed midget submarine attack on Sydney Harbour. The general feeling was that there were very seriously bad times ahead for us. The situation was so serious in January 1943 that commencement of schooling was suspended for several weeks. On top of the news, there was a steady flow of censored letters from troops fighting in New Guinea, to their parents and family in the district, that told of the life and death struggle going on to our north. News arrived of the death of Lieutenant Harold Salisbury, a local lad, at Milne Bay. Norman Houghton, who had worked for my aunts, was at the scene when Harold was shot by a Japanese sniper. Norman's letter with the news arrived to his parents before the official notification to the Salisbury family. The Houghtons kept the secret close for many days until the Salisburys were officially informed. This news spread quickly throughout the area.

A feature of the local war effort was that every man who enlisted for armed service was given a public farewell at a dance held for the specific purpose. Donations were collected to buy a wallet and some cash as a community memento of the occasion. There were sad scenes at the end of the dance when all present would stand in a circle and shake hands or kiss the departing soldier goodbye.

### Dances

The local ladies formed a branch of the Red Cross and set about sewing and knitting hundreds of garments for the sick and wounded as well as raising funds for soldier welfare. They mostly held dances to raise money. My mother was President of the Samsonvale branch for most of the war years so I saw much of the planning and preparations for these dances. Many loaves of bread would arrive from the baker in Samford or Dayboro and Dad, with a sharp carving knife, would cut these into slices. The sliced-bread era had not arrived then. Mum and my aunts or other helpers would mix milk with precious rationed butter to make it spread further. Fillings would be added to provide supper at the sit-down feast for up to 130 people. Other families would arrive at the dance with home-made cakes and tarts.

Percy Houghton managed the lighting system and cleaning of the hall. He would walk the mile (1.6 kms) to the hall well in advance of starting time and top up the pressure tank of the system with "Shellite" high-grade petrol. After screwing on the pressure cap he would

*Samsonvale hall - the social centre of the district*

pump the system up to about 20 pounds per square inch (140kpa) with a car-tyre pump. The seven lights that illuminated the hall were lit by climbing a step-ladder with a heater device. This would be soaked in methylated spirit lit with a match and held under the vaporiser stem of the light. When suitably hot a tap would be turned to allow liquid petrol to be forced from the tank through copper tube into the light. The controlled flow of petrol would vaporise and burst into light through an asbestos mesh mantle. The light was superior to kerosene lamps, but it would fade as the evening wore on due to lost pressure. It would be necessary for Percy to take to the pump from time to time to restore adequate pressure.

Dad's job was to provide plenty of tea for the supper. He would drag suitable firewood from our adjoining paddock before the event. Two four-gallon (18.2 litre) kerosene tins of water would be suspended from a rail above the open-air fireplace and a roaring fire started well ahead of supper time. The fireplace became a social focus for those who were not dancing. People would yarn away for hours as they gazed into the flames or turned their backsides to the fire for warmth on cold nights. There needed to be enough hot water after making several gallons of tea and to wash up plates and cups afterwards in an old tub placed on a table. As I recall these details 60 years on, it is interesting to note the advancement in facilities that are so taken for granted in the 1990s.

Music was provided by a three-piece orchestra. Miss Thelma Knight, daughter of the local station master, had received a good grounding in piano at the Mitchelton Convent and in her late teens was encouraged to play at dances. This developed into the basis of a very satisfactory dance band. Various local lads such as Hinton Austin, Sam Houghton, Colin and Wilf Kriesch learnt to play the drums. From time to time various people from Samsonvale or Dayboro made a third player with violin, saxophone or piano accordion. I seem to remember that Sid Barker from Dayboro played the violin; Phyllis McKenzie and Roderick Cruice played the accordion and Reg Kriesch Played the saxophone.

Imagine, today, music without electronic amplification! How did we manage? One important feature was that during the music those who were not dancing, such as older men and women who attended as a pleasant social outing, could carry on a conversation without being blasted into silence by the artists.

People came in a variety of vehicles ranging from motorcar to horse and sulky, saddle horse or bicycle. Dayboro people would come by railmotor.

During the 10 month period that the US Army was camped about four miles (6.4 kms) away, a strictly regulated number of soldiers would be released to attend. They would come in Jeeps and it was a big event for kids to score a free ride down the road and back in a Jeep. The soldiers seemed to give us kids a particularly good time. We loved to be treated to free Yankee Chewing Gum, which came in individually wrapped strips. Chewing gum was the bane of those who cared for the slippery dance floor because if dropped and stood upon it formed a black blob that spoilt the dancing surface and was very difficult to remove successfully.

Of course every member of a family would go to such evenings if possible. Babies would be wrapped up in a neat bundle and sometimes placed under a seat to sleep oblivious to the noise and excitement going on. There was a well-remembered night when one rather large family arrived home in their old truck to discover that the baby had been left behind in such a storage place. Various members had thought that another member was looking after the tiny one, who was eventually retrieved in the early hours of the morning sleeping peacefully in its bundle of blankets on the floor under the seat.

As kids we made our own entertainment while the adults danced. Mostly it was games of 'tiggy' outside the hall in the moonlight or spying on couples stealing a quick smooch in assumed privacy of the dark. Between dances we would take over the dance floor and practise skids up and down the very slippery surface. We would run about ten paces then lock our feet to assume a skating-like action while we used our inertia to produce a long gliding skid. Oh, what fun. This big game would be on when the adults were sitting down to supper in the adjoining room. There was no end to the pranks that could be invented as play on such a slippery floor. Often some adult would issue from the supper room to shout at us to quieten down so that those inside could carry on an audible conversation. All this relieved the tension of the overbearing war situation and Samsonvale people felt satisfied that they were in some way pulling their weight in the war effort through contributing the profits of these dances to the Red Cross. The last dance was planned to finish at midnight with a medley of the three most popular dances. Then all would stand to attention while singing" God Save The King". If someone was leaving the district we would all surround them in a circle and sing "Auld Lang Syne".

I was aware that there were official plans to evacuate women and children from the coastal front-lines in the event of a Japanese landing, while the menfolk remained on the farms to produce food. Mum, Jill and I were to go to Stanthorpe, where my mother's sister lived, in such an event.

We played soldiers using some old rifles that belonged to our parents and for which we were allowed no ammunition. One was a single-shot Martini Henry lever-action .303 and another was a Stevenson .32. A couple of .22 "pea rifles" were also carried around at times without any concern by our parents. There was a "Daisy" air rifle that was much in use. It actually worked, but we had no lead-ball ammunition or the tiny darts which that particular rifle fired. Before long we realised that the short barrel could be charged with soap or raw potato pellets and fired at targets or the backsides of one of the unsuspecting kids in the group. The result always seemed humorous unless oneself was the target. Now and again there would be a row and adult intervention would see the Daisy confiscated for a while. By and large we all became fairly good marksmen and it was no doubt one of the reasons that I became Champion Rifle Shot while in the Army Cadets a few years later.

*Ken and Bill - Would-be soldiers*

Bill and I wore hats with the side turned up and a bunch of peacock feathers attached, to resemble members of the Light Horse Company that travelled through the district about 1939. We even dug trenches and shot at imaginary enemy crawling about the farm.

As the war progressed we were exposed in the most exciting way when, as mentioned earlier, the US 1st Cavalry Division established its Camp Strathpine only four miles (6.4kms) away and proceeded to run training exercises across our farms. We met the GI troops who had strange accents and new words. They freely allowed us to examine all their field equipment including their "Walkie-Talkie" radios, field telephones, camping gear, food rations and firearms. We gladly accepted their chewing gum and were intrigued with their canned rations, which opened with a ring pull. We saw their military aircraft zooming close overhead and even touched a Piper Cub artillery spotter plane when it landed in the farm next-door. We wondered at the new invention called the Jeep. For 10 magic months we were exposed to something unimaginably exciting for country boys. When they suddenly disappeared we knew that their time had come to fight the Japanese back in such places as New Guinea and the Philippines.

My aunts were pressed into service as members of the Volunteer Air Observer Corps. Since they manned the post office they were asked to report every aeroplane that passed near that position. They were issued with charts that displayed the various makes of aircraft of the time, including a range of Japanese planes that might be observed. Every time a plane passed they had the duty of noting type, height and direction to a central control base in Brisbane per the telephone. At

*We inspect a US army aeroplane that landed on our farm*

times this task was quite demanding, for Samsonvale was on the route north from Archerfield airbase and also on the route for Avro Anson planes of the coastal waters surveillance operation based at Cressbrook as they kept a constant watch on sea lanes. There were a few exciting times when they were asked to check some unidentified plane or to answer questions about possible sightings of lost planes.

Perhaps the climax of the presence of the 1st Cavalry Division of the US Army was the final battle manoeuvres prior to their shipping out, in January 1944, to do battle in New Guinea. The force was divided into opposing groups to simulate a real war situation. One of the generals, in charge of one side of the battle force involving up to 30,000 men in the field, established his headquarters in the scrub near our houses and dairy. The paddocks were thick with troops in dugout trenches and the roads busy with vehicles and troops on foot. One side discovered that the HQ of the other was in our scrub, so planes were sent out to strafe the position at low level, not much above the rooftops of our houses. The battle continued for several days and I was sorry to miss some of it because I had agreed to travel to Toowoomba with my uncle for a few weeks' holidays. I remember hearing that the heavens burst with storms, that brought floods and added tropical realism to the exercise.

I recall a few months later going for a hike up to the head of Kobble Creek, in what is now Brisbane Forest Park. I discovering that the jungle was laced with tracks, battle control posts and other signs that the Army had done some very serious training there in preparation for the battles to come in the Pacific campaign, that took them through New Guinea, New Britain, Admiralty Islands and the Philippines.

One lasting benefit of the war and the US Army camping between Samsonvale and Strathpine was that the road was upgraded to bitumen surface many years before it would otherwise have been. Some of us made an exploration of the camp by pushbike some months after it was closed and found huts and cookhouses and offices already falling into disrepair.

Almost 40 years later it was my pleasure to meet former Major Bill Swan who had been a Lieutenant at the time he was at Samsonvale. He came back out of curiosity to look at his former training area. He had kept, all those years, the name and address of Harry Kriesch on whose farm he was stationed during the last big manoeuvre, before sailing to New Guinea. About 1984 he flew into Brisbane, looked Harry up in the phone book and drove out to Samsonvale to see him. I met him while visiting our bush block at Kobble Creek and took him on my tractor deeper into the valley, which he remembered with affection. Bill had set himself the task of recording the history of the 1st Cavalry Division during the camp Strathpine period and wished to speak to locals of that time regarding their memories of the period and their impressions of the 10 month "Invasion."

Glenda and I invited Bill home to stay with us for a few days to ask him of his experiences and learn what had happened to the division after it left Strathpine. Because of wartime security, the movements of the division had not been published and we had often wondered about their fate after Samsonvale. Bill made several more visits and we became good friends. He bought land here, intending to escape the cold northern winters. I had power of attorney for him in several real estate ventures that followed. Glenda and I visited him in Quogue, New York and enjoyed his returned hospitality. It was very satisfying to re-establish contact with our past in this way.

### Boy Scouts

As the Allied Forces built success upon success in the war a feeling of relative relief and great hope took over from the worry and fear of invasion that prevailed in 1942/43. Life in many ways became more relaxed. Such activities as Boy Scout camps on the creek flats of our farm resumed. Various Brisbane troops learnt of the choice camp site that Dad made freely available for their enjoyment. Of course the scouting scene impressed me greatly, especially the interesting uniforms.

Uncle Ted was connected with the Scout movement in Toowoomba and he sent me some copies of the scout magazine *Totem* to read. One copy had letters from Lone Scouts, which caught my interest. I eventually wrote to Scout HQ asking how I, Bill Houghton, Glen McLellan, Lyle Bennett and Athol Salisbury could become Lone Scouts. In reply I was told that I might consider forming a Lone Patrol and that the 1st Milton Troop was willing to adopt us as a remote part of that vigorous Group when we had turned 11 years old.

The Milton troop arranged to camp on our place to work out details of the adoption. So it was that under GSM "Tilji" Woodrow a bunch of raw bush boys began two years of most enjoyable and mind-broadening experiences. Indeed for Bill the love affair lasted for 40 years and found him a wife as well as later introducing his sons to the pleasures of the movement.

I seemed to become Patrol Leader by some automatic process and had to be the driving force of the group. That involved a degree of reading and letter-writing that I would not have ordinarily experienced. This may have set a pattern for a lifetime of such activity on many committees over the years.

Each week those of us local lads would meet at our place to teach ourselves from the Scout Book such things as Scout Law, knots and lashings, first aid, map work and so on. We were a pretty rough and undisciplined lot, but could hold our own at camp competitions, often because we had the advantage of local knowledge.

*The Curlew Lone Patrol*

Our first BIG adventure was to attend the Brisbane Districts Easter Camp held at Murphy's Creek. We travelled to Brisbane by railmotor on the Thursday morning, spent the day in the big city in our beautiful uniforms and visited the Scout Shop, where such wondrous things could be bought if one had the money. In the evening we boarded a special train with 300-400 other scouts and travelled to Murphy's Creek at the bottom of the Toowoomba Range, arriving about 8pm. Then in true Army style we marched raggedly with full packs to the camp ground for the weekend camp and a heap of new experiences in games, campfire concerts, open-air church parade. etc. Back to Brisbane by train came hundreds of tired but satisfied lads. Most of us stayed at Bill's grandmother's house in Milton and returned home like seasoned warriors on Tuesday's railmotor.

In 1945 our camp was at Wappa Falls near Yandina and this was equally enjoyable and beneficial as a training experience. Some warm, lingering experiences are of great campfire concerts. If we were camped locally our parents and friends were often invited and were evidently impressed. This reinforced their support for our venture. Experiments in cooking were also memorable. Planning menus and supplies was great training. The visits of possums to steal our food at night taught us that all does not go as planned at times.

I feel it is a pity that in modern life youth seem to shun participation in youth organisations that can be such fun and at the same time be a great training ground for later life. I truly believed in the high principles set for Boy Scouts by Lord Baden-Powell when he formed the movement in 1908. I am sure such beliefs have moulded the characters of millions of boys since.

### Piano Lessons

During this period I had the unusual distinction in our district at that time of being taught to play the piano. It had been noted that I had a small degree of musical talent when on finding a whistle with a sliding pitch-control rod in my Brisbane Show sample bag, I soon became able to turn out a tune such as *Home Sweet Home* in much the same way as people play sliding trombones. My father bought me a proper whistle called a Tonette to play with and later it was decided that I should learn to play the piano. My mother, her sister Olive and also their mother played the piano, as was fairly common before wireless and gramophones became widely used. Dad's sisters played the reed organ at church and home. Their father played the harmonium (a kind of pedal organ). So music was in the family.

Thelma Knight, who had been leader of the local dance band, agreed to teach me. She had learnt her skills at the Mitchelton Convent under the strict and able direction of the nuns. My progress must have seemed to be slow for my heart was not always in the compulsory hour of daily practice of scales and simple tunes. I would have two lessons per week at the railway house that the Knights occupied next to the station. One highlight of these lessons was the beaut big slice of cake and cold cordial that was provided before lessons started, about half an hour after school closed. As I recall the lessons, I developed the bad habit of learning tunes off by heart instead of following the printed music sheet. I much regret this now for I have never mastered reading music properly and impatiently resort to playing from something going on in my brain, that guides my fingers to the keys which produce memorised tunes. While this method can be entertaining it is also quite limiting in making any real progress.

I learnt for two years before going to boarding school when further lessons ceased. I hardly touched a keyboard for 30 years but often wished for the time to play again, especially on the great sounding electronic organs that had been invented in the meantime. About 1975, after a brief time in hospital with a duodenal ulcer, it was suggested by the doctor that I should take up some relaxing hobby to balance work pressures. On the way home from the hospital Glenda took me to a music shop and we bought a nice Wurlitzer electronic organ for $1200 and so began an enjoyable pasttime picking up where I had left off in 1945. It was interesting how much came quickly back to mind, including the sound basics of theory that Thelma taught me with much effort in my boyhood. She probably looked back on her labours on me as a lost effort. Often we do not realise that we can plant a seed that takes a long time to germinate. Thank you, Thelma, for making such pleasure come to life for me. Thelm's playing gave very many people great pleasure. Perhaps mine has cheered a few.

## *The End of the War*

Bill and I were being taken to see a circus at the RNA Showgrounds by one of my aunts when news of the Japanese surrender broke. We were on the railmotor at Ferny Grove or Newmarket when the stationmaster ran from his office to tell the good news to the driver as we arrived. The excitement and relief that spread through the little train was electric. I recall that when we arrived at Roma Street Station the city was in a state of near madness of celebration and release of pent-up feeling at the news. The circus, true to the best traditions of theatre, went ahead with the show and we were very impressed with the acts and the clowns.

We had arrived in the Atomic Age. The dropping of two atomic bombs on mainland Japan had precipitated surrender in a war that may have dragged on for many more months and cost Allied Forces many thousands of further casualties.

The clock was to tick away into a very different world and way of life for everyone. For me it was the end of primary school within a few months and the opening of the unimaginable excitement of secondary school in the big city.

*Samsonvale Railway Station*

*Samsonvale Presbyterian Church*

# Chapter 4.

# Boarding School

My parents do not appear to have made any firm plans for my secondary schooling and I seem to remember that after the Scholarship exam they tried to book a place for me as a boarder at Brisbane Grammar. Lists were full there, but Brisbane Boys' College was tried with success.

There were very few state high Schools in those days and the only one that could be reached from home by public transport was Brisbane State High in South Brisbane. This involved catching the railmotor at 8am, getting to Central Station about 9.15am, then taking a tram to South Brisbane. This meant the first period of the day was over before arrival. After school the railmotor left about 4.30pm and arrived back at Samsonvale after 6pm. Lyle Bennett from next-door attempted secondary studies this way, but worked under great difficulties and dropped out of the race before the end of the usual two-year course leading up to Junior Certificate exams.

*Off to boarding school in 1946*

Another neighbour, Bill Houghton, boarded with his grandmother and aunt at Milton and was able to get to State High by tram. Other classmates, David Joyner and Athol Salisbury, ended up in boarding schools as I did.

BBC at that time consisted of about 230 students. More than half were boarders from all over Queensland. I think the fees were about £100 ($200) per year for board and tuition. Considering the prices for farm produce at the time that was a fair sacrifice for parents to make.

The first few weeks were a mixture of dreadful homesickness mixed with exhilaration as we met with new experiences. *"Be it ever so humble there is no place like home"*. To be transplanted to communal eating and no-frills food; strict times for every feature of daily life; wearing collar and tie and shoes; making one's own bed; keeping track of one's clothes and possessions; being pushed around by a clique of older bully-type boys intent on "initiation" of timid new-comers; waiting for letters from home and coping with seven subjects taught by five different teachers was almost too much to bear. Even the water from the drinking fountain tasted dreadful compared to tank water. When it came to showers there was no hot water allowed. Some sadistic prefect took pleasure in pushing all new boys into the cold showers each morning as though he was dipping sheep.

On the other hand there were these wonderful new subjects of chemistry and physics, which began to explain how things worked. Once a week we went into the laboratories to do spectacular "experiments".

Being in a class of about 30 boys (no girls) and having a special teacher for each class was a big change from my Mt Samson one-teacher primary school experiences, as was having a different teacher for various subjects. I was drafted into the sub-junior class of IIB by reference to my State Scholarship Exam result. Lads with the best passes went to IIA and those with lower results than mine were allocated IIC. At the end of this first year we were all reassessed and I was proud to be upgraded to IIIA for the Junior Examination year.

In the post-war year of 1946 there was a shortage of classrooms and my class was housed in the assembly hall, which in later years was to become the St Andrew's Chapel. The old lino floor covering of the assembly hall was breaking up badly and replacement materials were out of the question due to wartime shortages. The floor was restored to serviceability by laying a timber floor over the original surface. This was rather noisy when there was any movement of feet or chairs. As I recall it there was no seating in those days for the morning assembly of every student. We stood for the whole session. When all the other boys left the hall IIB boys trundled out a stand-alone blackboard and took their seats at their desks to await the teacher for the first period.

Another novelty for a boy coming from a bush school was the sports sessions after school, with everyone in the team at the same age and size and using proper equipment. I swam in the Toowong Baths instead of Kobble Creek and found that at races I was not too bad at all in spite of no previous training. I was put in the team for the inter-school GPS swimming held after Easter that year.

*Cadet Marksman Ken*

On Saturdays we would be on the trams travelling through the big city to other schools to play cricket and in a sense finding our way in the new world; lapping up knowledge and experience and making new friends.

Then there was the Cadet Corps and the issue of army uniforms; learning to march carrying real Lee Enfield .303 rifles and receiving lectures on warfare from men who had recently returned from the fighting front of World War II. In that first year we had a week-long camp at Southport and the following year at Fraser's Paddock Army Barracks near Enoggera. We took part in sentry duty at night; watched movies about warfare techniques; fired rifles and Bren guns on the rifle range; did route marches and mock battles. This was terribly exciting for lads who had just emerged from childhood in which World War II was a vivid reality and in which many of our adult heroes were active soldiers.

There were four terms in a school year and boarders were allowed leave to go home at mid-term and between terms. I think my parents must have been glad to see me return to school after the first visit because I seem to remember talking nonstop about all the new things that were filling my life. Of course we were made to write home once each week, but most of us were rather poor letter-writers, I think. The news in one or two pages was rather inadequate to relate all that was happening in our lives.

Most of the new boarders were concentrated in Senior Dormitory and our friendships stemmed from this group more than from classmates and dayboys in our class. Some of those friendships from 1946 have lasted for more than 60 years.

Daily routine was rigid and began at 6.30am with the rising bell. No talk was permitted before this time. Indeed we were not allowed out of bed before this time unless for something special like swimming training. In the evening all had to be in bed by "Lights Out" at 9.30pm. Woe to anyone talking after that time. Duty Masters and Dormitory Prefects circulated constantly to enforce the rules and to punish rule-breakers by imposing "Lines". This involved writing some phrase like "I must not drop rubbish on floors", perhaps 50 or 100 times. Smart kids would hold three pencils at once when writing the boring directive, thus minimising the punishment if possible. This work would need to be handed to him by some appointed deadline. Some other onerous penalty like helping roll the cricket pitch or sweeping the tennis courts, might also be ordered.

Most of us discovered crystal radio fever in the first few months and if one had to pass some time in order to keep the silence rules we would put the headphones on and listen to Station 4BC, which was our nearest and loudest station.

One of our teachers, Tom Erskine (Tough Tom), was a science graduate. His radio-making skills were legend. He was an officer in the 8th Division in Malaya when the Japanese overran the country. He and many of his men had commandeered a cattle boat and escaped the Japanese at the last moment to avoid becoming prisoners of war. The boat ran out of fuel at Timor Island and beached short of their destination, Darwin. The men hid out in the hills when the Japs reached Timor. They would make night raids to various depots to steal food and equipment. Among the items stolen were radio parts which Tom made into a working radio set. With this radio, contact was made with Darwin to advise of the existence of the group and their need to be rescued. This was achieved in due course by submarine. I believe it is Tom's radio that is on display in the Canberra War Museum.

Tom and a few other daredevils stole a Jap plane one night, which was flown to Darwin. In the act of theft Tom collected several bullets in the back. We used to egg him on some nights to tell of his experiences and he said that two of the bullet fragments were still in his body, too near to his spine to be removed by surgery at that time. He always walked with a walking stick and a limp.

Well, Tom taught us how to build these simple radios that worked without batteries. We would get some earphones, variable tuning condensers and wire from one of the stores selling post-war army surplus equipment and some germanium crystal from a chemicals company. These would be assembled into a working radio. Some of the wire would be used for an aerial hitched to a tree branch near the dormitory; another length would be wrapped around some round wood to form a tuning coil. A fine wire would be arranged to just touch a sensitive spot of the germanium crystal to create a diode. That tricky bit was called the "Cat's Whisker" and was always the most troublesome component. The whisker had to touch the crystal "just right" or nothing happened. The slightest bump would cut the reception.

Following the rising bell all had to queue up for cold showers (in that first year), dress, make beds to a set style, tidy clothes lockers and be out of the dormitory before breakfast. A roster set aside two boys each day to do finishing touches such as sweeping floors, adjusting windows to a neat angle, straightening towels on bed ends and so on. Inspection by the Duty Master was at 8.45am and Morning Assembly followed at 9am.

Assembly began with a hymn displayed on a large cardboard sheet erected on a large easel at the front of the hall. There were about six or eight different hymns, which were rotated from day-to-day. Musical lead was by piano played by Keith Miller or in later years Ian Russell. Following this we would all read aloud a psalm from a small book that every student carried in his pocket. This was followed by prayers and the principal's address. This could be a mini-sermon or a talk on any relevant topic followed by announcements of any matters on the week's activities. Frequently there would be a guest speaker such as a famous Old Boy or a sportsman, or perhaps a moderator or president of one of the churches. Assembly took about half an hour and was followed by class. There would be two 40 minute periods before morning break, another two until lunch and three in the afternoon. A trusted student in the classroom adjoining the bell balcony was responsible for ringing the signal for the end of each period.

### Our Teachers

The entire staff of 14 could be seated on the stage at the northern end of the hall. I formed the impression that many of the older boys did not behave as the teachers would have liked and to some degree spoilt the tone of the school. This may have been a view coloured by my experience under the authoritarian rule of H.S. Smith at the one-teacher Mt Samson school. Nevertheless, I think that it had been difficult to retain experienced disciplinarian staff during the troubled days of the war and that school standards may have slipped somewhat. The principal, P.M. Hamilton, had seen a period of great difficulty in maintaining the school during those years. Apart from staffing problems there were shortages of various kinds, ranging from books to food, uniforms and money.

The year 1946 being the first after the end of the war saw the beginning of a rebuilding process. At least three of our teachers were returned servicemen and they in particular enforced strict discipline.

There is no doubt that the character and actions of our teachers had a bearing on our developing personalities and outlook as we grew up in the school community. This was especially so in the boarding house where we were separated from home influences. Perhaps it is appropriate to record my recollections of some of my teachers of that period.

Stanley Brown was deputy headmaster and a very hard-working second to P.M. Hamilton in administering much of the school activity in and out of class. I cannot remember him ever being still and relaxed. He seemed to always be busy on some aspect of school life, with books under his arm hurrying somewhere to tie up loose ends and keep the place running smoothly. He taught Maths and Physics and for good measure took adult classes for returned soldiers after school several afternoons per week as they struggled to attain Matriculation to the university under post-war rehabilitation schemes.

Claude Beales is recalled as one who taught softer subjects mainly to the Junior school and particularly Physical Education. He was English and is remembered for his exhortations to become manly and take the process of growing up seriously. He would recite the inscription on the bell at The Devon School, one of the older great public schools in England, to make his point – *"Boys come here to be made men."* In hindsight, that phrase was a very apt statement of the purpose of a good secondary school.

Mr. J.B. Campbell taught me Bookkeeping and in my view was an excellent teacher in that he explained the complex subject in such lucid detail and example in his neat blackboard handwriting.

Mr J. Edwards taught me Maths and as a former Squadron Leader was most formal and superior in his approach.

Tom Erskine has already been mentioned. He taught Science and Maths and could be diverted into periods of relating his war experiences. He once described the events of the Great Victorian Bushfire of the mid 1930s in which he was awarded the George Medal for civilian bravery. While he deserved his nickname of "Tough Tom" for his loud shouting at misbehaving boys, he was, no doubt, one of the favourites on staff.

Rev. A. Finch was occupied mainly in teaching Scripture to a largely unappreciative flock, although there were sometimes glimpses of devilment in his nature.

Mr R. Forsyth taught French and was a bit of a dandy. In later years I was told by a few pupils and fellow teachers that he had a secret weekend life that was quite amazing and definitely not in keeping with his outward appearances during the school week. However, like all his fellow teachers he put genuine effort into his classroom and Sports Master duties.

Mr J. Hardy was genuinely admired for his cricketing skills and serious approach to his work. He had a dreadful affliction of dermatitis that almost constantly disfigured his face.

Mr. A.E. McLucas taught English and History. He was nicknamed "Blah Blah" because he was an endless talker who could be diverted from the subject in hand to all manner of avenues not related to schoolwork. He had a problem with saliva and often ejected droplets onto the desks immediately in front of him as he spoke, much to the amusement of the class. He had been a teacher at BBC before the war. He joined the AIF and became Captain. He is remembered as an able organiser. He later served as Headmaster of Brisbane Boys' Grammar School.

Major A Stukeley, MC, BA, was ex-British Army from the 1st World War. He had a very gruff voice and manner and assisted the Cadet Corps after school hours. In spite of his gruffness he was well respected.

Mr H. Taylor came to BBC from Thornburgh College and was a terror for discipline and punishment. He wore rubber-soled shoes and could creep up, undetected, on scenes of misbehaviour. He was probably an effective teacher due to an element of fear that pervaded his presence, but he certainly was not a favourite.

Mr. W. Williams was a short and very slightly built man and was affectionately known as "Little Bill". He was my favourite teacher because he was such a gentleman, even to mere boys. He could be tough if necessary, but brought out the best in everyone with his genuine approach. He had been a student at old Clayfield College and came back to his old school after completing his BA at Queensland University. He taught Latin, Maths, Geography and Logic and so was an all-rounder. I used to think that if BBC had a "Mr Chips" it would be Little Bill. He was a bachelor and lived at the school like Forsyth, Erskine and Taylor. In that first year they acted as House Masters, having a large part to play in overseeing the boarding house meals, leave supervision, enforcement of dormitory and dress standards, roll call parades, etc.

Mrs J. Neish was the sole female staff member that year. She taught mainly in the Junior school, but pulled her weight in the extra-curricular activities of the school. One such activity was the monthly publication of a School Bulletin in later years.

Staff changed over the four years that I was at BBC and some people deserve mention.

In second term we received a teacher who was to be addressed as Doctor Roberts. The story was that he had been on the team that had developed the atomic bomb and had taken up teaching as a quieter peacetime occupation. He taught us Maths and Chemistry. His habits for a teacher were quite odd. He would often enter class and set some work and then, after a short time, disappear. Needless to say we did not make brilliant progress in those subjects. However, after end-of-term exams when marks were issued and class average was calculated there would be dismay at the low-level score. We would all be instructed to add 10 points to our results and then recalculate the new average. If the result was still too low to support the good reputation of Doctor Roberts and his pupils we would be told to add perhaps another five points to our results until a respectable level was reached. No-one complained about this generous procedure as the amended scores went on the report card sent to our parents.

I recall that he took an awful dislike to a lad called Don Booth and would cane him ruthlessly for slight reason. It was probably as an example to the rest of us not to give the slightest trouble. There was constantly a kind of gloating look on his face as he went about the school.

It appears that he went to great ends to impress his fellow staff members. He would leave telegrams of congratulation or of requests for his company to Parliament House or university functions and the like, lying casually on his desk or places where they were bound to be seen. It was later discovered that he had sent these to himself.

It was a surprise and a relief in some ways when he was not to be seen at the beginning of fourth term. It seems that he had just disappeared and everyone dropped to the truth that he was a con man. Many years later he was the subject of a *Courier-Mail* feature article in a series dealing with famous Australian confidence tricksters. He had apparently written a book that he entitled *A King of Con Men.* Many years later I mentioned his name in the presence of retired headmaster Dr. Ross McKenzie (BBC 1947-1955 and Sydney Knox Grammar). The same con man had spent three or four days as Doc's guest, posing as a visiting English Jurist with a special interest in GPS schools. He made a swift disappearance when" Doc" became suspicious of his bona fides.

Mr. W. Dancer joined the staff for the 1947 year. Immediately we noted that there was something different about his manner and movements. He appeared to be in late middle age and walked with a definite stoop. He could not move his head from side to side and thus had to turn his whole body to look to the left and right sides of the classroom and the blackboard. He had a strange shuffling way of walking. It was only a matter of days before he got the very unkind nickname "Creeping Jesus".

We soon learnt by drawing him out, as lads can do, during a maths class that he had been Professor of Mathematics at the Bangkok University and had been overrun by the Japanese invasion and interned in a civilian prison camp for four years. It was during this time that brutal beatings and lack of food had led to his pitiful physical condition. A few times he diverted to tell of his experiences. One was that he had seen the amazing sight of a "river of fire" when the authorities released the petrol from Bangkok's storage tanks into the river that flows through the city just prior to the arrival of the Japanese invaders. Somehow the petrol floating on the river surface caught fire and those present witnessed a rare sight.

That year another new staff member caused some concern. Mr G. Hubbard was appointed to teach Science and Maths subjects. He was different in some way that I was too young and inexperienced to understand. He was excellent at teaching his subjects, but seemed to have different attitudes to some of the school traditions and standards.

I was interested to read in Noel Quirk's history of the Presbyterian and Methodist Schools Association, *For the Good of the Community,* that someone had complained to the secretary that "Mr Hubbard was a Communist, that he was a house squatter, that he lived apart from his wife and conducted drinking parties".

Quirk records that the secretary investigated the matter and could find no grounds on which to take action. Mr Hubbard left after a short while and established a very successful study coaching academy in the city. I can well understand that he would have been able to assist people with study problems for he seemed to me to be able to teach successfully. However, his philosophy and manner seemed to be odds with the norm at BBC.

### A New Broom

The big change in 1947, however, was the arrival of Dr Ross McKenzie as Headmaster. While I was not aware of the unrest and drama in higher circles, it transpired that quite a lobby of influential people felt that P.M. Hamilton had let school standards slip to an unsatisfactory level and a decision had been made by the PMSA Council to replace him at the end of 1946. It seems that he was given notice about mid-year and that no reason for termination of his services was ever given to him. Most people that I spoke to said that he had had a most difficult time keeping the school functioning during the war due to shortages of suitable staff and supplies of every kind. They said that discipline and moral were bound to have suffered. It was a great ask to expect great recovery in the few months between war's end and the dismissal notice. As sub-junior students these matters were well above our heads and hardly mentioned.

The consequences, however, were very well recognised. Dr McKenzie set about straightening out the school in no uncertain manner. The old casual ways were brought abruptly to an end from the moment we arrived for first term. His very presence in an unusual white tunic with button-up collar such as dentists used to wear, his piercing eyes that seemed to see everything, his bald head and his commanding voice set him apart from ordinary men and struck fear and respectful obedience among we boys. It soon became obvious that best behaviour was the only means of avoiding punishment.

It seems that staff must have been told what was expected of them under a stricter leadership and they went along with the new broom approach. The cane got a lot of use in the Headmaster's office and on a few occasions a few boys were caned publicly before the whole assembly for serious misdemeanours. I recall that it was painfully

61

obvious that everyone had to toe the line or cop the consequences.

It seemed that prying eyes and ears were everywhere noting any infringement of the rules. I recall that I lost my money purse containing 2/10d (29c-30c) and that it was found and handed in. The rule book said that boarders must not carry more than two shillings (20c) at any time and I had a frightening time explaining the surplus 10 pence. On another occasion I had had a tooth extracted a few hours before the weekly Cadet parade. It was bleeding a bit and paining a lot, so I had asked the Duty Master for permission for exemption from parade-ground drill. The "boss" called for me and gave me a dressing-down about being soft and feeling sorry for myself before he relented and allowed me to sit it out for the afternoon.

However, along with the new order of strictness in relation to laws and standards of behaviour there was an introduction of words and activities that aimed at inculcating a philosophy of aiming for excellence in all things, to aspiring to live by good standards of morality, to widening our experiences and interests and to being involved in every activity offered by the school.

This was achieved through "pep talks" at daily Assembly and for the boarders, a Sunday night assembly that loosely resembled a church service.

I think it is safe to say that most of us younger lads assimilated these ideas and that the older boys who had had more years under a less rigorous regime were slower to change. Certainly within two years the general tone of the college had changed noticeably and we felt that as BBC boys we were highly regarded.

Generally our time was fully taken up with classes until 3.30pm followed by practice for sport of some kind. Wash up for evening meal and after about half an hour break we would go to a classroom to do "Prep" (homework) until 9pm. There was then half an hour until lights-out. There were frequent roll calls to ensure that all were present.

At weekends there was usually inter-school sport of some kind in the morning and time to relax or work at a hobby. On Saturdays we could get leave to go shopping, to see a movie, go riding on our bicycles or swim at the Toowong Baths. Such leave was strictly controlled by the duty House Master and times were set for reporting back. A dreaded form of punishment was to be "gated" or banned from such leave outings.

### *The getting of Culture*

Sunday brought the compulsory church parade. The boarding house was divided into two nearly equal groups according to the first letter of our surname. A to K would attend the service at the local Presbyterian church and LtoZ would attend the Methodist service. The groups would swap churches the following week

I preferred the Presbyterian church because Rev. Fred McKay was the minister from 1948 and his sermons often dealt with interesting subjects arising from his years as a padre with the Australian Inland Mission service, directed by Rev. John Flynn. He also told interesting stories concerning his years as RAAF Chaplain during the war.

The ministers of the local churches often visited the college and would conduct annual classes for membership of the church. It was under Fred McKay's instruction and encouragement that I became, in my final year at BBC, a member of the Presbyterian Church by Confession of Faith.

My faith was further fertilised by attendance at meetings of the Crusader Union at the college from time to time. This was an inter-denominational organisation for young men. Meetings centred on study and worship led by a Mr F.G. Costello, who would leave his work as Town Planner at the Brisbane City Council to lead the lunch-hour meetings. We all took special interest in the occasional meetings held in the home of a local member, because the meetings were followed by a great spread of cakes, tarts and soft drinks that had a special appeal for hungry boarders.

On Sunday afternoons I would often get leave and travel by tram for one penny (1c) per ride to visit various city relatives. Again there would be a fill-up on home cooking during these visits.

Doc McKenzie introduced drama to keep us busy on Saturday

evenings. Each year, under the direction of Mrs Nan McKenzie and Doc, we would produce one of Shakespeare's plays. This would take months of practice and demand effort by lads as stage hands and prop makers as well as actors. Interest in drama increased somewhat when some girls attended to play female roles. I recall being the out-of-sight prompter for the *Julius Caesar* production. The culmination of all this preparation would be two nights of public presentation to parents and friends with mention of the event in the *Courier-Mail*.

In my final year I was drafted with two younger lads to play a witch in *Macbeth*. I felt a bit of a dill doing that part, but the three of us had special coaching from Mrs McKenzie and public reaction to our final performance was flattering.

Another McKenzie introduction was choir singing by way of a select Glee Club for the older boys and a larger choir including younger soprano boys. This activity was led by Miss Betty Taylor, who taught in the junior school as well as some piano lessons.

Most of us could not read music efficiently, but we learnt our four-part harmony by hard work and practice and combined to produce a quite reasonable effort by all accounts. There would be an annual school concert at which the choir would play a leading part. There were many outings to youth concerts, speech nights, various special occasions and church visits as well as visits to sister schools to sing. The singing was enjoyable and the suppers that followed were even better.

Generally, music for enjoyment would not find its way into a boys' school list of activities apart from the rather laborious grind of formal learning of piano or violin for the brave few. The choir was an activity that most could join to find some pleasure and satisfaction and even surprise in achievement. I frequently look back on singing at BBC as a pleasant activity and I am often grateful, when enjoying music, for Betty Taylor's devotion to this extra-curricular activity. It was great to have the college Glee Club sing at our wedding in St Paul's Presbyterian Church in 1955.

Another extra-curricular activity that I greatly appreciated was the Camera Club. A Mr T Skinner from Kodak Supplies in the city would come to the school fortnightly, during lunch hour, to teach the mysteries of photography and to encourage us in our efforts with a camera. Some of us were able to convert a cleaners' cupboard into a dark room and produce a range of good to awful black and white results based on Mr Skinner's advice. Many of his instructions have stayed with me ever since and assisted in making photography an enjoyable lifetime hobby.

And so the happy years rolled busily along. We made lasting friendships, often spending part of our holidays with one of our school pals or taking home, for mid-term weekend, some pal from far away who would not otherwise get out for the weekend.

I was pleased to prove myself after failing the State Scholarship exam by passing the 1947 Junior Public exam with 2 As, 3 Bs and 2 Cs. About two-thirds of our year had to leave after Junior to join the workforce. I was fortunate indeed to be encouraged by my parents to continue towards the Senior Certificate. Only about 28 of us were that fortunate. That was the reality of those times.

### Responsibility

In other spheres I was appointed a House Senior in late 1947, a Probationary Prefect in 1948 and a Prefect in my final year. I thus gained experience in organisation, discipline and handling authority with responsibility, which was most useful in later years.

For the first three years the college tuck shop was run by a Mr Powell, the owner of the local general store. It would be open for mid-morning and lunch hour and sometimes for Saturday sports matches. He relinquished the lease in 1949 and Mr Graham Thomson, who had become the Senior Class Bookkeeping teacher, decided that conduct of the shop by some of the bookkeeping senior class would be a great grounding in commerce. I, along with H.J. Smith, from Mt Isa, was selected to supervise the venture.

We proceeded to purchase ice-cream, milk for popular milkshakes, chocolates and other sweets and to generally become shopkeepers. The task was time-consuming and chewed up our free time greatly. Two people found that they could not serve a mass of hungry customers in

65

the short periods available. The natural solution was to call in assistant labour. These very willing workers expected payment in kind, usually helping themselves. The drain on shop stocks of ice-cream, milkshakes and so forth by these "helpers" became an unmanageable drain on profits. After about five months it became most obvious that the venture was a loss leader for the college and the project was terminated. So ended my shopkeeping life.

Graham Thomson had been a student under Ross McKenzie at Thornburgh College and had come to BBC (in order to be near the university and take up part-time study for a Commerce Degree) to teach, coach sport and fulfil House Master duties. No doubt this shopkeeping venture was a valuable commerce lesson for him also. It is hazardous to allow your workers to pay themselves by generous access to the stock.

Graham was a very good-looking fellow in his early 20s and attained a place in the Queensland University Rugby Union team. He was a kind of hero to many of us. His good looks attracted the young female members of the Toowong Presbyterian Church and within a few years he married Barbara Gessner from that group. He was later appointed Principal of Thornburgh and Blackheath colleges in Charters Towers and in 1974 returned to BBC as Principal for a period of 15 years. At that time our son Paul was at BBC in Grade 11 and had as a classmate Graham and Barbara's son Ross. Their daughter was a classmate of our daughter Jennifer at Clayfield College.

In sport I had a go at everything, but was not a spectacular success at any. Early on I was appointed captain of the underage third cricket team, the DIIIs, but being a boy from the bush with little coaching and a basher attitude I did not become famous. Rowing was a novelty

*The Author as the bare-foot hurdler*

but the selectors failed to see much talent in me. Tennis was good as a social pasttime but I had no finesse to make any team. I was captain of the Second XV football team in 1948 and made it into the First XV football team in final year in the back line. We did not win many matches, but had a good time and learnt to take a beating with dignity. I got half colours for that.

I made it into the GPS swimming team for three years and achieved Open Champion for the school in 1948. As a non-competitive activity I also got a Bronze Medallion and Instructor's Certificate from the Royal Lifesaving Society.

I had a moment of glory when I got fifth place in the Open 110 yards Hurdles at the GPS Sports and won a point for the school. This entitled me to the special honour of full colours for Athletics and I graduated to the level of wearing both half and full colours pockets on my green, white and black striped blazer.

In 1949 rifle shooting was elevated to the status of sport and since I was fortunate enough to win Champion Shot of the school I had another full colours and a silver cup, presented by Little Bill Williams, for my mantlepiece.

In the Cadet Corps I attended training camps for examination and appointment as Sergeant and a year later to Commissioned rank of Cadet Lieutenant. The platoon that I commanded did well to win the Major-General Nimmo Cup for inter-platoon competition in 1949. In those days we had a small bore, 25 yard rifle range at BBC where we all got instruction and practice in small arms skills. I led the BBC team at the Earl Roberts Commonwealth Teams Rifle Shooting competition at the old Redbank Rifle Range in 1949.

*Cadet officers 1949 – Ken on far right*

*Discovering Girls*

On the social scene the subject of girls was never far from our minds. Being a boarder at a boys only college keeps a lad fairly isolated from the fairer sex. In that segregated estate imagination and fantasy can reach wondrous heights. There seems to have been a complete lack of education on the boy/girl subject as far as I can remember. I recall that there was a publication titled *Health and Vitality* in some newsagents and that occasionally someone would bravely buy a copy to circulate under the most secretive precautions. It contained pictures of nude women artistically posed, with darker parts blotted out. Wow! Just imagine.

It became a custom for Somerville House and Clayfield College to hold annual dances to which BBC boys would be invited on a more or less blind date basis. Lists of those wishing to go to these functions would be gathered by some seniors at each school and a meeting would be held to arrange the matchings. They would try to match tall with tall etc. Then the girl would write to the matched boy inviting him to the dance. The boy in turn would write a formal acceptance. All this was done under the strictest supervision at the girls' school where writing letters to boys was, under other circumstances, strictly forbidden. Occasionally a forbidden letter could be smuggled out from the boarding school to the world beyond by a brave daygirl when flights of romance ran strongly. Danger! Excitement!

On the big night the girls would be "dressed to kill" in their white church dresses (perfume but no lipstick) and the boys would arrive also dressed in their Sunday best. The excitement and high spirits can hardly be described. Senior girls would be appointed to conduct introductions and the night would proceed under the watchful eye of a group of schoolmistresses, who ensured that high spirits were not allowed to run wild. There would be letters of thanks afterwards and much talk about the adventure for several days.

On a few special occasions in our final year some of us got invitations to informal parties put on by some of the BBC dayboys or girls from St Aidans and Brisbane Girls Grammar, etc. The program consisted mostly of parlour games, perhaps some dancing, followed by supper. And thus boys began the transition into the social life of adulthood.

Eventually came the dreaded final exams. I had harboured the plan to become a surveyor after Senior Exams but as time drew to a close at school I was drawn to the idea that the farm pioneered by my grandfather, which was progressed by my father and that formed a rather special tie with me by virtue of the happy times I had spent there in growing up, should be kept in the family. I resolved to return to the farm and take up as the third generation to work the land selected by Henry Gold in 1868. I often look back on that decision and muse upon the critical decision that confronts school leavers and the vastly different paths that such decisions present to the student.

We were treated to a period of vocational guidance in our final year in which we carried out written tests and a series of problem-solving exercises. I understand the test was similar to one used to screen servicemen for talent when joining the armed forces. In the following interview I was told that I had an unusually high mechanical aptitude. The interviewer suggested that I might also try to become a medical doctor. I could not believe that I was in that class. In any case that meant six years of university in times when all but 200 of the brightest students in the State, who won Government Open Scholarships, had to pay full fees. My family certainly could not afford that.

I understand that in modern times older secondary students are given considerable assistance, including work experience, to assist them in choosing a career. The big change that I observe in comparing this situation now in 1995 with 1949 is that one could choose almost any career path in earlier times and be certain that one would get a job at the end of training. It puzzles me that in later supposedly more enlightened times we cannot guarantee a young school leaver that he or she will get a job of any kind, let alone one of their choosing, even after a university degree.

In 1949 Senior Exams were set by our only university and the Education Department and every student in Queensland sat the same test at the same time in each subject. The papers were assessed by a team of examiners and the results published in the newspapers just before Christmas. When I searched the *Courier-Mail* my name was missing from the list of students to pass the minimum four subjects. I was disappointed because I had worked fairly hard and done my best. Only in later years did I realise that my reading skills were much slower than average and this made the battle so much more difficult. Kids from various one-teacher schools must have often been at a similar disadvantage. However, I felt that I had done a fair paper in Bookkeeping and was surprised to have failed even though I had achieved an A in the subject for Junior Exams. I arranged for a re-mark of the paper and I was justified in my view when I was awarded a pass. With four subjects passed I had qualified for the coveted Senior Certificate.

The range of subjects offered in those times was rather limited, but I continue to be surprised at the use that I make of knowledge learnt in those basic areas of English, Maths, Geography, Physics, Chemistry and Bookkeeping. They were a good preparation for life in almost any calling one could choose. They were certainly most useful to a farmer and with that start one could continue to add detail and keep abreast of change in the fast-moving atomic age. In later life I found myself in an interesting job designing modern piggeries featuring new standards of hygiene, comfort and efficiency. When drawing plans and doing estimates I was amazed at the degree to which I was able to call on Maths, Physics and Chemistry principles learnt 40 years earlier.

After the exams I stayed on at BBC for about 10 days mainly to attend a party of teenage classmates and girls all about to go their separate ways after the most important phase of our lives to that date. All my boarder colleagues of the senior class had said their farewells and departed for their several "New Worlds" and I was left with a sense of loneliness and of good things coming inevitably to an end. While the rest of the school continued classes I decided to help the two members of the ground staff by mowing the Miskin Street oval. It had been built the year before and I had the privilege of playing in the first football game to take place on it. BBC played Warwick Scots College at a stage when there was almost no grass and during heavy rain. The leather ball became so slippery that it was almost impossible to handle.

Our clothes and faces became so covered in mud that it was impossible to tell friend from foe. After 90 minutes the score was 0-0, but a good time was had by players and spectators alike and the field was officially "opened".

I seem to remember that on my last day at BBC my parents came to pick me and all my belongings up in our 1936 Studebaker car and that they came early enough to do the unusual thing of sitting in on morning assembly. Dr McKenzie was gracious enough to say some very nice things about me in their presence and I think that in feeling proud of this, they felt that they had done the right thing in sending me to Brisbane Boys' College for four years.

Farewell old school. I have been able to retain contact with my old school and former pals across more than 60 years through the Old Collegians' Association reunions and similar gatherings. My son was also a boarder pupil there and his sons are currently going through their "growing into adult" phase at the old school under very much advanced conditions compared to my rather primitive experience there..

*It all ended with a 1949 version of schoolies week*

*First XV Rugby team 1949*

# Chapter 5.

# Becoming a Farmer

My father had closed the dairy while I was at BBC and maintained an income by trading in dairy cattle. When it was decided that I would join him in dairying he renovated the old dairy and the milking machines that had been installed many years earlier. He began the difficult task of breaking in a herd of young milking heifers that had formerly been raised as calves at foot. By the time I left school he was milking about 30 head with a four-unit milking machine.

I had not absorbed much detailed knowledge of farming practices before going to boarding school and now the real-life study began in the farming scene of 1950. Looking back it can be said that that time was about the beginning of quite a revolution in knowledge and practice in dairying in Queensland and across the world. It was exciting to be in the thick of it.

It has to be remembered that the 1930s were Depression years when everyone struggled to survive. Milk and butter prices were depressed and most people lived very frugally. There was not much spare cash to spend on the emerging range of machinery that was later to make the farmer's work much easier and to allow him to work more land with less labour. Following on from the 1930s came the war years with their scarcity of everything, including farm labour. I recall some old farmers discussing those years and the hardships they endured. I have always remembered their agreement that although they did not have much money or luxury, they always had plenty to eat from their land and good companionship among their fellow farmers.

It may be useful to record the farm's history and to describe it as I recall it at the time I returned from school in 1950. My grandfather, Henry Gold, had first set foot on that land 82 years earlier. In 1868 his first selection, Portion 26 Parish of Samsonvale, was a 160-acre (65 ha) block surveyed out of the original Samsonvale Cattle Station. The Joyner family lived in the station homestead about three miles (4.8kms) away and the block was reached by bridle track via the homestead or through the untouched bush to South Pine (now Strathpine). The block was unfenced and completely covered with native forest. For a time his only new settler neighbours were Leonard Deitz and his wife about two miles (3.2kms) away.

Henry Gold was one of three sons and two daughters born to Colonel Henry Yarborough Gold and wife Eleanor. He was born in South Africa while his father was on foreign posting and received some of his schooling in England, Guernsey Island (another army posting for his father) and at a boarding school in St Malo, France.

His mother insisted that the boys would break with family tradition by not becoming army officers like their father, uncles, grandfather and great-grandfather. After completion of schooling he travelled to Ceylon to work as aide-de-camp to his uncle who was the Colonial Governor at the time. There, at age 19, he made the decision to migrate to Australia. After being joined by his brother, Charles, they arrived in Melbourne in 1864 and soon after moved to Moreton Bay. He seems to have travelled soon after to the Moonie River district, south of Roma, where he was employed as a shepherd. In 1868 he came to the coast where surveyors were subdividing Joyner's original "Samson Vale" cattle station. It is said that he contracted to erect a trigonometry station on top of Mt Samson for use by the surveyors during this project. Perhaps this was undertaken before he officially applied for his land. Records show that Henry Gold lodged an application to select Portion 26 Parish of Samsonvale on 26th June 1869 at an annual rental of £7 ($14) for the block. It is believed that he arrived soon after Mr Leonard Deitz, who had also been working in the Roma district. they were thus the first selectors in the Joyner property break up.

On 12th November 1880 a Deed of Grant was passed giving Freehold Title after he had conformed to the various development and residential conditions and paid £70 ($140) in "rent" (time payment instalments) during the intervening period. Together with survey and other charges, the land cost 9 shillings and 8 pence per acre (97 cents in dollar equivalent terms) or 39 cents per hectare. The block can now be identified as the land either side of Golds Scrub Lane and includes land now used as the Samsonvale Cemetery.

Records from State Archives disclose two government inspections during the 10 year lease period. In 1876 Henry Massie, Bailiff of Crown Lands, stated that he had found that Henry Gold had erected and was living in a weatherboard house with shingle roof, consisting of three rooms and a veranda and a house yard, all estimated to be worth £60 ($120). He also had built a slab barn with shingle roof, a piggery, stock yard and calf yard. Four acres (1.6 ha) had been fenced with a three-rail fence and two acres (0.8 ha) were cultivated. The whole holding had been fenced with a two-rail fence and some cattle were grazing.

By 1880, C.J. Gold and J.J. Hogg attested that Henry Gold had fulfilled the conditions of his selection under the Crown Lands Alienation Act of 1868 by living continuously for more than two years on the selection and adding the following improvements:

| | |
|---|---|
| Four-bedroom cedar house, lined with cedar, shingle roof and verandah in front, valued at | £100/0/0 |
| Barn with shingle roof | 20/0/0 |
| Slab house with shingle roof | 10/0/0 |
| Slab school with paling roof and veranda in front | 15/0/0 |
| Stockyard and milking yard capped and divided | 30/0/0 |
| 45 rods of paling fence at 8 shillings per rod | 18/0/0 |
| 11 acres cleared and cultivated, £5 per acre growing maize and potatoes | 55/0/0 |
| ¾ acres Gardens fenced and planted | 25/0/0 |
| Total ………………………………… …………… ……. | £273/8/0 |

In order to provide grass for grazing cattle a large proportion of the trees on the block were ringbarked to let in light and preserve moisture. The ringbarked trees were left standing and old photos show them as a dense "stark, white, ringbarked forest" that eventually fell and supplied firewood for the kitchen stoves and the dairy boiler for almost a hundred years.

I recall that during the war, when fireworks were not available for the customary Guy Fawkes Night fun, Dad selected an old blue gum trunk that was hollow and had lost its smaller branches. He cut a window in it close to the ground and started a fire inside the hollow trunk. As the flames raged up inside the hollow tree we were treated to the best Roman Candle I have ever seen. The show went on well past bedtime with streams of red sparks shooting vigorously, high into the night sky through the many hollow limbs.

## Pioneering

Henry's first task was to build a hut to live in. This was erected near Kobble Creek about 100 metres north-west of the present Samsonvale Cemetery at about where the high water mark of the North Pine Dam is today. The first clearing for crops was on the nearby creek flats. Here maize was planted and no doubt vegetables and other cash crops. Fences were made laboriously from split post

*Grandfather Gold's home 1890's*

and rail. Galvanised steel wire and barbed wire were to become available many years later.

Grandfather spent over 50 years clearing, fencing and grassing his first block and the two adjoining blocks that he later added to his selection. To achieve cash flow he spent periods as a school teacher in various places as far away as Nebo near Mackay. His wife Janet, oldest daughter of John and Janet McKenzie of Terror's Creek (now Dayboro), would often hold the fort at home during these times. It seems that he was adept in photography and earnt an income with a camera and portable processing equipment while travelling.

Henry was joined in following years by another brother, William, who selected nearby land. No doubt there would have been teamwork

76

between the three brothers in their pioneering.

In their time my father and his brother, as partners, furthered the farm development work to the point where the farm was completely grassed with blue couch. About 20 acres (8 ha) of the flattest land had been stumped for ploughing and growing of crops by the time I joined Dad on the farm. Grandfather was way ahead of his time in conservation philosophy. He preserved 3 acres (1.2ha) of original hoop pine scrub during the clearing process. The area was fenced and secured from stock damage. It formed a valuable wind-break from the cold, gusty, westerly winds of winter both for the farm stock and buildings, that were constructed on the north-east perimeter of this clump of trees. That original hoop pine scrub still stands today and can be identified as "Golds Scrub" just west of the Samsonvale cemetery. Henry also took time to establish a garden of trees, shrubs and flowers covering almost an acre (0.4 ha) surrounding his house.

Grandfather had cut the rough bark ti-tree and other scrub species that lined the creek banks in his early clearing work. When the first flood arrived he realised that he had made a mistake in this strange new land. He witnessed soil erosion that he recognised as bad for the farm. Fortunately the ti-tree and some scrub species regrew thicker than ever along the creek banks. This well-forested Kobble Creek was a most attractive feature of the farm both for the aesthetic appeal of the place and from the point of view of the cattle, as it was a great place to shelter on hot days.

In 1950 there were several patches of native forest timber remaining for cattle shelter and a source of fencing materials in scattered clumps across the property. When Glenda and I were married there was enough mill timber on the place to build our entire house. When we became engaged I cut down a red cedar tree which yielded enough timber to provide us with dining room and bedroom furniture.

In 1919 the Dayboro Railway bisected the farm in almost equal parts. This with other fencing formed five grazing paddocks. Various gullies supplied almost permanent water for stock. Several areas of the light loam had been stumped to enable ploughing. Since the slopes dried out quickly most of the cultivation of crops was carried out on the heavier, alluvial soils of about 10 acres (4 ha) of creek flats.

It soon became evident that the process of waging battle with the bush was going to be a laborious one. This battle was still going on 80 years after Grandpa began the struggle. Every live tree produced an annual crop of seeds that would be carried on the wind on to clear pasture land and would germinate in the wet season. Birds would rest in the trees and their droppings would contain seeds from afar. These would germinate and the seedlings would have to be suppressed. This was done by digging out each individual seedling with a mattock or "grubber" there were many thousands to be dug out every year.

My father would impress on me the importance of this endless fight by pointing to various farms where the owners had failed to maintain the battle. The neglect of the second generation of pioneers had wasted the hard toil of their fathers. I was given to understand that this was a proper disgrace. One of my lifetime duties was made plain from the start and I did not much like the monotonous grubbing job that took up several weeks every year, but the struggle had to be maintained.

### An Inherited Trust

I began to absorb a kind of ethic that dictated that as the third generation to work that land I had some kind of sacred trust to look after it well. Serious responsibilities to be assumed included action to protect the creek banks; maintain the patch of hoop pine scrub; do not allow erosion to wash hillside cultivations away; keep grassland clear of regrowth forest; never let weeds seed and multiply; be careful with expenditure in good seasons for they will be followed by bad seasons; "waste not, want not" in everything; put in long hours of work for five days and if possible take things easier at sport and church attendance on the weekends.

A typical day started at 6am with a cup of tea and a few biscuits. Typical dress was shirt and long trousers held up with a belt on which hung a fob watch and a pocket knife that incorporated a splinter probe and tweezers. These were in leather pouches and worn on the hip. Hats were universal and of straw or army felt type. In wet weather heavy knee- length rubber boots replaced the leather hobnail boots. Since plastic had not reached the market raincoats came in various shapes made of rubberised cloth or an "oil skin" still used today in the Drizabone type of garment. For dairy farmers it was more common to simply get a sack bag and drape it around the shoulders with a piece of wire or a nail clasping two corners at the front. This seems crude by today's standards, but it was quite effective until it became overly wet. It was a simple matter to then grab another bag. Straw and felt hats soon became soaked and the brims drooped about the face. Some would resort to the good old hessian bag. By inverting one bottom corner inwards towards the other they would make a kind of hooded cape that was placed over the head. What a wondrous world it is where, today, we have various plasticised materials and such a range of wet-weather gear in which to go forth into the rain.

As time passed shorts became common and made summers more comfortable. Against the better instinctive judgement of our elders we also abandoned our shirts in summer and even abandoned our Jackie Howe singlets. Many younger farmers abandoned hats. The old

*Milking time at "The Pines"*

folk were proved to have had the greater wisdom in later years when most of us who worked in the sun like this developed sun cancers and skin complaints from overexposure to the UV rays.

Many farmers in the 1960s discovered the convenience of cotton overalls or boiler suits as worn by tradesmen. These were especially convenient to work in because there were no loose pieces to catch in machinery or barbed-wire fences. These could be put on over shorts and shirt on cold mornings and discarded later in the day as the temperature rose.

After the early morning snack there were two tasks to attend to.

First the milking cows had to be brought home from their night feeding paddock and be confined in the yard beside the milking shed. This was easier said than done at times. If it was still dark it was difficult to be sure that all had been found and driven home. If a cow had produced a new calf overnight, progress on the homeward journey could be painfully slow as the cow could resent one's presence near the calf, or the calf could be quite unstable on its new-found legs.

Cattle are habit-forming beasts and a herd settles into a routine related to the cycle of night and day. Most of the herd would sense when it was milking time and saunter towards the dairy as the regular milking time approached. There was a kind of mob consensus with a regular leader. However, there would always be the few that had to be "pushed" home.

We once bought a cow that had been reared on its own and served for some years as a pet house cow. She had never learnt the mob mentality. As an individual she did her own thing and was cursed hundreds of times for not turning up at milking time. She would be found at some far corner of a paddock eating away with no intention of socialising with other cows and coming home.

In the 1970s Queensland had a trial of daylight saving and the media and comedians had a great time making jokes about the cows getting upset with the change. It was a Country Party Government that established the trial in order that the public might make an assessment and express a wish in a referendum at the conclusion. Voting resulted in an expression by about 65% of residents that they did not want the innovation here in the tropics where the length of daylight does not vary greatly as compared with places in the higher latitudes. Nevertheless, the 2000 dairymen in the State were blamed for undue influence on the "bushie" Government for the idea being dropped.

However, it must be said that a one-hour change in routine did cause much confusion among the milking cows. They would not turn up for milking in accordance with the changed clock that farmers had to follow if they were to meet deadlines in their dealings with the rest of the world. Farmers had an arduous time changing cattle habits for about two to three weeks. It was a joking matter for the elite, but a pain in the neck for farmers.

On a lighter vein I relate an amusing incident associated with the cows coming home. In later years we granted a company of Boys' Brigade permission to have an Easter Camp on our land. We did not realise that these lads used a bugle to rouse their sleeping members at early dawn. On the first morning we were still in bed emerging slowly from our slumbers when an unearthly bellowing kind of noise rang out around the ridges. We leapt out of bed to see what was going on. It was some lad trying, unsuccessfully, to blast out the "wake up" Reveille. The more interesting aspect of the bugle call was that the cows that were beginning to saunter home to the dairy were electrified and broke into a panic-stricken gallop towards the campsite, obviously thinking that a member of their mob was in some kind of agonising trouble.

The bugler had a second try and it only intensified the reaction. The front runners in the investigation committee, with heads and tails raised and ears pricked forward, got closer and closer to the source of the anguished bellowing-like noise. Then one would lose its nerve and turn tail and run. Others would join the panic rush only to return for another look. It took 20 minutes and sustained silence to calm the situation down. I think the boys got more than they were bargaining for as well. They were not accustomed to being confronted by a herd of upset cows.

At the dairy the day began with some axe work as wood for the fire under the 16 gallon (72 litre) copper boiler was produced from a log dragged in from the paddock. In dairying one of the first lessons to be learnt was that of the continual fight against bacteria, which can breed so rapidly in milk and turn it sour. Hot water and washing soda were the tools for sterilisation of anything that came in contact with milk. A wood-fired boiler or even a steam-pressure "Jacko" steriliser were standard equipment.

In more recent times a variety of detergents and chemical sterilisers found their way into the dairy and extreme heat was not recommended.

Next came the starting of the stationary piston engine, which powered a vacuum pump for the milking machine. These hand-cranked engines sometimes developed a mind of their own and starting could be difficult if everything was not just right. On such occasions it was a great way to warm up on a cold morning when most starting problems arose. Our water-cooled Crosley three-horsepower engine was a massive thing with two 24 inch (600mm) flywheels and a 5 inch (125mm) bore horizontal piston. It probably weighed half a ton (500kg) and it ran at about 400 rpm. It was a delightful engineering achievement for its time. It ran so quietly as it turned a large piston-type vacuum pump with a flat belt.

Milking machines had been in vogue for about 30 years at this time and were quite efficient. With walk-through bails we were able to milk about 50 cows per hour with four sets of cups. It was a great advance on the hand milking that I had done as a school kid many years earlier.

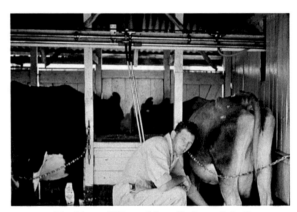

*Machine milking with walk-through bails*

Even at that time, 1950, there were some farmers in the district who had not graduated to machine milking, mainly due to the capital cost involved.

As milk was released from the machines it would be trickled over cooling coils to reduce the temperature and thus reduce bacterial multiplication. Tank water was circulated through the coils so the temperature reduction was never very great. An earlier version of cooling was achieved, particularly in-hand milking sheds, with a "beehive" cooler. This was a conical, tinned-steel tank filled with about 40 gallons (180 litres) of water. Atop the truncated cone was an open top 4 gallon (20 litre) cylinder with a row of small holes on its lower outside edge. When a bucket of milk was poured into the upper cylinder a flow of milk issued from the small holes to course down the outside of the water-filled cone. It would be aired and cooled as it descended to be collected by a gutter surrounding the bottom and piped into a can, through a filter. The filter was needed to extract stray hairs or dust or any other foreign matter that might find its way into the milk during extraction.

### The Horse and Cart Days

The next stage was transporting the milk to the roadside pickup point. This was done at our place, as at many others, with a horse and cart. It involved catching the draught-horse in a nearby paddock, fitting all the leather harness and backing the traction unit between the shafts of the spring cart. It always seemed to me to be a lot of work for a 10 minute trip.

Within a few years we graduated to a farm utility truck which was a great improvement. The incident that triggered the change may be of interest. We used a horse and spring-mounted cart to take four or five cans of milk to the roadside stop. This was also used to cart calves and pigs to the railway station at the southern end of our farm each Monday and to bring home any bought-in goods such as cow feed concentrate.

For some reason the best horse for this job was off duty one day and Punch, a far less reliable horse with a few bad habits, was pressed into duty to take some pigs to the station on goods train afternoon. The pigsty was at the crest of an 80 foot (24m) high embankment which fell away very steeply at about 45 degrees slope to the creek flat. The pigs were duly loaded amid much squealing, which was not much to Punch's liking in the first place. As he was given the order to "gee up" he started moving forward on level ground and then was given a gentle pull on the right rein to turn slightly uphill and exit the loading zone. As he turned uphill he did not like the extra load one little bit and decided to go no further. Dad gave him some loud "encouragement" and a whack on the backside with the free end of the reins to bring forth some more power and determination. Punch, being upset by all the noise and hassle tried the load again and decided to slip into reverse instead. Amid much shouting, bit by bit, in fits and starts, he backed the cart and load of five pigs towards the brink of the steep embankment. Panic set in all round and Dad jumped off the cart just as the whole lot went over the edge. To the sounds of crashing cart structure and squealing pigs, the rig went tumbling over and over down the steep slope. When the dust had settled, Punch stood up with his harness in disarray and two stumps of the broken shafts hanging forlornly at his sides. The pigs had disappeared from sight in the bushes, but came back to the sty at the next feeding time. Dad resolved to repair the wreck, but after a short time decided we could move up to light motor transport at last.

This was not the only time Punch disgraced himself. It was my duty one day to transport a breeding sow to Frank Austin's boar about a mile from home. On arrival the sow was keen to be unloaded and make love to the boar a few times while Frank and I chatted away and watched the making of another litter. However, when it came time to break up the party and load the sow on,to the cart again, there was a terrible noise of parting. The sow tried to extend the visit and squealed its lungs out as it was urged up to the cart, which was resting at the end of the loading ramp. Punch was wearing blinkers and unable to see what was going on behind him and twitched his ears nervously. We were fully occupied with the fractious sow, which would turn and dash back to the boar's pen. Suddenly it all became too much for Punch and he bolted at a gallop, around the fence of the small paddock beside the pigsty, with the driverless cart bouncing along behind.

When he got to the corner of the paddock he made an almighty jump and cleared the corner post and came to a standstill. Sadly the cart did not follow so well and it landed on top of the fence with a post sticking up through the shattered floor-boards. I was not sure whether I should laugh or cry. Frank was a rather serious old chap so I kept a straight face and proceeded to recover our transport system and make repairs. I remember that the sow had her wish of an extended sojourn with her male companion.

During my primary school days our milk was transported to Brisbane by the morning railmotor, but by the time I returned from boarding school this inefficient, outdated mode had been replaced by a road service using a specially constructed truck. It had the advantage of doing the journey more quickly with the perishable load. Since it went straight to the factory the labour and cost of transferring cans from Roma Street rail station to the South Brisbane factory was eliminated. By this time also, through increased population, there was opportunity to sell the afternoon milk as well as the morning supply and the truck supplied a service that the train did not.

If the milk factory was oversupplied with milk for current needs we would have to run the milk through a hand-turned cream separator. The cream would be sent to a butter factory to be churned and the skim milk would be fed to some pigs that were kept for the purpose of gainfully converting the valuable protein into pork or bacon. Looking back that seems such a waste. The protein was the most valuable component of the milk and it was being fed to pigs while the fat, that is so spurned these days, was fed to humans.

The milk transport business was run by a local-born man, Doug Clay. As he developed his run he undertook various other useful functions. He would deliver the *Courier-Mail*; bring regular supplies of bread and meat from Samford; carry mail for his customers and even carry emergency parcels from Brisbane on occasion. As milk supply increased, Doug was joined by his brother-in-law, Eric Fogg, with a second truck. They performed what must be truly classed as a faithful service in all sorts of weather. Not least of their useful services was the spreading of local news as they stopped at every farm gate for a few cans of milk and exchanged the latest gossip.

On return from the roadside pick-up, the returned cans had to be washed and sterilised along with the milking machines and equipment. There were usually some calves to be fed and then it would be time to return to the house for breakfast. Since we had been working for two or three hours by then we had developed healthy appetites for this meal. Time would be taken to browse through the morning paper before more work commenced.

One constant chore was to provide supplementary fodder for the cows in addition to what they could graze from the paddocks, especially in winter and during droughts. There were two forms. One was freshly cut crops such as corn, fodder sorghum, sugar cane, or legumes such as field peas. The other was field-dried hay of various kinds.

In those days it was all hard labour cutting daily supplies of green feed by reaping hook, scythe or cane knife; loading by hand onto horse-drawn wagon or slide; then carting to the barn where it would be fed into a chaff-cutter driven by a petrol engine. It was usual to provide one kerosene tin (4 gallons - 20 litres) per cow. The chaffed feed would be tipped into a trough at the head of each individual feeding stall in a line of 20. Cows would be admitted in batches of twenty to devour the treat. As an extra aid to milk production a meal concentrate consisting of crushed grain and a protein concentrate such as linseed or cottonseed meal would be poured over the chaff. Finally,

*Hand made stooks of lucerne hay drying*

the better cows such as freshly calved beasts or higher producers or maybe an old favourite might receive an added bonus to the above rations.

In dry times or in gaps between fresh crops hay would be fed through the chaff-cutter amid the production of much dust. At that time we still made hay the hard way. Lucerne was the preferred crop. It would be cut with a mower drawn by two horses and allowed to wilt for a day. Then with a horse-drawn dump-rake the crop would be raked into windrows for another day or two of drying. On the third or fourth day these windrows would be arranged into several stooks or round bundles with a pitchfork and tossed on to a horse-drawn wagon. The wagon would be loaded as high as we could toss the hay and carted to the hay shed, where it would be unloaded by hand into a shedded haystack.Should we get rain on the hay before it was dry enough to store in the shed we would have to continue to turn the windrows by hand with a pitchfork until the moisture content was acceptable. If it was stored too damp there was a risk of it heating and going mouldy. In the extreme case the heat could get so intense that the stack could catch fire, so great caution was observed.

These crops were all planted on ploughed and harrowed soil. Again this was done with two faithful old draught-horses. We had a single-furrow mould-board plough and peg tooth harrows for this land preparation. I cannot say that I ever liked this work with horses. It seemed so slow and laborious. It involved much shouting at the animals as they were turned at the end of rows or as one or the other failed to pull his share of the load. Then there was the process of removing weeds between rows of young corn. This was done with a scuffler, which consisted of a set of nine spring tines on racks mounted between two wheels. The driver sat on a steel seat and guided the horses, which pulled on either side of a central pole. The tines would uproot weeds and leave a loose moisture-retentive bed between the rows.

All this seems to be perfectly logical and efficient. However if the horses were clumsy, or slow to respond to the guiding reins or shouted commands of the driver, the result was quite the opposite. The beasts could trample all over the young plants and crush them and if they did not walk a straight course the gap in the tines at the centre point of the machine would be where it was never meant to be. The tines would rip out the very plants that were meant to be pampered and protected from weeds. The driver would soon get bad-tempered and the horses would get upset by the shouting and rein yanking of the driver. There had to be a better way.

The above work was very much a daily routine, but there were other tasks to fill in the days. I recall that we spent a lot of time fencing. Many of the fences that my grandfather had erected needed replacing. It was recognised that grazing and grass quality would be improved if we had more and smaller paddocks in order that grazed plots could be rested and re-grow in a systematic rotation. To build a new fence we first found a suitable stringy-bark tree. It was well known by then that stringy-bark posts lasted longest and were most resistant to damage by bush-fire. Another advantage was that they split into posts more easily than most other trees. The tree would be felled by two people pulling on a crosscut saw. It would be cut into 6 foot

(1.8m) lengths and these in turn would be split from one end to the other using steel wedges and a wooden maul. With the right skills, posts of the desired thickness could be backed off with ease and some satisfaction.

Hauled into line, these posts would be stood in the ground by digging a hole with a crowbar and shovel, lining them up neatly with the aid of some sight sticks, before ramming the earth back into the hole to secure the upright post. Finally the barbed wire with staples or holes would be bored through the posts with an auger and the wire threaded through prior to tensioning and tying off,

What a break it was to later get a chainsaw to replace the two-man crosscut saw and a tractor-mounted post-hole digger to stand the posts. The continuing story of the next 25 years of farming was the advance in mechanisation and improved technology. Not only did these reduce the drudgery of the heavy work, but they increased output remarkably and led in many ways to increased production from the same amount of land. Mechanisation was a factor in reducing the use of hired farm labourers.

### Winds of Change

As farmers with a direct market in metropolitan Brisbane the arrival of tens of thousands of troops during the WW11 extended our local dairymen greatly and ushered in a new dimension to management. The US forces were accustomed to milk that was certified free of tuberculosis bacteria. Our herds had never been tested for this disease so every animal was included in a thorough testing program. While our herd had no reactors, some of the best herds in the district were found to include cows with this disease. These were condemned to slaughter and turned into fertiliser. The test program continued annually for many years until the whole area was declared disease free. In later years testing was extended to include brucellosis. Eventually the whole Australian continent was cleared of these serious diseases of bovine animals.

In the pioneering days, farm labour was relatively plentiful. Most farms employed a permanent worker or two. There was usually a pool of casual labour in the district to call on in times of special need. In two world wars this labour pool dried up so to some extent farm upkeep suffered and farmers had to work harder and longer to keep up standards. After WWII it was obvious that returning servicemen elected to find employment in the cities rather than settle down to the farm labour scene that they had left a few years earlier. This shift was probably a catalyst in the mechanical and technological changes that I saw and lived through in the 1950s and 1960s.

Other changes that had great effect on small farming were in progress also. In the mid-1930s I can just recall great concern in my father's conversation with friends and neighbours concerning the state of the milk section of the dairy industry. It should be pointed out that dairying consisted mainly of producing milk for the purpose of separating the cream and selling that for butter making to meet a ready export market. The protein-rich skim milk was fed to pigs along with corn and other homegrown feed. Fresh milk for the city was originally supplied by a multitude of farms on the city fringe. These farmers would deliver the milk to the customer's door by horse and cart. The customer would provide a jug and the delivery person would draw milk from one of the cans in his cart and pour it into the customer's jug.

As the city grew this system became inadequate. About the same time the health advantages of pasteurising milk were being stressed. A number of small milk pasteurising and bottling plants were established. Farmers within 49 or 50 miles (64kms-80kms) of Brisbane gained an outlet for fresh milk to these factories. It was not long before the management of these plants were hard at it cutting costs, particularly in relation to the prices they offered to farmers for their milk. There was often more milk available than was needed and prices would be low. However, when there was a drought, supply would be scarce and prices would rise. For their part farmers found themselves in a precarious position, caught between being cream farmers and whole milk suppliers. They were quite irate about the heartless approach of factory managements as they played off one group of farmers against another in relation to supply and price.

### The Dairy Farmers Strike

The situation reached a head in the mid-1930s as farmers began to band together to resist these tactics. They formed the Country Milk Association and some of its bravest members took a lead in advocating a milk strike. Divisions developed among farmers who favoured a strike for better terms of business and those who were meek enough to endure the tough trading tactics of the factories. Eventually the strike did take place in all the districts surrounding the city. Milk trucks continued to run to collect from those not prepared to strike. I can remember my father supporting the strike and telling of some incident where a milk truck was stopped by strikers. While talks went on with the driver others got into the back of his truck and put junket tablets into the milk he was carrying. No doubt it was curdled by the time it reached the factory.

All this created great news and attracted sufficient attention from the Forgan-Smith Labor Government of the time to cause it to step in and establish the Brisbane Milk Board in 1938. Its duties were to supervise a quota system of sharing entitlement to supply between all farmers in selected districts near Brisbane; to control the issue of transport licences and prices; to supervise hygiene aspects of milk production; monitor milk quality and to fix the price of milk supplied with reference to the fair cost of production through good and bad seasons. This brought in a new era of stability and also demonstrated to farmers that united action could bring results. The Country Milk Association evolved into a larger group called the Metropolitan Milk Producers' Association to speak for members on a range of issues. A few years later the Government established the Queensland Dairymen's Organisation under the Primary Producers Organisation and Marketing Act, which compulsorily embraced the nearly 25,000 dairy farmers in Queensland at that time.

For several years there was rivalry between the two organisations, but eventually the QDO, the Government's recognised voice of the farmers, prevailed.

The QDO and the Brisbane Milk Board were to be all important in setting standards and smoothing disputes for all the 25 years that I was a dairy farmer. I was active in the Samsonvale branch (several years as Secretary and delegate to District and State Conferences). For many years our farm was used by the Milk Board as one of the sample group to determine the fair cost of production that formed the basis for price fixing.

As I write this I am sad to record that the wheel has turned full circle. The industry, nation-wide, has long been divided on the issue of equal access to the city milk market. Those nearest to cities claimed they had the right through historical attachment and geographical location to supply their local cities at prices that were set by Milk Boards and reflected the cost of producing milk every day of the year. Others, mainly in Victoria, which had a great surplus of milk after satisfying local fresh milk markets and who produce on a largely seasonal basis, claimed this allocation was unfair. With government help they decided to attack the orderly marketing system across state borders under the protection of Section 92 of the Constitution. They would use the advent of fast, reliable road transport to crash into interstate cities with cheap milk. The Federal Government had established the Competition Authority to free up trade and outlaw restrictive trade practices throughout the business world. Eventually it turned its attention to Primary Producer boards and warned State governments that it would no longer tolerate the Milk Boards set up to regulate supply and price. Who were the private milk-processing giants (some by now owned by foreign interests) to resist an open slather in finding cheap supply? Milk retailing had evolved largely from door to door delivery of unpasteurised bulk milk by dairymen, to door-to-door delivery of pasteurised milk in returnable bottles or disposable cartons. Predominantly, the current position is that a few big supermarket chains with their very powerful bargaining power retail most of the product. Door to door delivery is extinct.

As the deregulation of the dairy industry unfolds it appears that the consumer is paying 15c or 20c per litre more for their milk while the farmer is being offered 10c or 15c less for his product, with every prospect of much further reductions in pay in the near future. When challenged with this result of deregulation a Competition Authority spokesman was heard to say that it was not supposed to work like that. Well, in spite of pleadings by people who were in a position to forecast the disaster forced on the industry it did happen. As a result it appears that in 2012 less than 500 dairies are now operating in Queensland. A milk price-cutting war brought on between Woolworths and Coles has further reduced the price paid to farmers. A consequent reduction in profit margins is currently accelerating the exodus from dairy farming.

Dairying was the activity that assisted so greatly in pioneering the closer settlement of this nation. When I joined my father on our dairy farm there were 30 farms in Samsonvale. By 1998 there were none. The Samford district had slightly more farms at this time. It now has none. The Dayboro district, which had enough farms (about 200) to support its own farmer co-operative processing plant in 1950, has in 2012 only three dairies surviving.

Returning to the daily routine, I recall that harvesting and chaffing supplementary feed crops took up most of the morning and we would retire to the house for lunch and some time off. One essential part of this break from toil was listening to the Australian Broadcasting Commission Country Hour on 4QG. During this lunchtime hour we could hear weather reports and forecasts, market reports and discussions on all manner of subjects relevant to farmers. This session was guaranteed to keep us up to date with the latest research and best practice for that time. This hour was followed by a quarter-hour radio drama that nobody dared miss. *Blue Hills* brought to us a reflection of our own country-based lives as it dealt with farm problems, family and community relationships and the ebb and flow of the seasons with their attendant problems.

This midday rest would be followed by three hours of odd jobs such as mending or building fences, grubbing out regrowth seedlings with a mattock, general repairs and the like. By 4pm the cows would be seen sauntering towards the dairy for the evening milking, which began after a substantial afternoon tea. Milking took about 1½ hours. In summer this left a short time before darkness fell (in winter it was dark when we finished). In this period there might be time to take a look at the dry stock and the heifers in a far paddock. I would usually carry my rifle in case I met the occasional dingo that liked to attack the calves, or perhaps I would see some hares that had a habit of destroying the freshly shot seeds of one of the newly planted fodder crops.

Farms do not exist in isolation and it was necessary to travel to the city regularly to conduct business such as banking and to buy supplies of cow feed concentrates, such as pollard or special mixes to enhance the diets of milking cows. There was need to buy parts for the milking machines, tools, fencing materials, household supplies, clothes, etc. Such trips were undertaken at least monthly. They had to be fitted in between the times of milking. Those two important daily operations bound a dairyman to his property and his herd most strongly, unless there were family members who stayed at home to do that work. It must be recorded that the farmer's wife and children often carried the day when the male was away on business.

We banked at the old National Bank building on the corner of Queen and Creek Streets. In those days one could park a car free of charge (no parking meters) within a few hundred yards of any business house in the inner city of Brisbane. Our milking-machine supplier was in Adelaide Street, tools and engine parts were bought at IBC in Ann Street and ESCA in Mary Street. Amid today's hustle and bustle it is strange to recall central Brisbane as the shopping centre for the surrounding farming community.

Roma Street was perhaps the hub of farm trade with its many stockp-feed suppliers. One enterprise stands out above others. That was "Red Comb", or more properly, The Poultry Farmers' Co-Operative Association. It was driven by vigorous management which expanded its trade to encompass all farming needs, including stock feed, fertilisers, seed, hardware, clothing and a cafeteria. The group occupied a continuous stretch of the southern side of Roma Street from Makerston Street almost to Countess Street. And there could be no doubt in studying the people and the vehicles that crowded that area, that this was farmer business territory.

Farming activities generated some paperwork, of course. On discovering some old records recently I was amazed at the small bundle that covered a whole year's activity, as compared with the piles that seem necessary to struggle through a business year these days. Business life was certainly simpler in the 1950s. In these days of endless statistical returns, registrations, applications, permits and official directives, the situation then seems unbelievably simple and one wonders what real benefit farmers have gained from all the paperwork burden now placed upon them. It seems that the only annual returns then were the simple tax form that farmers could manage without the assistance and cost of an accountant and a short series of questions for the Statistics Department.

So that is a sketch of the scene I became part of on leaving school and beginning a career in farming.

*I saw the end of the horse and wagon days*

# Chapter 6.

## A Country Home

It may be of interest to describe our farm home of the late 1930s and during the war years and to note the progress in living conditions that followed that period. It is so easy to forget the limited resources that the average farming wife had to work with in her separate toil of caring for her man and her family.

Our house stood on high stumps and was surrounded by a high garden fence of split palings. Mum was a keen gardener and managed to keep a vigorous display of shrubs and flowers growing by sheer hard work. There was no water laid on and every drop of bath, laundry and kitchen wash-up water was saved to distribute by bucket on those beloved plants.

The entire water supply for the house came from two tanks of 1000 gallons (4500 litres) each. These were supplied by rainwater falling on the roof. There was never any doubt that this water was safe to drink. In extended dry seasons everyone was under orders to be especially careful with water use. The quantity of water remaining in the tank could be gauged by tapping one's knuckles on the various rims of the tank. Those below water level returned a dull sound while those above the water line gave out a louder hollow sound. As a drought continued relentlessly on this tapping became more frequent and progressively more serious. The last of the water would be reserved for cooking and drinking. Water for washing would have to be drawn from the creek or a well.

Hot water was in very short supply. It came from a three-gallon copper tank attached to the side of the wood stove in the kitchen and was drawn off from the sole tap on the bottom of the tank. There was no such thing as long daily, hot showers. A daily mop down from a dish and a weekly wallow in a few inches of warm water in the bottom of the bath was the rule. The warm water was obtained by carrying hot water from the stove tank to the bathroom in a bucket.

It can be imagined how much we all appreciated the time when prosperity and a windmill allowed us to pump water from a well several hundred yards away, down by the creek, to allow watering by hose and installation of a shower. It was possible to eventually replace the old earth-closet dunny with a septic system. Many readers will find it difficult to envisage these conditions in these days of affluence. There will be some who remember them all too well and recall humble beginnings when money and resources were scarce for most farmers.

The area under the high-set house was enclosed with thin, spaced battens. One part was partitioned to accommodate our open tourer car and another area had a small concrete floor with a set of wash tubs comprising the laundry. Outside but nearby was a brick fireplace incorporating a 16 gallon (79 litre), wood-fired, copper boiler vessel in which the clothes were boiled with soap on wash day (almost always Monday). The clothes would be dragged from the boiler and rinsed in clean water by hand in the tub. They would then be wrung by hand and hung on a clothes-line strung between two trees near the house to dry. Mum would be able to reach the line by lowering the light sapling that comprised the "clothes prop". When the clothes were pegged to the line the prop would be hoisted to a higher position that would elevate the wet clothes well above the ground where they were able to flap in the drying wind.

Other areas under the house were used for storage of a variety of possessions and there was always space to play out of the hot sun or the driving rain. Since the floor was earth it was ideal for mud pies or for roads for our toy cars. Most farmers discovered that this space under the house was the coolest place on a hot day and chairs or a hammock were often installed under the very practical Queenslander house.

There were verandas on three sides of the house and these too were favourite places for the squatter's chair and the rocker chair. Mum decorated these spaces with pot plants and ferns to present a homely effect.

The kitchen was rather spartan with two small built-in cupboards, a table with four chairs and a dresser. A dresser consists of a lower cupboard about 4 feet 6 inches (1.5 metres) wide and 3 feet (0.9 metres) high and was used to store the grocery supplies. Above this was attached a set of open shelves about 20cm wide. A small ledge on these allows plates to be arranged on their edge in a side-by-side display. To some shelves were attached rows of hooks on which cups were hung by their handles.

### Before Electricity

The floor was covered in lino and the same material was used to cover the table top. The stove was made of cast iron and stood on a fibrous cement floor in a corrugated-iron recess that extended outwards from the house wall. Its chimney extended upwards through the roof of the recess. Close at hand, beside the stove, was a wooden box holding the firewood. Under the stove sat a cut-down kerosene tin containing kindling wood for starting the fire.

In one of the nearby cupboards were three "Ma Pots" irons. On ironing day these were placed on the hottest part of the stove-top to heat up for use on the clothes. As the one in use cooled it would be replaced on the stove and another would be latched on to the detachable insulated handle to continue the process.

The stove was a "Crown" made at Stones Corner in Brisbane and had some chrome areas on its front. The cast-iron surfaces were kept attractive-looking by brushing with black stove polish at regular intervals. This gave the stove an attractive low black sheen. The fire compartment was on the upper left of the stove and under it was an ashtray to catch the products of burning wood. On the right was a full-height oven. One can only wonder at the skill of the housewives of the time in coping with all the intricacies of lighting and controlling the fire in these stoves. Without temperature gauges they used their senses to judge the correct oven heat to turn out delicious cakes and roast meals in their stride. I am sure that it would be completely beyond most modern cooks.

Rather than use the sink for washing up, my father and mother preferred a tin wash-up dish because it used less water. After the hand-wash the water could be sparingly distributed to various plants in the garden.

Several kinds of fresh food would be stored in a ventilated cabinet with gauze sides. Such food would be attractive to ants. To spoil their efforts to reach the food, the four legs of the cabinet would be stood in specially designed saucers with a water-filled moat.

In 1950 we bought our first refrigerator. It was a *Defender* and achieved cooling by burning kerosene continuously in a lamp compartment at floor level. A one-gallon (4½ litre) tank would provide flame for a week. Somehow the heat from the lamp boiled a mixture of ammonia and other liquids into a vapour that was condensed into liquid at the top of the unit. Here it was evaporated by an ingenious arrangement of lowered pressure. In the process this caused enough coolness to freeze water in the ice-block chamber and to cool the whole food cabinet sufficiently to store food for some time. The unit was not capable of producing temperatures in the deep-freeze range, but it was so very far advanced from the formerly used ice chest and the Coolgardie cooler or the old meat safe, which gained its modest cooling effect from evaporation of water-soaked cloth or hessian draped around the steel-mesh cabinet.

Drinking water had been cooled at home and often on the job around the farm in a canvas waterbag where the evaporation principle was employed. By comparison, the cold water from the new fridge was positively freezing. We take home refrigeration and deep freezers for granted now, but farm people, without electricity, regarded it as a luxury well into the 1950s.

Lighting at night came from kerosene lights. In the kitchen we had an Aladdin lamp which produced brilliant light (perhaps equivalent to a 75-watt electric bulb) by playing the flame from a round wick on to a conical asbestos mesh or mantle. This glowed white hot and shed a superior light to the ordinary kerosene lamp. The latter consisted of a flame burning on a lit flat wick in a removable globe and consuming kerosene soaking up from a glass reservoir at its base. This type of portable lamp was used in our bedrooms.

After the evening meal we would retire to the sitting room taking the Aladdin lamp with us. There we would read or listen to the battery radio. There were five Brisbane stations available on the AM band. FM and stereo were not in use until many years later. At night broadcasts from more distant stations could be tuned but for the most part reception would wax and wane and was unsatisfactory. The ABC 7 pm news was always most important to start the evening then there would be lighter entertainment led by nationally famous presenters. In conversation with neighbours and friends the recall of such programmes and comment on them was an important part of socialising.

I recall Jack Davey's Quiz shows which always began with his signature "Hi-Ho Everybody." There were similar sessions led by Bob Dyer and his wife Dolly under the banner of the "Atlantic Half Hour" I think that the long-running "Australian Amateur Hour" was still running in 1950. Weekly, this brought a great range of singers, musicians, bird-song mimics and elocutionists to compete for the prize decided by audience vote. Everyone knew John Dease and "The Quiz Kids". A radio adaption of Steele Rudd's series concerning "Dad and Dave" would have us in stitches of laughter as would the antics of comedians Roy Rene and Mo McCackie.

At bed-time an alarm clock would be wound by hand and set for the morning and last chores attended to. This included a trip to the dunny about 30 yards from the back steps. For those likely to need it during the night, there was a "jerry" or "bedroom cup" of about half-gallon (2.2 litre) capacity shoved under the bed. This would save that long trip to the outhouse, particularly in the rain or cold wind. To add discomfort to the short cross-country trips it should be recalled that there was no such thing as fine toilet paper in our area. A torn-off section of the *Courier-Mail* or an old mail-order catalogue, cut to size, served the essential purpose. In these days of comfort and convenience it is too easy to forget some of the most inconvenient aspects of living everyday life before flush toilets and mains power. One of the most disliked tasks to be addressed was the frequent digging of holes and the burying of "night soil" from the traditional Australian dunny.

Our house was graced by a piano, which my mother played for entertainment. We did not own a wind-up gramophone and collection of bakelite, 78rpm records. These were common place in those days.

We were proud of a bedroom suite made from a red cedar and also a silky oak dining room suite consisting of an oval table, six chairs and a sideboard with high back and an oval mirror. These were manufactured for Mum and Dad from trees harvested from the farm.

Soon after I returned from boarding school I decided that we should have home-produced electricity. It was reasonably common for farms to have a set of car type batteries connected in series to produce 32 volts. These were charged by generator and petrol engine. We installed such a system and had the house wired to a standard that would cope with mains power if it ever came our way. What a difference that made to life after work. We had light in every room at the flick of a switch and could actually read in bed.

### Mains Electric Power

In 1952 we were visited by a representative of the City Electric Light Company who enquired about our reaction to possible connection of mains power and to what extent we would use it in the home and on the farm generally. Along with almost everyone else in the district we were over the moon about the prospect. The survey showed that there was more than sufficient demand to justify an extension of the lines from Winn's sawmill to Kobble Creek and southwards to link up with Samford. Work proceeded quickly with men digging the holes 4 feet 91.2 Metres) deep by hand and other crews erecting the poles and hanging the wires. Since the lines traversed mostly private land we received a one-off payment of £1 ($2) for every pole on our land.

On Christmas Eve 1952 our dreams came true when the switch was thrown and we were connected. In readiness for the event we had purchased such luxuries as an electric jug for making tea and heating water when the wood stove was not burning; an electric toaster to replace holding slices of bread impaled on a toasting fork over the burning embers of the stove; and a Sunbeam Mixmaster to replace the laboriously operated cake whisk. With an electric refrigerator and the Sunbeam we could even make ice-cream. Dad and Mum were reluctant to part with their faithful wood stove for some years. It was so nice to sit around on winter nights. Instead they bought an electric hot plate to harness the convenience of the new wonder power that had at last arrived in our part of the bush. Then came the Sunbeam frying pan and a radio that did not rely on batteries.

My aunts conducted the Samsonvale telephone exchange in the old homestead about 110 yards ( 100 metres) from our house and for many years my father felt that we did not need a phone in our house. We could walk across the paddock if we wanted to make a call. Incoming messages would be taken by my aunts and relayed to us. A "cooee" from an aunt meant that we should walk across and get the message. By the time I left school the exchange had been passed to Max Hedge and we had our own phone installed. To make a call we would turn a handle that would drop open our numbered shutter on the control panel at the post office exchange and ring a bell to signal an incoming call. The postal service and the telephone service were both run the by the Postmaster-General's Department at that time. Max or one of his family would answer the bell that signalled our call and they would initiate the connection to a local subscriber or to some distant exchange, which would make the final connection by hand. If the trunk lines were busy we would have to wait for a call back when a connection became possible.

Owning a phone in the house was another big step into the brave new world that seemed to gather so much speed in the post-war years. Truly the 1950s were a turning point for us in the great burgeoning of economic and scientific progress that followed quickly upon the difficult years of the Depression and the rationed years of the WW11.

Who could have imagined that in our lifetime, phones would be carried in our pocket and would not only convey phone calls wherever we go, but would also carry a real time picture of the caller. Could we imagine that we could search the world for information on any subject via something called "the net" using that hand held wireless device.

# Chapter 7.

## Social Life

A wise old saying claims that "all work and no play makes Jack a dull boy". If you lived in Samsonvale in its early days there was no excuse for Jack to be dull. There was always opportunity to leave behind toil on the farm or in the kitchen and mix with neighbours and friends in some social activity. My father has described some of these early activities in his history of Samsonvale. As the third generation of a Samsonvale selector I would like to describe the situation in my time from the 1950s to 1973.

On returning from boarding school I certainly felt the lack of company of people my own age. There was already in existence a branch of the Presbyterian Fellowship Association loosely attached to the local church. It met fortnightly in the hall on a weeknight. While the constitution of the PFA described it as a youth organisation, attendance at Samsonvale usually included several parents who would drive their youngsters to the meetings. Many of those who gathered on weeknights had only tenuous connections with the local church, which met each Sunday. Most knew each other very well. For the most part we had all gone to Mt Samson Primary School. Some had proceeded directly to work with parents on the farm after the Scholarship Exams at Grade Seven. Others of us had been to various secondary schools and were back to the home farm to start another phase of life.

The program would commence with a devotional period in which choruses would be sung and a leader would deliver a Bible reading and a sermon. Then would follow a range of boisterous games and a concluding supper. The leader was officially the Presbyterian minister of the time who would live in Dayboro. However, these men were usually student ministers and would normally be at the Theological Hall in Brisbane at midweek. Noel Hedge, who was a lay preacher and student of scripture, acted as leader of the group for about 15 years. Membership would range in number from 15 to 30 people.

There was no doubt that the games segment of the program was the highlight and main attraction for attendees. Everyone enjoys a romp and some friendly competition as a change from work and these games were played with immense gusto. People living a mile (1.6 km) away would comment that they could hear the shrieks of joy and laughter originating in the hall on a quiet night. Usually there would be two teams picked in turn by mutually agreed captains; the teams would include males and females of various ages, but mostly in the teens or 20s years. There is no doubt that the meetings provided a place for boy/girl relationships to develop. They simply threw people together in a fun atmosphere where there were no social obligations or expectations arising from being there.

By far the most popular game was Duster Hockey. Having picked two teams and numbered off, they would line up at each end of the dance floor of the hall and an umpire would call a number. The corresponding players from each team would race to the other end of the hall, grab a 2 foot (60cm) length of broomstick and return to the middle where an old rag would represent the "ball". Unimaginable twists, turns and gymnastics would follow as players tried to put the rag into a box at their team's end.

There would be team games such as passing a ball using only feet while team members sat side-by-side in opposing lines; relay races where "runners" were required to step only on two pieces of cardboard, that would be moved as quickly as possible by another team member; and relay races where the runner would be required to keep a balloon in the air with a stick as they proceeded from one end of the hall to the other.

Another popular game was called "winks". In this, girls would sit in two rows facing each other and a boy would stand behind each girl with his hands behind his back. One boy would have no partner and he would try to steal the girl from one of the boys by winking at her. The girl would try to leave her seat quickly and her boy was allowed to try to stop her by releasing his hands from behind his back and grasping his girl by the shoulders. This seems a simple thing to do successfully, but it requires concentration and speed of action and escapes are often successful, especially if the lonesome boy winks at several girls in quick succession. After a time the roles would be changed and the girls would do the winking.

No function would be complete unless tea was brewed and home-made cakes were consumed over lively conversation and swapping of news. Looking back from the busy and complicated times of the 21st century, life seemed to be much simpler and the things that gave us pleasure seem to have been of our own making and inexpensive.

## *Junior Farmers*

After boarding school several school pals would exchange an occasional letter to tell of their post-school activities. One of my friends told in his letter of having joined a group called the Junior Farmers Organisation. It sounded as though that might be an interesting group to get involved with. It seems that the organisation had been established as a form of continuing education for those many young country kids who were not able to go on to secondary studies for various reasons. For a start very few country kids lived within convenient travel distance of a State secondary school. There simply were not many high schools in country areas and road transport was not as well developed as it is today. Some were fortunate if their parents could send them to the State's only Agricultural College at Gatton. For others their only course was to go to the city and board either with relatives or friends or at a private boarding school.

For more than 20 years various citizens had been advocating some form of post-school agricultural education initiative for both boys and girls. As a ground-breaking initiative the RNA had introduced Show Camps for selected youths over the age of 12. A committee appointed by the Government in 1945 noted that NSW had some time previously established an organisation based on a club system in that State. At that time there were 370 clubs in NSW with up to 13,000 members. It pointed to similar organisations in Victoria Europe and USA.

In 1947 the State Government decided to follow these initiatives and appointed a Mr Thomas Lewis Williams to bring a similar organisation into being in Queensland. He had been a teacher in early life and an agricultural journalist before entering the Queensland Parliament, where he had served for years as Minister for Agriculture and Minister for Public Instruction (Education). As a consequence of internal ALP rivalries he had lost endorsement for his seat and was looking for a challenging occupation. He had been involved in discussions on the need for a post-scholarship movement in rural areas for many years and had been involved with the RNA camps.

The first club was formed near Gatton and in the following two years about 30 clubs had been formed. Tom Williams had an office and a secretary in the top floor of the Treasury Building which has since become the Treasury Casino. However he spent most of his time travelling by train around the state, forming clubs and revisiting those already formed. He carried a portable typewriter as he travelled by train on his First Class, ex-politicians Gold Pass and typed most of his correspondence with the machine balanced on his knees.

He would be met at various railway stations by club members who would provide accommodation in their homes and take him to the night-time meetings. Having encouraged and taught each small group Tom would catch the next train to the next centre. On the way he would be back on his typewriter recording any new ideas for activities or news of some interest to other clubs. These would form the basis of his monthly newsletter to all members.

It was expected that a club would rally about 12 or more members who paid a five shillings (50 cents) membership fee. Each club was required to elect an adult Advisory Committee, which would assist members to learn meeting procedure, program planning, organising guest speakers, field days, record-keeping, social activities and keep activities on an even keel.

These committees were comprised mainly of parents who, in the days when very few teenagers owned cars, would transport members to the meeting place anyhow. If there were professionals such as school teachers, bank managers or agricultural extension officers available, these were often invited to be on the Advisory Committee. Many clubs could be thankful for the unstinting assistance that such people gave in helping country youth to bridge the gap between school and young adulthood.

It was no time before adjacent clubs would get together for debates, field days, educational tours, sports days, ploughing competitions, cooking and dressmaking demonstrations, picnics and dances. In all these events youth would be widening their horizons and experiencing valuable social interaction to prepare them for adult life.

### Samsonvale Junior Farmers Club

In mid 1950 I contacted Tom Williams and told him that Samsonvale had enough eligible young people to form a club. In no time he arrived on the Dayboro railmotor by arrangement and stayed with my father and mother overnight. We gathered about 15 members and proceeded with the formation of the Samsonvale club and the election of an Advisory Committee.

*Tom Williams forms the Samsonvale JFC*

As I recall the night, I became the Club Leader, Lyle Bennett accepted duty as Secretary and Raymond Bennett became Treasurer. Others who joined in the first year or so included Marlene and Ian Clay, Herb, Alan and Ron Carr, Doug and Bernice Pinsker, Bruce Southwell, Jack and Bob Greensill, Val and Neville Clark, Les Kunde, Joyce and Fay Schmidt, Jack McLellan, John Barke, Brian and Shirley Magher, David and Peter Schacher, Mary Burley, June Hedge, John Bradshaw, Raymond Bennett, Barbara and Errol Herron, Phil and Stan Taylor, Ian Johnson, Wally Henderson, Alan O'Hara, Frank Williams and no doubt there are several I have forgotten.

This group formed the first circle of friends that continued for the next eight years as we entered exhibits of produce in the Pine Rivers Show; held dances; listened to a range of guest speakers from fertiliser companies, machinery agents, banks, accountants, the Department of Agriculture and specialists from many fields; held movie evenings and organised fun debates. In these days I am amazed that so many high-profile people were voluntarily willing to give up their nights or weekends to travel over dusty, corrugated roads to Samsonvale in order to support club activities. As might be expected the Advisory Committee, consisting mainly of parents, put themselves out for what they saw as a worthwhile cause involving their children. They often commented that there was never such a worthwhile organisation when they were youths and naturally backed it and in many subtle ways guided and safeguarded its progress.

When Samsonvale Club came into existence there were already clubs at Wamuran (where names such as John Grigg, Roger Murant and Adrian Scott come to mind) and Kallangur (where names such as Ron and Sid Bray, Bernie Hetterick, Charley Dohle, Fred, Norm and Joe Kruger and the Morris brothers are remembered).

*Samsonvale Junior Farmers Club 1954*

It was not too long before a club started in Strathpine and we all added Lorraine, Kevin and Nola Turtin, Joe and Betty Peterson, Barry and Vera Stanton, the Turnbull sisters, along with others, to our circle of friends. Clubs followed at Ferny Grove, Redcliffe, Caboolture and Elimbah.

Within a few years the organisation had grown to the extent that extra staff organisers were added. Tom Williams retired and John Park replaced him to continue expansion to about 2000 members and perhaps 160 clubs. An annual State Conference was initiated to which clubs sent delegates, who debated development plans and voted in a Constitution in true democratic fashion. Eight zones were established for more convenient organisation of activities. We formed part of the South East Zone and added to our already large circle of friends with clubs at Redland Bay, Russell Island, Indooroopilly, Beaudesert and Woodford. As time passed clubs were established in Dayboro, Brisbane (which catered largely for country members who came to the city to find work), Kilcoy and Tamrookum.

I was never at a loss for somewhere to go or some Junior Farmer Club duty to complete. The Australian Broadcasting Commission Rural Department, which filled many hours each week with special programs for farmers and rural people, in 1952 devised a radio program entitled "The Junior Farmers Leadership Competition". It took the form of a radio quiz and interview of eleven finalists. I cannot recall how one made it into the team but I found myself among the select group and went on air one evening to a very large, pre-television-era audience. I was surprised

*The ABC Rural Radio Leadership contestants 1952*

to find that I had been placed second and that my old Brisbane Boys' College friend, John Wedemeyer, had won. John later went to Sydney where he won the Australian competition and then to New Zealand to contest and win the Australasian prize.

These days I wonder at the amount of goodwill, attention and opportunity that was directed to country youths through the Junior Farmer or the Rural Youth organisation as it was later named. That was a time when the whole nation had a much higher regard for its farmers and the people who produced food and fibre for their city cousins and for export income for the nation. It was a time when so many city dwellers could claim that they were born and grew up in the country, or they had relatives who were from or on the land. Many knew themselves to be part of the great population movement that was known at the time as "the drift to the city". They had a much better appreciation of the relatively harsh situation of farmers and approved of government efforts to bring in improvements to the rural situation.

### Some Notable Honours

As consolation prize in the radio contest I was awarded a free trip to the Adelaide Show camp where I mixed with Junior Farmers from other States and rural SA. The long trip on my own by train and plane at age 20 years was a very great stimulating experience for a boy from the farm at little Samsonvale.

There were more honours to come for me in Junior Farmers. Tom Williams had been working on the idea of introducing international travel and in 1953 it was announced that an invitation had been received from the Young Farmers Club organisation in Great Britain to join in an international farm youth exchange program. As a first step one member would be selected from each Australian State to travel to England by ship to be guests of the Young Farmers Club organisation in England and Wales. They would be away for a period of four months plus the five weeks cruise time each way. All was to be free apart from personal expenses.

Initial entry was by essay competition. From these a small panel of finalists was to be chosen and the final winner selected by interview with a panel of three judges. I wrote an entry essay and then decided not to post it to HQ due to my mother's illness at that time and the need for her and Dad to be away from the farm frequently. The local postmaster, Max Hedge, phoned me on the last day for entry and asked if I had sent the letter because he had not noticed it pass over his counter. When I told him that I had decided to pull out he began urging me to reconsider. He offered to personally deliver the letter to a city post box in order that the letter could arrive on time. I relented and gave him my essay. Surprise and dismay! I was included in the finalists. At the interview on 28th February 1953 I was amazed to be declared the winner! On 28th March, only weeks after my 21st birthday, I was on my way to Sydney by train to join the SS *Otranto* for its cruise to London.

Preparations were hectic and in many ways I was poorly prepared, in the short time available, for the adventure of my life. I met the NSW exchangee in Sydney and we embarked for the cruise to Melbourne where we were joined by members from Victoria and Tasmania. In Adelaide we were joined by the only girl in the group and the team was completed when we called at Fremantle. Our journey passed close to the Cocos Islands on the way to Colombo where we had a day ashore exploring our first-ever foreign country. Then followed an evening in Aden where we were exposed to the Arab culture and real bargaining in its many shops. Onward through the dreadfully hot Red Sea to Suez where some of us took the opportunity to visit Cairo and the Pyramids while the ship was making its slow passage through the Suez Canal to Port Said and the point where we rejoined the ship. Thence we sailed to Naples, Marseille and Gibraltar to Tilbury Docks, London.

*Our view of the Coronation procession*

The journey took five weeks and for a young country dairy farmer it would be difficult to imagine a more stimulating experience. From the posh Russell Hotel in London's West End we were introduced to more of London's sights and the Young Farmers Clubs organisation of Great Britain under the kindly hand of their international secretary, Miss Barbara Tylden, who had supervised our various itineraries and travel arrangements for the next four months. In pairs we were soon on our way to the counties where we were guests of club members on various farms. The exchange concept was for us to work and learn within the farm family and

*Australian JFC Exchangees off to England 1953*

exchange information and culture. In reality we were star guests and spent much time visiting leading farms, factories, markets, shows, field days and Young Farmer Club events. At meetings with leading citizens such as the mayor or the local lord we were expected to make appropriate speeches. At club meetings we were asked to talk at length about Australia and our home farm scene.

It so happened that 1953 was the year of the Coronation of Queen Elizabeth II and we were caught up in the unimaginable excitement of that event, which came as a climactic release for the British people after the long, hard years of WWII and the painful post war recovery. Our group was given a comfortable balcony on the third floor of a building in Pall Mall from which to view the unforgettable parade that followed the Crowning Ceremony at Westminster Abbey. During the service we were given our first exposure to a wonder of the times - black and white television on a small roundish, 15 inch (38 cm) screen. How could we adequately describe all this other world experience to the folks back home?

During our visits to London we were involved in gatherings of young farmers from other Commonwealth countries and from several European Young Farmer organisations at a variety of conferences and events such as conducted tours of Westminster Houses of Parliament, Mansion House as guests of the Lord Mayor of London, a reception at which we shook hands and spoke to the Prime Minister of Malta and Viscountess Mountbatten, a visit to the farm of the Duke of Gloucester, met the Australian High Commissioner and were driven about London in his Daimler (registration plate AUST 1) seeing the sights in real style.

I stayed on eight farms during four months, making friendships that have lasted over 60 years through regular Christmas cards and letters. Friendships with other exchangees from several countries have also continued and in later life it has been a great pleasure through travel to revisit families in Great Britain and Canada. In turn some of my hosts or their children have visited my family in Australia.

At the end of the official itinerary our group was free to do some private touring. The member from Tasmania and I decided that it would be a good idea to buy pushbikes and tour through Europe. We took the "Flying Scotsman" train to Newcastle where a small passenger boat took us to Esbjerg in Denmark. From there we pedalled our way to Copenhagen to take in the sights before taking a ferry to Germany. At Lubeck we examined the grim "Iron Curtain" border between free West Germany and Communist East Germany. Making day-to-day decisions we followed a vague plan that took us to Holland and Belgium, staying at youth hostels each night and lapping up the scenery along the way. On our best day we covered 205km. In the evenings we mixed with young explorers from all manner of places and somehow we

*Working on an English farm*

managed with only the English language to exchange information and ideas. In hindsight the venture was somewhat audacious, but we were having the adventure of our lives. As the Alps loomed ahead we sold the bikes and took trains to Luxembourg, Switzerland, Austria and finally to Italy, where after 21 days on the road we met up with our ship, the RMS *Oronsay* in Naples for the four-week cruise home.

This segment was somewhat of an anti-climax after the excitement of the previous five months. The passenger list included a large proportion of British migrants on the £10 ($20) subsidised passage supported by our government at the time. These folk were naturally sad and anxious concerning their departure from home and the unknown future ahead of them. This resulted in a quite different mood on board compared to the spirited activity of the Aussies going to adventures in England and Europe on the forward journey.

I had taken £200 ($400) with me for spending on items outside our hosted tour. In those days credit cards had not been invented. The money was stored on a piece of paper called a "Letter of Credit", which was in effect a travelling ledger account that could be drawn on at certain banks in the countries we visited. We also carried travellers' cheques for expenses along the way. After six and a half months abroad I arrived back in Brisbane with two shillings (20c) in my pocket. I have often looked back in amazement at that kind of "living dangerously". But what a series of experiences this was for a 21year-old dairy farmer of the time.

Settling back to the routine of the farm after all that took quite some effort and our way of farming seemed somewhat unsophisticated after what I had seen in England, where mechanisation was years ahead of Australia due to government subsidies there. Labour seemed to be so much more plentiful there, prices for farm produce were much higher and the reliability of rainfall so much better. While there was not much from British agriculture that could be directly applied in the Queensland climate, there were many systems, methods and attitudes that might be adapted in time. One significant practice was artificial insemination of dairy cattle, of which I will write later.

The exchange trip came with a "cost" that I had not counted on. The State Director of Junior Farmers wished me to travel to a large number of clubs scattered throughout Queensland to talk about the experience and to show coloured slides taken during the trip. In all, by undertaking several trips away by train, I covered 55 clubs telling the story. This took me to many parts of the State that I had not seen before. As I was billeted with a large number of families along the way I came to know a large circle of friends and became known to a very large number of Junior Farmers and club advisors. It was a kind of fame that lasted for many years and led to opportunities and expectations that widened my horizons in public life.

The Junior Farmer Organisation continued to grow at a rapid rate and counted in excess of 2000 members in the 1950s. To cope with the numbers the organisation was divided into several zones and I became the inaugural Zone chairman for the south-east of the State. This involved considerable travel between clubs spread between Kilcoy,

Elimbah, Beaudesert, Indooroopilly and Redland Bay and Russell Island to foster well-rounded programs and to encourage inter-club activity. The Zone bravely undertook to enter a new competitive District Exhibit of produce at the RNA show in 1954, which was just half the size of the current RNA District display. As winners we learnt a lot about teamwork and showmanship under time pressures.

*A Junior Farmer field- day teaching tractor operation*

Once each year up to 200 members from across the State would converge on a campsite for a great event, the Annual State Conference. This gathering in true democratic style decided policy and instituted a series of competitions such as debating, needle-work, cooking and various farm practices. The event was a great mixing point for members and many new friendships and even marriages resulted.

The Samsonvale Club formed an important focus for local youth between the ages of 15 and 26 for eight years. Then an historic thing happened that marked the end of an era. Sons and often daughters would return to the farm after schooling and join their father and other siblings in the farm project. Farm produce prices, being fairly low, were usually insufficient to

*Our club on tour. Our "coach" a 2 ton truck.*

114

give all the family much more than pocket money. A few lads and lasses found that they could get comparatively "huge" wages in nearby Brisbane city. One chap became the owner of a beautiful new motor-cycle after a few months working in the milk factory where his dad sold his milk. It seemed that in a matter of less than a year most of the club had joined the "drift to the city" and this left too few people to run weeknight activities successfully. The Club folded in 1958.

### *The Coming of Television*

The following year television came to Brisbane. What a wonder that was. In the first few months of the new invention's use in Brisbane it was common for electrical stores to place a TV set in their front window where it would play until transmission closed about 11 pm. People without a set or those curious to learn what TV was all about would come out of their homes with chairs and stools and settle down on the footpath for a night's entertainment. It became quite a community thing and no doubt generated sales for the shop.

The first black and white receivers which look so archaic 50 years later, quickly became common in Samsonvale homes, where the signal from Mt Coot-tha was strong and mostly clear. People became almost addicted to this new form of entertainment and conversation when people met would invariably focus on the latest programs. However, there was a price to pay. Attendance at regular dances that formed such an important part of the social fabric of the district quickly waned and to a large extent the dances were abandoned. Before television a visit to a picture show involved a drive to a theatre at Kallangur, Dayboro, Strathpine or Chermside or to a drive-in at Aspley. Now there were four programs available at home, the movie picture theatre industry declined and in most places died with the coming of TV.

There had always been a healthy social structure in Samsonvale where folk gathered for company and recreation. This had taken the form of church, concerts, dances, rifle club, cricket, annual sports days, picnics, Masonic Lodge and occasional expeditions to climb Mount Samson or tour to the beach at Redcliffe. By the time I returned from boarding school tennis and dancing were the main distractions.

The two tennis courts that were built beside our old homestead were still in operation in spite of the shortages of the war years and I fell in with the regular Saturday afternoon activity. The events were largely under the leadership of my three maiden aunts who, being strong supporters of Protestant church beliefs of the time, would not consider sport on Sundays. Up to 25 people would gather at about 1 pm carrying a cake for afternoon tea. Many did not come to play but to have a good yarn with friends. As a school kid I would be allowed to have a go at using a racquet along with other kids on the second court when the adults were taking a rest or eating. As a school leaver I was able to participate fully along with my former school pals. We were not very talented players since we lacked any kind of coaching. We just followed others and had a go. The pleasure was probably no less than that enjoyed by experts. Occasionally we would arrange a competitive tournament with some similar group from another district. An organised competition worked throughout the Upper Pine Rivers districts on Sundays, but I was never part of this or a similar cricket competition.

Following the very wet year of 1950 when we measured 68 inches (1727mm) of rain at our farm, the skies turned blue and dry into a very severe drought. By the end of 1951 we were struggling to find feed for our cattle and many of us had to make special arrangements for even drinking water for stock. Tennis was abandoned for a greater priority. It seems that most of us fell into the bad habit of working all day on Saturday for some years after this. Tennis ceased at our place. Some years later regular tennis was revived at the new courts at the Mount Samson State Primary School, but the days never seemed to regain the sense of social outing that had existed when the game was played on Golds' courts.

### Dances

I have described the Samsonvale dances elsewhere, mainly from the viewpoint of a school lad in the 1940s. In the 1950s I was more involved in organising these. They were always run with some profit in mind, either for the Junior Farmers Club, The Dayboro Ambulance Centre or for the Samsonvale Public Hall Committee, which was responsible for maintenance and improvements to the building handed down to my generation by our elders. Organisation always required a meeting to choose a date, a band, general program and ensure a good supper. My father as one of the trustees was Chairman for many years and Mr Ernie Bennett kept hand-written minutes in his distinctive, flourishing copperplate style for half his lifetime. He faithfully held post at the door collecting admission fees at dances. In doing so he gained a wonderful collection of news from his customers, who would come by car or truck from centres all over the shire and beyond.

Choice of a popular band (usually three musicians) was most important because folk were very particular about rhythm, tempo, selection of tunes and short breaks between dances. A Mr Tom Gilvear served as MC for decades and was followed by one of the Carr brothers, who took their dancing more seriously than most.

As for the patrons, they were simply out for company. In some cases they were out for particular company, namely a special boy or girl of their dreams. Many a lad would stand at the door or the back of the hall trying to pluck up courage to ask his special heart-throb for a dance. Likewise many a girl sat, hoping intensely, that a particular bloke would ask her to dance with him. The last dance of the night was always a medley of three dances and was of special significance because it meant that the bloke, following the courtesy of the time, would walk his partner back to her seat. With a bit of luck he might walk her to her car and even score a goodnight peck or more serious smooch. That is how romances and enduring marriages began in those days.

Of course all these activities were under the eagle eyes of several elders, because dances were an all-age gathering, even if many people did not dance. It could be tricky for young lovers at dances.

The fabric of a district involved several other activities involving evening meetings. In the early 1950s Carrie Gold led a move to establish a branch of the Queensland Country Women's Association in Samsonvale. The organisation, which fosters the special needs of country women, had been in existence since 1922. Samsonvale women had been very active through the Red Cross during two world wars. With the cessation of war and the closure of the local branch there was a void which could be met by the CWA as it fostered crafts, cooking,

117

welfare issues and companionship.

### *Committees*

For men of the district dairy farming was of foremost interest. Soon after the gazettal of the Queensland Dairymen's Organisation as the long-awaited official representative body for the 24,000 dairy farmers in the State, a branch was formed in Samsonvale. Almost monthly farmers would gather at the hall to discuss problems that might be addressed by the State Council or debated at the annual East Moreton District Conference of the QDO. I recall my father chairing meetings for a time and later I became a delegate to conferences, putting the case for some reform or other with vigour and perhaps more force than was appropriate. Our pleas would be for such things as better prices, lower taxes, increased milk quotas, improved government services and so on. The local branch would also put pressure on the shire council to improve roads. It would handle delicate discussions regarding milk cartage fees to be negotiated with carriers, who were really our friends, since they were the people who brought us mail, bread, meat and newspapers as a daily service.

Little did I think during the time that I attended meetings that one day I would become a District Councillor through elections or that this would extend to joint committees with officers of the Department of Primary Industries concerning farm advisory services and distribution of dairy pasture subsidies in the late 1960s. It would have seemed even more unlikely that one day I would be assistant to the State Secretary of the organisation following resumption of our farm for the North Pine Dam in 1973.

Schools have a special place in country communities. Before the fall in population of rural areas and centralisation of education centres there were numerous State primary schools throughout Queensland. Mostly these were one or two-teacher posts. While the department provided buildings and teachers there were always less essential items missing from the establishment. To fill these needs Parents' and Citizens' committees were very common. They worked with the teachers to solve problems as they might arise and raised funds to supply extras such as sporting equipment, radios for school broadcasts, radiograms for music instruction or marching, movie projectors, garden equipment and the most important "break-up" picnic.

I recall that my father was chairman of the Mount Samson P & C most of the time that I was at school. A generation later, as my children approached school age, I was pressured to become Chairman for a period of about eight years. Here was another regular meeting and more reason to be on the telephone, steering committee affairs along.

At one stage in the 1950s some newcomers to the district convinced the old-timers that the area needed a Progress Association to thrust the community into a new modern era. A group was formed and proceeded to put increased pressure on the shire council for road improvements such as more regular grading and even a start to extending the bitumen seal from beyond the old US Army camp at Bullockie's Rest, towards Samsonvale. There were also moves to make the area more attractive to tourists on their Sunday drives. Progress was disappointing and the initiative folded after a few years. In some respects that was a blessing. There was one less meeting to attend after a day's work.

### Church

The Presbyterian Church in the Upper North Pine was based in Dayboro where there was a minister's residence. Congregations meeting in churches at Samsonvale and Closeburn were serviced from Dayboro as well as groups meeting in the Mount Pleasant Hall and sometimes in private houses. Church committees in each centre raised funds for the ministry and attended to church maintenance. I had been home from school only two months when my dad told me there was to be a local committee meeting and that I had better come along. Within a few minutes of starting I was told that I was the best educated person present and that I had better take the minute book and be Secretary. The job lasted in various forms for the next 23 years. Quite a few minute books were filled concerning building maintenance, the parsons' motorcars and fundraising in that time. There was a permanent shortage of money in spite of fetes and appeals.

For those interested in church history it is worth noting a

revolution in relation to church finances in Australia, which was ushered in by the appearance of the Wells Organisation from USA. This commercially based group specialised in revival of church finances by unashamedly challenging people to assess their fair responsibility to maintain a healthy and active church in their area. Their method was to list everyone connected with the church in any way and to challenge them to consider their responsibility to their God and the local church as His agent for good in the district and to give generously as instructed in the Holy Bible.

The results were amazing for those who had been struggling to make ends meet for so long. In many centres the Wells method made it possible to replace dilapidated churches, provide halls for community use, provide counselling and other social services unimaginable in former times. Fifty years later the benefits of frankness in highlighting needs and presenting challenges lingers on in Australian churches as they undertake a tremendous and increasing load of social work and service in the community.

As well as the Management Committees, which dealt with finance and property matters the Presbyterian Church had a committee called the Kirk Session consisting of several elders. These were people of good reputation elected by the congregation to oversee the more spiritual matters of the parish, such as admissions of new members, keeping of rolls, pastoral care, Sunday schools and youth groups, organisation of Holy Communion and matters relating to ministers' activities. When I was about 30 I was asked to accept duty as an elder and was duly elected to office. Thus began another duty involving meetings, minute books, phone calls and visits to parish members. It also led to becoming a Sunday school teacher at Samsonvale and Dayboro for almost 20 years. Combined with activity within the other committees in the district these duties made me truly a member of the fabric of the district in a way that I suspect has been lost in later years as the North Pine Dam encroached on so many farms, others were subdivided and the population of new residents held a more city-based outlook.

## Politics

Being a farmer naturally led me to be active in the political party that represented the special interests of people on the land. This was the Country Party at the time. Our State Member of Parliament was David Nicholson, representing the State electorate of Murrumba (the name derived from the name of Tom Petrie's homestead on the hill at Petrie where the convent now stands). Our Federal Member was Charles Adermann. Both were later knighted. Dave Nicholson was Speaker of State Parliament for many years and Charlie Adermann served farmers well as Minister for Agriculture for several terms. I joined the party just before I turned 21, the then legal age for inclusion on the voters' roll. There was a branch at Samford, which held meetings about four or five times per year. Our politicians would attend quite frequently as they put themselves out to be available to the grass roots of the party. Members felt that they were being kept in the picture and that their aspirations and needs were being attended to.

Occasionally it would be my duty and privilege to represent the branch at annual State Conferences. In the late 1950s the party formed the Young Country Party and I attended meetings at Kallangur along with several people that I knew from Junior Farmer activities.

One of my duties on election days was to ensure that there was a supply of "how to vote" cards freely available at Samsonvale and Mt Samson booths. That was originally a simple task. I would take a stool or box to the booth, place a fistful of cards on the box next to the entrance and place a rock on the pile to resist the wind. Voters helped themselves. There were no competing cards to worry about in the farming district.

About 1965 I did the usual early morning run with cards before opening time, to be confronted with helpers for the opposing candidates, personally handing out cards with a smile. What new development was this that had come to our patch? Did I have to stand there all day personally handing cards to voters like these strangers were doing? I was still dressed in my cow milking clothes complete with gum-boots and had not had breakfast at this hour. I had to race home, take a few bites, shower and dress respectably and return to the booth for an all-day session of unprecedented electioneering.

At the end of the day I lined up with two other scrutineers to see about 125 votes counted. There was one Liberal vote. It was obviously the vote of the scrutineer present. There were about 7 Labor votes and the remaining 117 were for Dave Nicholson. Imagine my embarrassment when one of the scrutineers (a local farmer) said to the other when finalising the Labor total, "Now, who would they be?" He then proceeded to name those among our community that might have voted for other than the Country Party.

When Sir David Nicholson retired he sent nomination forms to a circle of party members who he encouraged to enter the selection process for his successor. It was an honour to receive his encouragement to" have a go". In hindsight it was probably fortunate that I was unsuccessful because the life of a conscientious politician is not at all attractive.

Looking back over 60 years of membership of the party, which changed its name to National Party in the 1970s, there seem to have been so many days taken up with handing out how to vote cards, raising campaign funds, attending branch, electorate, divisional and State Conference meetings, all in the cause of having a say in the governance of the State and nation along the lines of the conservative philosophy. It has always seemed to me that if we value our freedom and democracy we should be active in its functioning, even at some personal cost. When this kind of interest and activity fails so will our valued way of life deteriorate. It was with some surprise that I was presented with Life Membership of the National Party at State Conference in 2005. Upon amalgamation of the national and Liberal Parties that honour was transferred to the LNP.

### Historical Society

In 1969 Shire Chairman, John Bray, convened a meeting of interested residents to consider celebrating the 200th anniversary of Captain Cook's voyage of discovery that passed nearby as he sailed northwards along the east coast of Australia. The Government encouraged a general movement along the coast to mark one of our national milestones. The meeting was held in the old hall that housed the Pine Shire offices of the day and having been invited I joined a variety of citizens to consider a suitable tribute to the occasion which was to occur in 1970. We considered such things as commemorative plaques, tree plantings and street namings without much fervour until I mentioned something that had been on my mind for some time. It had seemed to me since my Junior Farmer trip to England that we as Australians had not recorded our history nearly enough. I asserted that such preservation of memories, achievements and artifacts of the 200 years since Cook passed by would be best achieved by establishment of a Historical Society for the Pine Shire. This suggestion received enthusiastic support and became an important part of the celebrations.

Some old notes from the time suggest that there might have been a small group of Strathpine people already active in collecting information and recollections of old residents under the leadership of Mr Norm Reilly, the head teacher of the Strathpine State Primary School for many years.

If being a good citizen means being involved in community groups and going to their meetings I feel that I might have qualified. To some extent my family suffered by the man of the house being out so many nights when he might have been assisting with homework and other family activities.

Since I had introduced the idea it seems that I was voted in as President of the new group, which gathered monthly. Mrs. Nola McCullagh became secretary and Miss Marg Reynolds became Treasurer. Some members that are still remembered were Councillor John Scott, Jack Mitchell and Dr Elizabeth Marks from Samford; Tom Gleeson, my wife Glenda from Samsonvale; John Bray, Rolo Petrie, Paul Jackson, Merv Ewart, Norm Reilly and Carol Parkinson from Petrie.

We met monthly in the Petrie School of Arts to plan a way forward. Progress was slow at first. It seemed that we needed a headquarters and one suggestion was to gain a shed on the farm that the Shire Council was acquiring from the Hyde Brothers at Sidling Creek. This transaction was meeting with some legal difficulties and the uncertain future of the deal prevented this from happening at that time. The construction of the North Pine Dam had begun, farmers were moving out and buildings and items of historical value were becoming available and needed a storage place. John Bray pointed out that there was an old slab shed behind his house on neighbouring land that could be a temporary storage. The land had recently been bought by Stirling Quarries for gravel extraction and the manager gave verbal approval for the use of this shed.

I borrowed a truck from Winn Brothers' sawmill and delivered two loads consisting of a German wagon and tip dray, along with much old farm and domestic equipment from the farms of Dot Mason and the Golds just prior to our vacating. Other items were probably added to the collection. It came as a severe disappointment to learn many years later that a new manager for the quarry group, not knowing about the original storage agreement, assumed that the stuff was left over from the farm acquisition and belonged to the company. He sold it to a collector or dealer in Sydney! Not quite the result that the history group had intended.

As Steve Kriesch vacated his farm at Samsonvale it was recognised that there was a small shed of historical note that might be simply demolished in preparation for dam flooding. The Society arranged for this to be dismantled and re-erected on a council reserve near the Petrie Court House. The building was not really secure at that site and was never used as a storage place or a museum. Many years later, when the Hyde farm came into the full possession of the council, this shed was moved to the farm, where it stands today. I understand that while the council had gained title to the farm in the 1970s it had been agreed that the Hyde brothers would reside on the farm and have agricultural use of the property while they lived. The council had planned to use their farm as a source of gravel along the river flats. It appears that this extraction never occurred.

Meanwhile, our family had to move out and we became resident in the western suburb of Kenmore to start a new life. We had no easy way of continuing our contact with the Pine Rivers Historical Society. It continued for many years under the leadership of Paul Jackson, one of the family of Gordon Jackson, who as proprietor of a small village garage in Petrie, grew the business into the thriving North Pine

Motors. Merv Ewart was foremost in research and accumulation of knowledge of the shire's history. He had a remarkable grasp of the facts and events of our past. We can thank him in particular for much of the basic information now carefully preserved and catalogued within the Historical section of the Pine Rivers Library. He worked closely with Nicola Geeson, the first specialist historian employed by the library, as well as with her successor Leith Barter.

It is gratifying that the early intention taken in 1969 to preserve our history has grown into the comprehensive resource that is represented today by the historical section of the library at Strathpine, the expansive historical village on Hyde Farm and, more recently, the Historical Museum on that site. Continued featuring of past achievements of early settlers through special days and through annual pioneer family feature displays at the museum are beyond the dreams of those few of us who gathered in the shire hall many years ago. For all this achievement the community can be proud of the long sighted councillors who have backed this enterprise with rate payer funds.

# Chapter 8.

## The Changing Farm Scene

I was the third generation to farm the block selected by Henry Gold at Samsonvale at the age of 24. He subsequently added blocks that became available and spent his life fencing, ring barking, stumping and cultivating his selections. My father, along with his brother, spent his life further developing the block through subdivision of paddocks, treating forest regrowth, digging out stumps and roots to expand areas that were possible to plough and crop. He also improved his farm buildings. In turn, my trust was to take this development process further.

There was a phenomenon recognised among bankers and businessmen called "Third Generation Syndrome", which referred to an often observed happening wherein the third generation rested on the hard toil of preceding generations. They were often lazy, lacked vision or got expensive, high-flying ideas that wasted all the achievements of their pioneering forebears, even to the point of bankruptcy. I was aware of this situation and determined from an early point to avoid the shameful possibility.

From the time that I returned to the farm my father included me as a full partner in the business. He gave me the responsibility of handling the bookkeeping, but gave plenty of advice and examples of how to be successful and how one could fail. He was very conservative where new ideas were concerned, especially where spending money was concerned. It has to be remembered that he had lived through the Depression years of the 1930s and appreciated that hard work and thrift had pulled most farmers through those desperate times. He, no doubt, had inherited similar teaching from his father arising from his lifetime experiences.

The years following WWII saw rapid change in all aspects of life across the world. The war caused a great leap forward in research, technology and scientific knowledge and some of this culture found its way into agriculture. I was to see significant advances in the way our farm was equipped and run during the next 25 years.

### *Replacing the Draught Horse*

I began my farming life using horses. We had three draught horses to pull the spring cart or German wagon or home-made slide. These would be employed to transport fodder such as sorghum, corn, field peas and sugarcane from the cultivations to the barn, where they would be made into finely chopped cow feed by a petrol-powered engine and chaff cutter.

This feed would be enriched by adding a few pounds of ground grain and protein-rich concentrate such as meat and bone meal, coconut meal, cotton-seed meal or a proprietary mixture. These came from Brisbane by train in bags weighing 112 pounds (one "hundredweight" or 50 kilograms). Transport of these bags from rail station to the barn was done by horse-drawn vehicle and was a time-consuming job.

Every Monday evening the goods train from Dayboro to Brisbane carried pigs and calves for sale at Cannon Hill Auction Yards on Tuesday. Harry Kriesch acted as receiving agent for the auctioneers and farmers would congregate at the railway trucking yards in a variety of horse-drawn carts. This was a time-consuming journey involving catching and harnessing the horses and travelling at about 5 or 8 kilometres per hour to the station. In those more laid-back times it would be standard practice to stop on the road to talk to every fellow traveller encountered on the journey.

Enter the motorised age. More and more farmers were obtaining motor utilities consisting of modified open tourer cars. The farm utility or "ute" was coming into popular use. As farmers gradually increased their wealth following the Depression they were able to make this time-saving investment.

Some even bought new factory-made utilities that came on the market during the 1930s and were further advanced in design during and after WWII. We followed the trend by converting a 1932 Morris Cowley open tourer that had been in the family since new. Following the pattern of others I removed the rear bodywork consisting of the rear seat and doors and replaced them with a timber tray and sides. Now the task of carting milk to the road-side pickup point, transporting cow feed, market pigs and calves and even shopping expeditions involving bulky goods could be done with so much less effort and a great saving in time. However, something was lost when the motorised versions took to the road and proceeded to destinations with all possible speed. There seemed to be no time to suspend progress for a yarn and exchange of news as in the days of the horse.

As time progressed this new motorised dray served to carry a surprising variety of cargo and served our family as a second set of wheels, including social outings when required. It was eventually sold for £25 ($50) to friends who got several more years out of the faithful old work wagon. I often feel sorry that I did not keep the old Morris for restoration and sentimentality. It had been de-registered and put on blocks during the war when petrol was rationed to four gallons (18 litres) per month. At about age nine or ten I would unlatch the door of the old shingle-roof garage and creep in to the driver's seat to do some imaginary driving. I would produce the engine noises and go through the gear shifts, braking and imaginary steering to my heart's content.

When I was 16 and the car was back on the road my Aunt Caroline took me for driving lessons around the paddock and farm tracks and eventually out onto the road on short trips to the shop or the railway station. There were no such items as Learner's Permits then. One day it was decided that I was ready to apply for a licence and I drove Aunt Carrie to the Dayboro Police Station. When we arrived and announced our business, Sergeant Doug Gregory asked my aunt if I could drive OK and if I had driven up from Samsonvale satisfactorily. On her positive assurance he sat down to his old typewriter and produced a licence forthwith. I think there was no charge and at that time it was issued for life.

We replaced the Morris with a more modern Vanguard utility bought at a government auction. This offered more comfort, room for our two children and security from the weather. Later yet we bought another second-hand Vanguard offering greater load capacity and modern technology. Looking back it seems that most of my equipment upgrade purchases were second-hand. This probably related back to my father's warning to shun debt. It was also also a recognition that often the greatest depreciation losses for machinery are incurred in the first few years and that well maintained machines are just as effective even though they are a few years old.

### The Tractor

Pre-war tractors were big, heavy, cumbersome beasts. They were not really suitable for the small paddocks and tight corners typical of land in coastal dairy districts. Their cost meant that most farms did not have the new invention that could replace horses. However, developments in England during and immediately after the war were bound to herald big changes. An agricultural engineer named Harry Ferguson had conceived a machine that would carry its implements rather than simply drag them behind as did most tractors of the time. He introduced a hydraulic pump

*The revolutionary Ferguson TE20 tractor*

within the gearbox that used its generous supply of oil to power a ram that was controlled by a small lever beside the driver's seat. The three-point linkage had arrived to revolutionise tractor design.

A variety of implements such as ploughs, harrows, tillers, mowers, post hole diggers, lifting hoists, soil scoops, grader blades and a transport platform called a "carry all" were hitched to the rear of the new concept tractor by a three-point linkage system. Every standardised implement fitted to two main lifting bars and a third upper linkage and were secured for work by small spring loaded lock pins in a matter of a few minutes. The driver could lift the implement and drive to the starting point of a job and by simply moving the control lever beside the seat, could lower the implement to the ground

129

and start ploughing a furrow or some other job. After a few yards the correct depth setting of the lever could be determined and a simple wing nut could be used to set the correct position in order to return to that setting for subsequent furrows. An inbuilt draft-control mechanism ensured that the plough maintained its set depth even though the soil conditions might change as the plough progressed. If the plough hooked on a buried root or stump the traction of the wheels was immediately diminished to a point where no damage would be caused to the plough.

A rotating shaft that became known as the PTO (power take off) was also powered by the engine and could drive equipment such as mowers, hay rakes and post-hole diggers. By bolting on an external gearbox and belt pulley such machinery as irrigation pumps, wood saws, grain grinders and chaff cutters could be powered with easily varied speeds and the 20 horsepower produced by the engine of Ferguson's TE20 tractor

This grey-coloured TE20 tractor was powered by a four cylinder engine that was used by the Standard Motor Company of England to power its Vanguard range of cars and was modified for agricultural work with a different carburettor and a large oil-bath air filter to cope with dust. One model ran on petrol; another was started on petrol and switched to power kerosene when it reached working temperature. Another less popular model had a diesel engine and being more expensive was not a big seller in those days.

This system was so far advanced from any machine that had been marketed before that it was immediately seen to be just what the doctor ordered for small farms. It was unbelievably more suitable and the time saving or additional work that could be achieved by one man with the little grey "Fergie" was a dream come true. Whenever there was an Agricultural Show or a Field Day the Ferguson and its ever-increasing range of implements would be the main centre of attention. Dealerships sprung up all over the country and it was said that 70,000 were sold in Queensland in a decade.

Gordon Jackson of North Pine Motors added the Ferguson dealership to his burgeoning Holden dealership at Petrie and the company flourished to become a household name in the Pine Shire. It is a lesson in business acumen and drive to recall how a typical country garage, with a staff of three, selling petrol and doing motor repairs on the corner of Gympie Road and Dayboro Road, could be grown to such a large and well respected family business. The invention of the little Ferguson tractor was a large factor in this growth.

I was never kindly disposed to working with farm horses. They seemed to be so slow and troublesome. I was mad keen to get one of these new inventions. My father, who had managed well enough with horses all his life, was not impressed, however. He said that tractors cost too much (about £650 [$1300] in the 1950s) and that we would always have our hands in our pockets buying fuel and paying for repairs. He said that he would be much more impressed when tractors gained the ability to breed their replacement generation like horses. It must also be recognised that there was a strong bond between most farmers and their faithful servant horses that was every bit as strong as their feelings for their dog or favourite cow. I did not seem to develop that bond as far as our horses were concerned and I do not think they liked me that much either. Perhaps I was too impatient or shouted unkind words at them when they were confused at what I wanted from them.

I kept up the tractor campaign for a few years, pointing out at every opportunity the feats of some tractor owner or the merits of some new attachment. I eventually wore Dad down and we bought a second-hand kerosene model, together with some implements, from Edgar Kopp at Closeburn for a rather attractive price of £325 ($650). A new era had begun and it seemed that we were able to achieve so much more with our time and labour. Work seemed more tolerable when done with a tractor. We had more energy to spare at the end of the day.

It was a feature of our district that friends and neighbours would borrow a variety of the attachable implements from each other. In this way no-one had to buy a large range of machinery to be used only infrequently. Sometimes it could take a while to track down one's own gear for it would be lent on to third and fourth parties. Alas, there would be times when the lent item would have to be repaired before it was fit to use again. However, generally speaking, this casual arrangement worked surprisingly well in a community where most people were very friendly and co-operative.

The three-point linkage patent quickly became standard on all makes of tractor and eventually the big US firm of Massey Harris merged with Ferguson to form the well- known Massey-Ferguson brand. In the matter of a few years the original was improved for small farms by raising horsepower from 20 to 35. The trend towards greater horsepower continued and diesel became the standard engine type due to its superior torque characteristics for farm work, extended engine life and for convenience and comparatively lower cost of the fuel type in those days. I graduated to a brand-new diesel model in 1964 and still own that tractor, in excellent condition, today.

Fuel for our cars and the tractor would be obtained from 44 gallon (200 litres) drums delivered by one of various agents servicing the district. It would be hand pumped from drum to fuel tank with a degree of effort.

North Pine Motors obtained a bulk fuel agency for Shell products and began another innovation that made farm management easier. We received a monthly delivery of bulk fuels and lubricants right to our farm storage tanks. As the bill would arrive by post Dad would remind me at times that he never paid a penny for horse fuel. They grazed their own fuel in the paddock. So while we were making technical progress it came with some cheque-book disadvantages.

### Stock Horses Overshadowed

Since our farm was over a mile from north to south a riding horse was frequently used to inspect fences, check on dry stock and muster various paddocks on days when cattle needed to be dipped for cattle-tick infestation. Once again the task of catching one of the riding horses could take some time, especially if the nag was not feeling like work. We would think twice about saddling up to travel to some small job if time was short. About 1960 I got an idea that a motorcycle would be much more convenient for jobs like collecting the mail, attending to shifting of irrigation pipes, inspecting and repairing fences and inspecting cattle in distant paddocks. By this time our land was relatively clear of stumps and logs and it appeared that a motor bike could save much time and inconvenience.

I commissioned my brother-in-law, who lived in the city, to scout out a suitable machine. He selected a 1949 BSA 250cc street machine that cost a whole £10 ($20) and I taught myself to ride it on a solo journey from Ashgrove to Samsonvale. I did not have a licence endorsement for a motor-bike at that stage, but felt that that detail was not very important. As I was passing the Mitchelton Police Station a wayward dog ran out in front of me and I discovered, as a raw learner, that I could not readily locate the brakes. There was instant panic. My heart was in my mouth and I still do not know how I missed that dog and a buster right in front of the police station and with no licence!

I spent the following weeks trying this new idea and found that it was a marvellous improvement as a means of getting about. I was doing about 70 miles (112 kms) a week on various farm jobs. I must admit that the street bike was a bit heavy for the job and with no springing on the rear wheel it was rather rough over some paddocks. After a few weeks there was no going back. A motor-bike was bound to be a part of the scene for ever, even if most of my neighbours and friends thought that I was slightly crazy.

As I was in the intensive learning phase there was considerable talk in our household about the new invention and my need to get a licence. My son, Paul, noted adult talk about my going out on the road to get the mail from the post office. Through my association with various committees the Dayboro police officer would call in for a yarn from time to time on his motor-cycle and side-car. About this time, he turned up and was greeted by four-year-old Paul at the garden gate. "Good-day, my father has got a motor-bike now. He hasn't got a licence yet and he has gone down the road to get the mail." Friendship overcame a sense of duty and nothing bad followed. I was issued with a licence the following week.

There followed three more street bikes. The 80cc Suzuki was a little small, but the kids quickly learnt to ride on it. The old BSA Bantam two-stroke was almost ideal, but not quite up to the rough work it was asked to perform. These were progressively sold on to other farmers in the district who were catching on to the idea that bikes and farming mixed well. Then came the Suzuki TC90, a bike specially made for farm work and I bought the first one to arrive at the agent's shop, sight unseen, apart from the coloured brochure. What a dream machine for my kind of work. With eight gears it could tail a mob of cattle at slow walking pace, but out on the road it could run messages at 70 or 80 kph. It was most economical to run and with its knobby tyres and deep-acting springs could climb steep hills and handle rough terrain with ease.

After five or six years of my pioneering the motor-bike in farming in our area and the arrival of a purpose-built farm bike, the craze seemed to catch on and within a year or so practically every farm had to have one.

### Water

At home and at the dairy the supply of water was confined to rain-water collected off roofs and stored in 1000 gallon (4546 litre) tanks. Obviously this limited source had to be used very sparingly and in extended dry seasons we would be reduced to digging a hole in the dry gravel bed of Kobble Creek and bailing the water, which seeped into the hole, into milk cans that would be carted to the house or dairy for daily use.

Since there seemed to be permanent water below the gravel bed it seemed reasonable to assume that a well could be dug down to that source, below the creek flat about 55 yards (50 metres) from the stream. With crowbar and shovel, windlass and bucket my cousin, John Barke, and I proved this theory to be true. The hole was lined with concrete well rings and an old second-hand windmill was set up to pump water up to the dairy through a galvanised pipeline. What a pleasure it was to have an endless supply for washing dairy equipment, cleaning floors, watering a vegetable garden and providing drinking water within the cattleyards and the pigsty. The innovation seems so simple today, but dairy farms in the 1950s were only emerging from the poverty-stricken conditions forced on them by the grim decade of the Depression and years of shortages during and after WWII.

Advances in technology brought a wide range of improved equipment onto the market at affordable prices and farmers grasped the new era with enthusiasm.

Polythene pipe was invented about this time and its cheapness enabled us to extend this supply of crystal-clear, soft water to our houses. Flower gardens were never so well cared for and now we could go a step further in living standards by installing a home septic system. Some would say that the replacement of the old dunny down the back with a WC was one of the most progressive and appreciated advances to enrich our lives.

Having proved this reliable water supply it was natural to move into irrigation of crops about 80 years after Henry Gold settled his selection. It had been disappointing to plant a crop on moist soil only to see it wither for want of rain weeks later. We needed to make hay for storage until lean times and lucerne was reckoned to be the best crop for this purpose. In warm weather with enough moisture we could mow every four weeks. However, if there was no rain this frequency would decrease greatly and the weight of yield would be much lower.

Irrigation pipes up until the early 1950s were typically made of galvanised pipe similar to plumbers' downpipe. They were connected into an extended line by cumbersome brass couplings that were prone to leaking if the pipes were not fairly precisely lined up, one with another. Moving a line after wetting a strip of crop was a rather laborious task. Then came lightweight aluminium tube and a variety of snap couplings that could tolerate misalignment over uneven ground. No doubt much of the aluminium came from melted down wartime aeroplanes. Lengths were up to 30 feet (9 metres), which was a better spacing for sprinklers. A new range of rotating sprinklers that could reach up to a radius of 90 feet (28 metres) really improved the whole irrigation scene. These pipes were quick and easy to shift as compared with the old type.

We dug a new well in a more suitable position for our main lucerne growing area and powered a centrifugal pump with a stationary kerosene engine. One more modernisation step was in place to improve our business. Irrigating throughout a drought is a demanding chore, but we were able to cope with such work due to the time and hard labour savings that flowed from mechanisation of many old practices.

Changes came thick and fast throughout the 50s and made life most challenging and interesting. The process involved reading everything relevant that one could set eyes on, listening to *ABC Country Hour*, attending Field Days and listening to guest speakers at Junior Farmer meetings, undertaking correspondence study courses and vowing to keep up with the times.

*Irrigating fodder crops*

### *Electricity*

In 1952 the City Electric Light Company visited every farm in the district to survey the possibility of extending mains supply from Winn's Sawmill, where it had terminated in 1939. Most of Samsonvale had no electricity supply. The result of the study was a very pleasant surprise. We were to get connected by the end of the year without minimum usage guarantee fees.

On Christmas Eve the inspector passed our wiring installation and switched on three-phase power. Now, one flick of a switch started the motor that drove the milking machine and chaff cutter. Hot water was constantly on hand for dairy cleaning. There were bright lights to assist work in the early morning or late afternoon. We could use power tools and even a welder. Flat batteries could be charged and electric fences more easily managed. In due course the irrigation pump was electrically driven and its run time controlled by an electric time switch. The windmill was retired in favour of an electric pump that did not falter when wind failed to blow.

Electricity enabled another significant advance in achieving improved milk quality by means of refrigeration. Once milk is extracted from the cow it is exposed to bacteria, which eventually cause milk to turn sour. In spite of thorough sterilisation of equipment and elimination of dust at the dairy, a few damaging bacteria will make contact with the milk, which happens to be a perfect medium for the massive multiplication of its kind. Fortunately, Mr. Pasteur discovered that these could be killed by raising the temperature to 37°C for a short time before cooling again. It became standard practice to treat all milk destined for human consumption by this pasteurisation process as soon as possible after production.

It is also fortunate that the rate of multiplication of these bacteria is spectacularly retarded if the milk can be cooled as soon as it leaves the cow and kept at a temperature just above freezing. With electricity we could conveniently run a specially designed commercial refrigerator. This consisted of a large insulated cabinet with a hinged lid on the top and lined with copper. Being watertight it was half filled with water, that was cooled to about two degrees C. When milking commenced the fresh milk would trickle down a series of tinned copper tubes through which the cold water was circulated by pump. This acted as a heat exchanger. The milk would be cooled to a relatively low temperature in seconds before dropping into standard 10-gallon (45 litre) milk cans.

The evening production after shock cooling would be immersed in the water in the cabinet overnight. Each full can weighed about 120 pounds (55kg) and we had a rope and pulley hoist to lift each can in and out, through the top-opening door of this storage. Now we had a means of eliminating the afternoon run of the milk transport truck with resultant savings in time and cost. The shock cooling of milk as soon as it was extracted improved quality

*The shock cooler and the old metal milk cans*

137

and keeping time in the consumer's fridge dramatically.

Towards the end of the 1960s this innovation took a further leap forward when bulk storage vats were introduced throughout dairying districts. With more powerful electric refrigeration units at work, milk was dropped directly into a large stainless-steel vat to come immediately into contact with the cold inner walls and floor of the vat. Here it would be kept at a closely controlled temperature, being stirred at regular intervals to prevent cream from rising to the surface. An insulated stainless-steel tanker would call right at the dairy door to pick up on alternate days. Here was more efficiency and improvement in quality, even though the capital outlay for the relatively expensive equipment and the cost of upgrading farm roads to all-weather standard for heavy trucks was a considerable hurdle for those contemplating conversion. For some years it was necessary to maintain the old can transport service to allow smaller producers to meet these outlays. At the customer end of the supply chain there had been remarkable improvement in the keeping life of milk thanks mainly to temperature control of the product. There was considerable Government effort to ensure good quality and for this purpose there was a Dairy Inspector who was charged with the task of monitoring milk quality. Laboratory tests could reveal the extent of contamination with undesirable bacteria and poor results would ensure a special visit to sort out the problem and warn careless suppliers to pull their socks up in the hygiene area. He would also visit regularly to ensure that cleanliness and building standards were ever maintained or improved.

While milking machines were driven by the new energy source the actual design of the milking machine changed little over the years. The basic principle remained the same and manufacturers invented a variety of gadgetry of increasing cost to do the same job. Stainless-steel construction became universal and rendered cleaning easier. Plastic replaced rubber in places and rubber improved in durability.

The significant change in the dairy was in the design of the milking area. Initially our forefathers constructed bails requiring the cow to walk in and be locked in place at the neck by a hinged batten. One leg would be drawn back with a leg rope and restrained from kicking by attachment to a post. When milking was complete the leg rope and head lock would be released and the cow would back out and move out, via a side gate, to the paddock to graze again.

A later version was called the "walk through bail". In this design the cow walked into a stall with a full-length wall on one side and a half-length wall on the milking side. She would be secured with a chain drawn round her rump and hooked to the edge of the half- wall. The leg rope was attached as in the old method and the milking machine attached from the half exposed-side. At the conclusion of milking the milker would release a door in front of the cow with a locking rod above his head and the cow would walk out forward, leaving a vacant space for the next cow.

All this involved the milker sitting on a stool to wash the udder and apply the teat cups of the milking machine. There was much sitting and standing (at least twice per cow for each of two milkings per day). Up to the time that I had to vacate the farm this is the system I used. The exercise kept us rather fit.

In the 1960s the next innovation was to have the cows walk into the shed in two rows. Due to the arrangement of steel rails, they stood rib-to-rib in a herringbone pattern so that the back half of each cow was accessible to the milker, who worked, standing uprigh in a pit between the rows. The pit was such that applying and removing the teat cups was carried out at waist height. No more tiresome sitting and standing. The time saving was also significant and it was found that one person could manage as many cows as two workers under the old system.

The ultimate system in operation on farms milking large numbers of cattle consists of a type of carousel where the cows walk on to a slowly rotating circular platform and are milked as they make the one revolution-ride. The

*Strip grazing with a movable electric fence*

139

milker stands in one place applying the teat cups while a device automatically removes the cups when the milk flow ceases.

In all these stages each innovation reflected the need to handle ever-increasing herd sizes, which have become the feature of economic survival. The other improvement that a long- term observer would notice is the use of greater areas of concrete and pressure-hose cleaning of these after the cattle have been processed. All this progress because mains electricity came to the farm.

With a mains-powered battery charger we could conveniently employ a single-wire electric fence. These units would convert a six-volt battery supply into a pulsing harmless, 2000-volt jolt similar to the shock produced for the spark plug of a car engine. Animals touching the wire received an alarming shock every second. Few actually stayed long enough for the second bolt. Now it was possible to quickly and economically erect a fence to contain cattle in a particular zone in a paddock. Lightweight steel posts with rubber or plastic clip-on insulators could be relocated almost as fast as one could walk and the wire run out from a small portable reel to suit any length. Livestock learnt very quickly to avoid brushing against this lively wire barrier. It was amazing to watch some cows grazing within a few centimetres of the wire, but seldom getting a shock.

Early in our introduction of the electric fence I recall with some mirth its introduction to old Punch, the draught horse. He walked down the paddock as was his habit to find that a section had been excluded from grazing that week by this new single wire. He walked up to it and put his nose on it as if to examine it with an exploratory sniff. Just then the unit in the shed gave out a pulse of volts. Old Punch got such a fright he slipped into reverse so quickly that with a snort he sat fair on his tail and ever afterwards avoided the single wire. We had a rather cocky cattle dog that would trot around the place with tail high in the air. Imagine the scene when passing under the fence one day the tip of its tail contacted the wire at precisely the time that the power unit ticked its pulse. The dog went from casual trot to racing greyhound speed in an instant. After about 20 breathless metres he stopped, turned to face the fence and began to bark in a very perplexed way. Another lesson learned. We were all tempted to introduce unwitting visitors to the charms of the electric fence by one way or another. If they could be induced to touch the innocent- looking wire or to brush against it there would always be a spectacular but harmless reaction.

These fences had one weakness in those days. If a stem of moist grass or a green twig touched the wire it would short the voltage pulse to earth and there would be little or no sting. If one wanted to test whether the fence was live a long straw of grass or oats could be held in the hand and touched to the wire. If it was working a rather reduced electric pulse, much less than the real thing, could be felt. If there was any doubt the length of the straw between the hand and the fence could be reduced and the pulse intensity would increase. In later years the problem of shorts to earth was overcome with the introduction of the high-impedance unit. The shock from this was much more severe but they could energise many kilometres of wire and overcome a fair amount of leakages to earth. The ultimate was a unit powered by a solar cell and was capable of mounting in remote paddocks.

This simple piece of equipment brought a big change in the method of feeding cattle. Whereas we used to laboriously cut, cart, chaff and hand-feed the milking herd in stalls it was possible to run the temporary electric fence across a cultivated fodder crop and allow the cows to graze the crop for themselves. After an hour or so they would be driven out and the fence would be advanced a few yards into the standing crop for next day's grazing session. With this change we learnt to adapt the variety of crops from ones that suited mechanical harvesting to varieties that suited grazing. Imagine the saving in time and effort to achieve the same result.

## Technological Advances

While all these physical advances were being made on the ground there were other changes at work, driven mainly by a band of devoted officers within the Department of Primary Industries and the CSIRO. Governments of all persuasions held the strong opinion that Australia as a very significant exporter of farm produce needed to encourage eve-increasing production to balance our trade account. There was a

141

common belief at the time that the world would not be able to produce enough food to meet rapidly growing human needs.

Shortages of food in many countries during the war had stimulated a great leap forward in agricultural research. The early effects of this were being spread throughout the land. It was public policy to inform farmers of the latest findings in improved animal husbandry and crop production and protection. Soil conservation became a live issue and literally hundreds of departmental officers set about practical experiments that tested latest theories. Extension officers passed on proven improvements to farmers, who for the most part were quick to adopt improved technology.

One early step at our farm was to join a Herd Recording Group of about 20 farms. In time there were hundreds of such groups across Queensland. The system was not new. but its expansion to a greatly increased number of herds at the time was part of the new wind blowing through rural areas. The daily production of every milking cow would be measured once each month and sent to a central record office for processing and reporting back to the farmer. The total quantity of milk and butterfat produced by each individual cow would be meticulously calculated and this data allowed the farmer, for the first time, to compare the productivity of one cow against another and against the average for his herd. The total herd results for each member of the farmer group and the average for each district in the State were also available and assisted a farmer to compare his efficiency with other unnamed farmers.

Cows were found to vary greatly in their capacity to convert grass and supplementary feed into milk. It was obvious that the low-producing cows should be culled and that herd replacements should be bred only from the top group in the herd. The scheme went further in that it became possible to identify cows across the State that had been bred from common ancestors. Certain cattle families with above average genetic value began to be identified and farmers, in choosing a bull for breeding future generations, sought out these families.

In practical detail the process involved the Herd Recording Officer visiting and staying overnight once a month. He brought equipment to attach to the milking machines to measure the quantity of milk from each cow and to trap a representative sample of the milk which was tested on farm for butterfat percentage. These men through their regular visits became good friends and a source of entertainment and local gossip.

I have seen a diary entry recorded by Mr Joyner of Samsonvale Cattle Station that indicated that my grandfather bought cattle from the owners in the 1870s. They were probably the foundation stock of our farm and were of the British Shorthorn breed. This breed was known as a dual-purpose breed in that it gave reasonable amounts of milk and at slaughter the carcass yielded quite satisfactory cuts of beef. In time farmers in the Illawarra district of NSW began a breeding program that concentrated on high milk- production families and disregarded their beef characteristics. A new breed of red and white or sometimes roan cattle was called the Australian Illawarra Shorthorn (AIS). It became popular throughout dairying areas and our family converted to this type by buying AIS bulls from multiplier stud breeders.

On my Junior Farmer exchange trip to England I was impressed with the production and popularity of the Friesian breed. It seemed that there was a national swing to these black and white cattle that originated in Holland. At the time they were a minor breed in Australia but as I studied the herd recording summaries of breeds in Queensland there appeared to be sound evidence that the Friesian breed had been underrated. We bought a bull from the Yarrabine Friesian Stud in Kingaroy about 1954 and began a conversion through crossbreeding.

In this we were a bit ahead of the pack because eventually there was an enormous swing throughout Australia to Friesians, mainly because of their ability to produce, on average, greater quantities of milk per animal. However, the solids content and butterfat percentage of their milk could sometimes be a worry as they bordered on the legal minimums. In retrospect I feel the decision was a wise move and our farm production improved by it.

*Artificial Insemination*

The importance of genetics continued to be driven home by our respected DPI advisors. They in turn were turning to another development that I first saw and took notice of while on Junior Farmer exchange in England. While herd recording data was discovering a few sires with superior breeding merit it was impossible, under natural methods, to have these animals sire much more than a 100 or so calves per year. Half of these would be males whose breeding merit may or may not be as good as their fathers. The holy grail of cattle breeding would be a technique whereby these superior bulls could father thousands of calves per year. Veterinary research found a new way, even though horse breeders of the Middle East had been doing something similar a few thousand years earlier.

Scientists invented a technique during a simulated mating to divert the ejaculated bull semen into a test tube. This was then diluted many hundreds of times with egg-white and buffers and packed in glass ampoules each of which contained enough sperm to produce a calf. Top-rated bulls could now sire up to 20,000 calves throughout thousands of herds per year. Genetic advancement of herds could now be speeded up to an unimaginable degree.

The next step to be solved was storage and implantation of this semen in commercial cattle. It was found that fresh semen could be effectively stored for only a few days before use, but that controlled cooling to about freezing point lengthened its useful life. Then it was found that cooling at a precise rate well below freezing would allow semen to be stored almost indefinitely. At first dry ice mixed with methylated spirits was used for storage at minus 79 degrees C in insulated boxes. Later still liquid nitrogen contained in stainless-steel vacuum insulated tanks at even lower temperature was found to be a more convenient storage method. Progressively, transport and storage of semen for delayed use in remote places and even overseas countries became ever more possible.

The best practice required to achieve conception also evolved. This involved inserting the small sample, through a fine plastic tube, directly into the uterus of the cow at the height of her fertile cycle.

This required a high degree of skill and training. Our Queensland Government Department of Primary Industries was quick to foster the new technique at all its stages. Technicians learnt the various skills needed and began to establish stations for semen production at Atherton Tablelands and at Wacol. An Inseminator Technician training course was established at Wacol and Samford.

As these steps were being taken Eric Brander, the very energetic manager of the Dayboro Dairy Co-operative Association at the time, asked me what I had learnt concerning artificial insemination while I was on my Junior Farmer exchange trip to Great Britain in 1953. I was able to lend him some booklets on the practice that had been collected from the Milk Marketing Board Centre, Thames Ditton, during that trip. Soon several interested farmers were attending a meeting called for the purpose of considering the establishment of an artificial insemination service based in Dayboro. DPI officers told of their progress towards a basic support system. Directors of the Co-Op promised £10,000 ($20,000) as repayable seed capital to establish a Co-operative Artificial Breeding Association open to all farmers within reasonable travelling distance of Dayboro.

A Board of Directors was nominated with members drawn from Dayboro and surrounding districts. Mr Win Henzell as Chairman of the Dairy Co-Op Board and his deputy, Gordon Kenman, were Chairman and Deputy of the new Association. Other directors were Keith Bryce of Strathpine, Vic Britten of Mt Mee, Walter O'Hara of Bald Hills and myself. As years passed other men to serve on the board were Dick Biggs (Nambour), Evan Evans (Maleny), Morrie Duncombe (Nerangba), Pat Rowley (Dayboro), Jeff Newton (Upper Caboolture), Morrie Thomason (Mt Mee); Bruce Brittain (Stanmore) and Alan Lawley (Maleny).

Applications were called by newspaper advertisements for an AI Technician. Recent British migrant, Mr Clifford Wilding, was chosen mainly due to his involvement with AI on English farms. He duly completed the Technician course at Wacol and Samford and was issued with Queensland AI Technician's Licence No1. Cliff took to the road in his Datsun utility on 1$^{st}$ June 1961 in response to telephoned calls for service from several farmers who had joined the Co-Op by buying 10 shares at £1 ($2) each.

Actual service figures seem to have been lost over the years but Cliff was kept very busy meeting the calls from farmers who were keen to take up the new technology. He travelled 44,000km in his first 10 months. He probably performed close to 5000 inseminations in that first year. By the winter of 1962 he needed part-time assistance so Mervyn McKenzie of Dayboro was trained and employed to cope with rising demand during the main mating season.

When a cow was observed in season, members would phone in by 8.30am and Cliff would begin his rounds, taking care to practise strict hygiene as he went from farm to farm. The farmer had a list of available bulls in each dairy breed and also a beef breed where the farmer did not intend to raise the resulting calf for dairy purposes. The cost was £1/10/0 ($3) per cow for a first insemination with two free repeat services in an effort to achieve pregnancy. At first conception rates were 60% for first service rising to 95% by the third service. With experience and improvements in equipment and technology these figures increased, with first service achieving near to 70%.

The first AI conceived calf was born on Stan Peters' farm in Lacey's Creek. It was a great curiosity and taken to the Dayboro Show that year for all to see. Many were surprised that it looked just like any ordinary calf, even though it had been produced by such unnatural means. The concept caught on quickly and success of the new venture was assured at an early date.

At first most of the bulls were stationed at production units of the New South Wales Milk Board at Aberdeen and Berry. Included on their list were a few high reputation bulls that had been imported from Canada. Soon semen produced at the Queensland Department of Primary Industries AI Centre at Wacol came available and the progeny of the calves derived from local bulls entered a wide ranging production comparison survey. Eventually there was a list of proven bulls available whose daughters were found to be higher producers than their mothers over a wide range of farms and conditions. Proven sires were allocated a Predicted Breeding Value as a guide to farmers and the semen was priced according to this indicator score. Now another new technology was available to farmers to drive efficiency gains and change the face of dairying.

For some the new technique was most timely in that a venereal disease had begun to affect fertility in many herds and bulls were passing this disease from cow to cow. There had been a rash of abortions of five-month-old foetuses in infected herds and these had upset the production

*Pam, a crossbred Friesian by Artificial Insemenation*

timetable, which called for regular, yearly calving of cows. The disease was treated seriously by the DPI and farms found to be infected were placed in quarantine. Unfortunately a straying bull from a nearby cattle dealer infected our herd. AI was the answer, just in time, to curtailing a serious herd health problem.

As word spread there were requests for service from adjoining districts and in 1963 the board employed Mervyn McKenzie full time in Dayboro to cope with demand. The company was requested to extend service to the Maleny area and this was initiated by employing a locally stationed technician.

Initially semen was packaged in one-cubic-centimetre glass ampoules that needed to be thawed gently and accessed by breaking the top off the tiny bottle. In 1965 these were phased out in favour of fine plastic straws, which thawed more easily and whose contents could be delivered by means of an improved injector system directly from straw into the uterus.

Up until the late 1960s semen supplies were restricted to bulls born in Australia or imported from approved countries via the Cocos Island

Quarantine Station. History was made again in the '60s when Kevin Hickey of Samford imported semen by air freight from Canada and Great Britain for use in his Stud Friesian herd.

By 1970 the Co-Op was employing five full-time and two part-time inseminators who daily serviced cattle, including many house cows, from Pinkenba and Myrtletown in the south to North Arm, Eumundi and Bli Bli in the north. A service was extended west to the Kilcoy area and through a sub-branch arrangement with Bob Fogg, to a group surrounding Toogoolawah. A February 1973 report reveals that 19,079 inseminations were carried out during the preceding 12 months. The Board demonstrated a degree of progressive thinking for those times when it employed female inseminators Robyn McPherson and Lyndal Stoddart.

Eric Brander must be credited with the vision and energy that got this initiative up and running. Upon the closure of the Dayboro Co-operative Dairy Company and Eric's retirement, I took on the task of Secretary of the group for a few years until Max Kuhn, who had been doing the statistical and accounting work of the group, took on secretarial duties as well.

After 12 years as a board member and a few as Secretary I resigned with fond memories and a sense of having helped to achieve something significantly good for dairying in the area. Our farm, along with 26 others that used the AI service, was included in the area resumed for the construction of the North Pine Dam. In 1973 the closure of these farms caused a significant dent in the business.

The winds of change blew strongly in other ways over the next few years. For financial and social reasons the steady decline in dairyfarm numbers continued to accelerate. It became popular for farmers to obtain the technical training required to personally practise AI on their own cattle. They achieved a degree of independence and financial savings by buying their own storage units and equipment. Over time a reduced demand for Co-Op services caused increased travel costs. This forced the Board to increase fees and this in turn hastened the trend to "do-it-yourself" AI on farms. The Board was forced into a relentless contraction phase and finally ceased the service in 1978.

Mr Harry Griffin, the last person to serve as Secretary-Accountant, managed the closure of the venture by distributing residual funds to remaining shareholders. In place of the pioneer service there arose another opportunity. Those farmers who converted to do-it-yourself service required regular liquid nitrogen top-up of their storage units and supply of semen and other equipment. One such supplier who seized the opportunity was one of our early women technicians. Lyndal Stoddart, who had married John Kenman, son of our long-serving Chairman, filled this need through regular farm visits. She is continuing in that role at time of writing this chapter (2004).

Cliff Wilding, who started his working life as a herdsman on an English farm of Sir Reginald Rootes in 1976, took the proud step of buying a farm of his own at Kandanga after 17 dedicated years of faithful service through many ups and downs. It was good to see him realise his dream to own and work a farm in partnership with his wife Dorothy.

### *Animal Health*

Wherever there are animals there are health problems. About 1905 the dreaded Cattle Tick reached Samsonvale and there was much suffering and death from "red water fever". These ticks had gained entry to Australia on a shipment of Indonesian buffalo said to have been a gift of Queen Victoria. They had relentlessly spread from the Northern Territory over several years. Cattle were immunised against tick fever by a crude practice of injecting vulnerable animals with blood from recovered and now immune animals. Calves reared by mothers that had gained immunity seemed to become immune without further action. Immunisation did not affect the prevalence of the fast-breeding tick and its blood-sucking habit. They could be present on animals in their thousands and had to be controlled for the comfort and wellbeing of cattle, which even though immune could die from loss of blood.

Initially ticks were killed by application of a liquid containing a relatively low concentration of Arsenic Pentoxide. They were mostly forced to plunge into a dip, become completely immersed, swim to the exit ramp and stand in a draining yard for a few minutes while surplus liquid drained back into the 2000 gallon (9000 litre) pool. This process would have to be repeated every seventeen days during the warm months of the year when ticks were active. It was always said that frost had one favourable aspect. It sent the problem insect into recess for winter. Since the life cycle of a tick is nineteen days it was preferable to dip more frequently than this to head off breeding of the next generation as much as possible. Eggs and nymph ticks would reside in grass and attach to cattle as they grazed. Millions have been spent on research, but to this day the cattle tick problem has not been solved.

About 1960 we were finding that ticks seemed to have built up resistance to arsenic. Even though the concentration was increased to the point where the tender skin of cattle was being scalded, the ticks seemed to be increasing. There was a universal change to DDT, which killed ticks quickly and in such numbers as had never been seen before. We thought we had a new lease of life in this battle. However, it seemed to be only about four years before DDT was banned and we moved on to another family of tickacides known as chlorinated hydrocarbons. Alarm! It appeared that the tick was able to resist these new poisons one by one in a matter of five or six years and the fight to keep one step ahead continues.

Keen observers had noted long ago that cattle breeds from Asia had apparently developed over thousands of years the ability to repel ticks with a naturally

*Herding cattle through a plunge dip to kill their ticks*

produced substance exuded from their skin wherever a tick attempted to attach itself. The CSIRO and the Queensland Department of Primary Industries began cross-breeding projects aimed at achieving the dream genetic combination of high milk production and tick resistance. Considerable success was achieved. It seemed unbelievable that a Labor Government, in an effort to save finance, decided to abandon this successful 20 year project. Meanwhile the tick remains one of the problems that has not changed very much in my time.

There were other spectacular success stories, however. Pleuro Pneumonia, an often deadly disease like influenza, became widespread in Tropical Australia. I can just remember the vaccination campaign carried out in our herd when I was a boy. Australia is effectively free of the disease today. Similar big-thinking schemes eliminated bovine brucellosis and bovine tuberculosis across Australia during the time I was farming. These schemes involved patient cooperation by farmers and vets in whole-herd screening and vigilance at meatworks over many years. All involved can feel proud to have carried this work to a successful conclusion. Similar eradication has been achieved in very few countries throughout the world and we can never relax our quarantine vigilance regarding animal or vegetable pests. Our almost unique trade advantage deriving from the health status of our animal and plant industries is worth billions of dollars to our nation.

During my time as a farmer and worker in agro-business it has been pleasing to see the rise of the availability and sophistication of veterinary services. In earlier times the value of an animal was relatively low and this mitigated against calling one of a relatively few vets from far away to attend to a sick animal. The fee could be more than the animal was worth and one would do one's best for the stricken beast with the relatively crude methods in common practice at the time. Just as the discovery of antibiotics revolutionised the treatment of infections in humans, it also saved farm animals from much pain and suffering. As vets got to know their clients they often prescribed, without actually seeing the beast, these wonder drugs for use by trusted farmers and this saved much time and expense in dealing with animal sickness.

Mastitis has always been a problem infection of milking cows. Defective milking machines appeared to be a cause of some infection and also a means of spreading the organisms from cow to cow. The advent of penicillin and other antibiotics made a dramatic improvement in saving affected cows from much misery and even from culling due to permanent damage to the udder.

The establishment of a Faculty of Veterinary Science at the University of Queensland in the 1950s resulted in an increase in the number of vets available. Schemes such as the eradication of TB resulted in regular visits to farms by vets who gained the confidence and respect of farmers. This flowed on to increased use of the vet. The swag of new- generation drugs, especially antibiotics, for treatment of infections also led to an improved life for farm animals. Like most farmers I found it necessary to study as much as I could understand about new innovations in vaccination and treatment of numerous animal health problems. The vets I had dealings with were always patient, unselfish and co-operative in my education.

### Pasture Improvement

Another aspect of dairy farming in those two exciting post-war decades related to improvement in animal nutrition through pasture improvement. Governments of that time were confident that Australia's financial future depended greatly on grazing animals. Significant government funding was allocated to research that would stimulate animal production in the beef, dairy and wool industries. Most of the fundamental work was allocated to the Commonwealth Scientific and Industrial Research Organisation (CSIRO). Leading scientists recognised that the native grasses of Australia were mostly poor quality when assessed as cattle fodder. Native species were mostly low in protein and very high in fibre. They had a quick response to rain, but quickly matured and lost value for beef, milk and sheep production. Over the years since European settlement many foreign species were introduced and changed the face of grazing practice, especially in Southern Australia where clover-type legumes and soft European grasses thrived, particularly if soil chemicals were brought to balance with superphosphate and trace elements. Winter rains produced a climate in the south that was similar to Mediterranean areas. Pasture-improvement practices had been copied from these areas.

Improving pastures in the summer rainfall tropics and the subtropics was not so easily achieved, even though early attempts with such species as Paspalum and Rhodes Grass from Africa had been a limited success. There were large tracts of land with a generous rainfall that

*Preparing land for new species of grass*

were unproductive only because soil conditions were not suitable. A large team of very talented researchers was assembled to solve some of these difficulties. Research facilities were set up near the University of Queensland (Cunningham Laboratory) and a 600 acre (245 ha) field station at Samford. Further field stations were set up in Central and North Queensland.

At these, soil chemistry was extensively studied and introduced collections of grass seeds from every tropical and subtropical part of the world were propagated for assessment. The best performers were refined and improved by patient cross-breeding and selection.

As results began to be released for farm trial there was great excitement among farmers and graziers. Farmer press and radio services were alive with the latest findings and with success stories based on farm trials.

There had always been a slight culture of distrust among farmers regarding academic knowledge, but it must be said that the practical work of the CSIRO men was universally supported and admired. They were most keen to pass on their latest findings and to talk to farmers on their own level. A feature of this time was the number of well-attended field days at which every aspect of the new forward thrust was discussed. At this level the State Department of Primary Industries was most active. I doubt that there was ever a closer relationship and mood of respect between farmers, DPI and CSIRO.

I was digesting this scene and making trials on our farm to gain experience in new age pastures when the State Government made a bold move to promote practical use of the new research. A Dairy Pasture Subsidy scheme was announced under which a cash grant would be paid for every acre of new pasture that was established.

*Improved pasture for our grazing cows*

This was to partly offset the cost of ploughing, fertilising and seeding undeveloped land that could boost dairy production.

It had been established that our land at Samsonvale needed two bags (100 kg) of super- phosphate and one bag (50 kg) of potash per acre (0.4 ha) for optimum production. The ploughing phase was heavy going since the apparently clear paddocks still harboured the roots of giant trees from my grandfather's time. The plough would suddenly hook one of these and bring progress to a sudden, jolting stop. After ploughing there followed harrowing of the rough sods, spreading the fertiliser in measured quantity by tractor-mounted spreader and finally sowing seed or grass cuttings.

I had decided that the best-performing grass for our sandy soil was Pangola, one of the hundreds of varieties of couch grass collected overseas for testing here. Cleared land along the east coast of Australia had been colonised by common Blue Couch grass decades ago. It had proved to be very palatable and nutritious for grazing animals. Its close-rooted runners made excellent protection against erosion. Unlike many of the new pasture grasses, it withstood drought and very close grazing. Among all the new species coming on to the market Pangola grass seemed to me to be closest to the faithful old Blue Couch and it produced far more feed. Unlike impressive species such as Seteria and improved Rhodes strains it bore no viable seed and had to be propagated laboriously from cuttings. I obtained some runners from

Mr Wyn Henzell of Mt Pleasant, who had established a trial plot from runners obtained from the CSIRO. I sectioned off a nursery area from which I could multiply future planting material.

It was my practice to prepare the land by mid-summer and await soaking rain. I would rake this propagation plot with a set of tines and masses of runners would be torn from the tangled mass. I would enlist any local kids who wanted some pocket money to load the runners on to a trailer. On reaching the prepared land the kids would grab armfuls of the runners, spread out each side of the trailer and sprinkle runners as evenly as possible over the surface as the tractor moved along very slowly. That done, a disc harrow would be used to partly bury the runners, which under ideal conditions would take root and sprout leaf and runners that could cover the ground completely in six to eight weeks. Every year I would add 10 or 20 acres (4 to 8 ha). The resulting increased quality grazing would result in increased milk production. The Government subsidy for doing this work was most helpful for the few years that it was applied. It was instrumental in popularising the new pasture revolution.

A most important aspect of this pasture revolution was the discovery and development of suitable legumes to plant with the grass. Plant growth is dependent on three main essential ingredients, Nitrogen, Phosphorous and Potash (NPK). While the latter two must be bought, it is fortunate that nature has provided legumes that have the ability to fix nitrogen from the air through the action of special bacteria that attaches to their roots. This is stored in organic form in nodules on the roots. When these decompose other crops can take up that growth promoting nitrogen. Legumes are themselves high in protein and enhance the pasture as cattle feed.

Unfortunately, the subtropical climate is mostly unfavourable for the growth of clover, which is the main legume component of temperate and Mediterranean pastures. Again CSIRO came up with some answers. Collections from Indonesia, Africa and Central and South America were screened and cross-bred with success. Siratro, Desmodium and Lotononus proved suitable for the Samford area. One or more of these were planted with any grasses used in the establishment of new pasture.

155

Improved production from old land that had been grazed constantly for up to 80years was gratifying. The innovation was just in time, for a rather unpalatable, poor-quality variety of paspalum known as "mat grass" had invaded our couch grass paddocks. There was also overdue need for replacement of minerals that had been taken from the soil through grazing over the years.

We were now in a program that would produce much more nutritious grass, but one that would also require us to apply phosphate fertiliser on an annual basis. Doing this by means of a tractor-mounted fertiliser spreader became an arduous task over our increasing area of improved pasture. It was time to step up to another innovation. Fertiliser companies began to copy a New Zealand practice of spreading fertiliser from aircraft. Some of us examined the proposition for our district. The company arranged for the contractor who owned a super-phosphate spreading aeroplane to visit and inspect sites for a possible airstrip. We found that it would be possible to build an 800 yard (740 metre) strip on the flat at the southern end of the Postman's Track. It was owned at the time by George Lever and had once been owned by my father's uncle, William Gold. During the 1930s and '40s it had also belonged to Dad's sisters. George was willing to allow construction of the strip and for it to be used a few days each year at no cost. Ian Johnson, the local bulldozer contractor, was able to clear remaining stumps and smooth some rough places in a few hours. The boundaries were marked with old car tyres, painted white for easy recognition by the pilot.

The fertiliser was delivered by tip truck and simply dumped on the ground and covered with a tarpaulin. A few days later the plane arrived and a specially constructed loader was on hand to fill the plane's bin with carefully weighed

*Loading super phosphate for the fertiliser drop*

amounts of fertiliser. The experienced pilot was able to calculate his speed and drop rate to a fine degree of accuracy as required for each contract. On our part we were required to have a person with a conspicuous flag at each end of the drop paddock as a marker for the pilot. Each time he passed we would endure a shower of fertiliser pellets, then march a designated number of paces along the fence line as a guide for the next pass. No doubt there would be some inaccuracy in this method of spreading, but it was quick and practical. I get a degree of satisfaction as I drive through my old farm 40 years later to see that those pastures continue to thrive. The yellow-flowered Lotononus legume has spread by traffic along the roadside between Dayboro and Samford and can be seen in the spring months. Setaria seed has floated far and wide on the waters of the dam to establish at water's edge for miles. The pasture revolution continues.

## *Pineapples*

In the late '50s it seemed that we could increase our cash flow by establishing a small pineapple plantation. Mechanisation and improved methods had freed us from formerly labour-intensive work and would allow such a project. We planted about 2.4 acres (1 ha) of the Ripley Queen (thorny) variety, which were in strong demand on the fresh fruit market. This

*Our' Ripley' variety pineapple plantation*

proved a success and added welcome additional income. The labour of suppressing weeds and harvesting among the prickles was somewhat daunting, however. Harvesting under natural flowering methods took place in mid-summer and again in spring. Picking had to be done between morning and evening milkings. We would deliver the fruit to the agent's selling floor at Roma Street Markets in the evenings. Since the unloading and grading for size had to be done by hand in those

157

days, it was a two- person job. Glenda usually accompanied me on these trips and often our children would be asleep on the bench seat between us.

All this farming activity was exciting and absorbing. It was almost a satisfying end in itself, with financial results a secondary consideration. In the early days it seemed enough to simply check the bank balance to discover how well the business was doing from time to time. We simply worked hard to produce as much as possible and exercised restraint in spending.

My father had relied on me to keep financial records and handle finances from the time I left school. This included preparation of our annual Statistical and Taxation Returns. As time passed it became evident that the formal business side of our enterprise should become more sophisticated.

The first improvement came when the Brisbane Milk Board approached us to become one of the sample farms that it would use to assess the cost of production of milk for the metropolitan market. One of its responsibilities was to regulate the share of the bottled-milk market among quota-holding farmers and to set the price paid to farmers for that quota milk. It also was responsible for controlling the margins allowed to processors and retailers.

The fair cost of production was determined by analysis of actual farm costs from a representative sample of suppliers. We were chosen as one of the sample farms and this entailed keeping detailed records. This responsibility represented one step up in record- keeping and in month-by-month monitoring of farming as a business rather than a way of life. As a co-operating unit we received feedback from the Board with useful data on which to base decisions. Such information naturally turned one's thoughts along business lines and targets.

It was a small step in later years to join the free and voluntary Farm Management Accounting Scheme fostered by the Department of Primary Industries. This scheme collected similar data and produced more detailed feedback. It also enabled us to compare our costs and production data with other unidentified members of the scheme state-wide. Extension Officers would hold annual meetings of participating farmers where a wide range of management factors would be examined and discussed. In return the Department was able to gain useful, detailed economic information on farming practice across the State.

What changes we saw in those 20 years. The future appeared to hold much promise now that modern science had solved so many problems for us and made our labours somewhat lighter. The farm labour force had shrunk considerably to a point where there were few paid workers on the farms and only a few share-farmer arrangements in force. Most farms relied on family labour only. The financial rewards had grown to a level that our predecessors would not have dreamt of. Unfortunately, change is ever present and in a later chapter I will outline some other developments that rather dented the optimism that accompanied so many advances that flooded into the farming scene of the '50s and '60s.

### Unwelcome Changes

Prior to 1962 we knew about the cane toad but felt pleased that it had not invaded Samsonvale. It had a reputation for being poisonous to small domestic animals and poultry and it was ugly. One evening I was surprised to hear the distinctive sound of a single cylinder engine running in the distance somewhere south of our house. It came in bursts and had me puzzled because I knew that none of my neighbours had such an engine. It was some days before I discovered that this new sound was being generated by a big fat toad in our water-lily pond as he called for female company. They had arrived.

I must say that we did not experience many of the promised, dreadful side effects of the toads arrival, except for the antics of a silly dog which could not resist bighting any toad that he found. The poison was obviously very distasteful because he went around trying to wipe his tongue free of some dreadful taste and frothing at the mouth in the process. However, he did not appear to suffer any other adverse symptoms.

After a few years fellow farmers began to comment that they had not seen any black snakes about during the usual summer showing. We assumed that these snakes, which prefer wet areas where frogs and toads abound as food, had eaten too many poisonous, young toads and had been greatly reduced in numbers. We noticed a reduction in the number of the green frogs that were common in our area and assumed that they had also fallen victim of the cane toads. Some observers say that there are fewer iguanas to be seen these days and that they may be dying from eating cane toads. Perhaps that might be the cause of these reduced numbers. One thoughtful farmer suggested that this led to an increase in the scrub turkey population because the iguana loves to raid incubating turkey eggs in their leaf-litter mounds.

Forty years later it appears that there may be less toads about than in those early invasion days. Keen observers have told me that they have seen crows flipping toads on their backs and eating part of their innards while at the same time avoiding the poison glands behind their heads. Trust the cunning crow to work out how to get an easy feed. Perhaps nature is working out its self balancing phenomenon. It would be interesting to see these theories tested by scientifically devised research.

In the many years that I lived in Samsonvale I never saw or heard of the presence of the eastern brown snake. Since the building of Lake Samsonvale it is reported that they abound throughout the district. I ponder why that should be so.

*A stock water dam in every paddock*

*Building a pigsty*

# Chapter 9.

## Family Life

When I returned from boarding school to live with my father and mother my sister Jill was employed as a typist at Union Trustees in Queen Street. Like many farm girls, she boarded in Brisbane and came home by rail-otor for weekends.

Dad had three unmarried sisters who lived in the big house built by my grandfather in 1900. This low-set house had large rooms with high ceilings and verandas on three sides. It had been built in stages over the years and contained boards of red cedar, beech and hoop pine which had originally formed part of the original house nearer to Kobble Creek. It stood in about half an acre (0.2 ha) of gardens which included palms, mango, macadamia, a huge red bougainvillea clump as well as various garden beds. Like my parents' garden there were extensive couch grass lawns and growing boys were required to push an old cylinder mower over these lawns many times each summer.

Two tennis courts adjoined the garden and at one stage we had an emu and brolga within the garden enclosure. The aunts had a liking for birds and the garden featured an aviary about 33 feet long by 10 feet and 10 feet high(10 metres long by 3 metres wide and 3 metres high). It had a covered section with night perches at one end. Bird species included many of the natives that frequented the district, such as various parrots, doves, pigeons, bower birds and an old, talkative sulphur-crested cockatoo called "Cocky". These were generously fed and with suitable nesting material they bred freely. The satin and regent bower birds even built a playground bower on occasions.

Farm life flowed from day-to-day in a mixture of essential work and family life, which was enhanced from time-to-time by visits from relatives and friends from the city. Dad's brothers were frequent visitors for they never quite got the country and the home farm out of their blood. Family ties with my mother's sisters and her mother also meant that frequent weekend visitors were greatly appreciated as they took tea on the veranda and led animated conversation.

I have written earlier of the social life off the farm, centring around church, Junior Farmers and fundraising dances for a variety of community causes. In this situation it is only natural for a young man to develop a special attraction to a particular girl. It all started when Laurie Stubbings, a boy who had been at Brisbane Boys College with me,

*Our first date*

introduced me to his sister at one of these dances. As time passed there was a need to secure a partner to attend Old Collegian Balls in the city and Glenda Stubbings asked me to partner her at one such ball. Soon after I asked her to partner me at a ball sponsored by my old school and so a friendship strengthened into something more serious over a few years. Glenda's family were dairy farmers at Mt Pleasant and like the Golds were descended from pioneer settlers. The Stubbings, Williams, Strains and Juffs families came to the district as far back as the late 1860s. We belonged to the same church and our families shared the same conservative values and traditions.

After about three years and the interruption of the JF exchange trip to Great Britain there was a proposal, an acceptance and an approval by Glenda's parents in the tradition of the day. We announced our engagement on Glenda's 23rd birthday, October 24th 1954.

Next came the need for a house. Finances being rather slim (I had £500 [$1,000] in the bank) the design had to be less expansive than those of my father and grandfather. We played with some crude drawings and approached George Turton, a builder we knew through Junior Farmer Club contact, who drew these up into a bluerint for presentation to the Pine Shire Council for approval. The lodgement consisted of just one sheet of paper and an accompanying sheet answering a few details regarding the materials, etc. Total area including two verandas was about twelve hundred square feet (111 square metres). The Council building application fee was £1/17/6 ($3.75).

Since I needed finance to proceed, Dad agreed to raise a mortgage on the farm which at the time was free of debt. I recall that everyone was on their best behaviour at morning tea when the Inspector from the National Bank at 308 Queen Street, Brisbane, visited to assess the application. Approval was given on the spot for a floating overdraft of £2000 ($4000) to be paid off as soon as reasonably possible.

In preparation for the construction it was agreed that I would use some of the standing trees on the farm for timber. There were several shelter breaks around the property that contained trees large enough for sawmilling. These were mainly eucalyptus hardwoods, which when removed would simply allow smaller, nearby trees greater opportunity for increased growth which

*One of our pine trees formed the floor of our house*

would soon fill the newly available space and thus retain the amenity of the shelter for cattle from the heat of the day and from cold wind and rain. One very large bunya pine planted by my grandfather about eighty years earlier provided enough material for the whole internal floor. Some small hoop-pine trees which had fallen in a violent windstorm some months previously produced all the mouldings. My father, who was an ardent tree lover, suggested that I cut a red cedar tree near the creek in order that I might do as he had done when he became engaged – season cabinet timber to convert into furniture at a later stage.

With the help of my cousin, John Barke, who worked for us for several teenage years, the required number of trees were felled with a crosscut saw and the logs were dragged to a loading bank with our

164

little Ferguson tractor. Winn Brothers, the local sawmillers, carried the logs to their mill and sawed the logs into the various sizes and lengths in accordance with the quantity list prepared by the builder. Some of the boards were taken to a city mill to be dressed for flooring and wall cladding.

On 26th September 1955, seven weeks prior to our appointed wedding date, a brief 20 line agreement was signed with George Turton of Strathpine to provide labour for construction at 10 shillings ($1) per hour for himself and his tradesman son, Kevin. George charged five shillings (50c) per hour for his apprentice, Joe Peterson. I was to pay the contracting electrician and plumber separately on a supply and install basis. I was also responsible for supplying all materials.

It was agreed that John, Dad and I would assist the carpenters wherever possible. Gravel was carted from the creek and mixed by shovel to pour the house stumps in situ using hand-made moulds and steel reinforcement bars from the farm dump.

After five weeks the team produced a modern house to the stage where we could complete the finishing touches without the leadership of the three carpenters. Such items as a water supply, painting, garden fence and laundry fit-out were worked into the farm schedule over the following months.

Old records reveal that the total cash outlay was £1274 ($2548) comprised as under.

| | |
|---|---|
| Sawmilling | $423 |
| Roof iron and labour | 215 |
| Electrical Installation | 51 |
| Doors and windows | 86 |
| General hardware | 167 |
| Floor sanding | 16 |
| Carpenters' wages | 276 |
| Paint | 40 |

As wedding presents Glenda's parents gave us a refrigerator and my parents gave us a Rayburn slow combustion stove, which incorporated a facility for a hot-water system on tap. Free and unlimited hot water was somewhat of a luxury on farms at that time.

As the appointed wedding day, 19th November 1955, approached, Glenda and I went shopping for basic household items, including blankets (£12), blinds (£20), kitchenware in addition to gifts given by friends at pre-wedding parties (£9), linoleum (£30), mattress (£28), cost of custom-made furniture (£133). Total £232 ($464).

By the wedding day we were reasonably ready for occupancy after what seemed to be months of frantic work. There was still work such as cleaning up, completion of laundry facilities, garden fence, clothesline and items such as curtains and floor coverings to complete. The toilet consisted of a typical

*Our house on our wedding day*

dunny of the time situated 40 yards (36 metres) across the paddock. Unfortunately it had not been furnished with a door at that stage. Glenda was not very impressed with that particular arrangement. However, each week there would be some homemaker improvement. Each little new item came in its time with much appreciation as we gradually achieved our dream. We were conscious of the farm overdraft and the need to balance our desire for comfort and amenity with the need to meet a promise to reduce the overdraft. It seemed to take about four years to pay off the bank and a few more years to make up to my parents for their advances out of their share of farm profits in order to pay the overdraft off at the earliest possible time.

Glenda had grown up on the family dairy farm at Mount Pleasant. Her father had grown up on the Stubbings' dairy farm in Lacey's

Creek and at adulthood began banana growing at "The Settlement" at the top end of the Mt Pleasant valley. Banana growing at that location struggled in the mid 1920s due to the virus disease "Bunchy Top". Sam had married Laura (Lilly) Williams of Mt Pleasant and to adapt to the changed situation they gradually got into dairyfarming and became suppliers to the Dayboro Co-Operative Dairy Association factory. Glenda was their second daughter and had a younger brother. Her childhood was similar to mine in that we were part of the typical farm scene, went to one-teacher schools and at age 14 were sent off to boarding schools in order to take part in secondary school education. Glenda followed her sister as a student at Moreton Bay College at Wynnum. This rather small school had been started as a young ladies' college by the Green sisters and had been included in later years in a scattered group of boarding schools run by the Presbyterian and Methodist Schools Association. Boarding away from home along with many other young people from a variety of backgrounds; being exposed to many new experiences; having to adopt a new sense of independence and taking part in competitive sport with people of similar age was as much a life-changing experience for Glenda as it had been for me.

Glenda returned to the family farm after her Junior exams. She was needed at home to assist her father on the farm. Herding the cows home for milking, assisting with milking, feeding and cleaning up twice per day became her constant routine. Housework alongside her mother consumed much of the rest of the day. Lilly was a keen cook and needlewoman and she passed on these skills to Glenda. She was also very outgoing and just had to take an important role in the Church Ladies' Guild, the Country Women's Association, the Ambulance Auxiliary, the Dayboro Show Society and the like. Glenda was taught to drive as soon as she was old enough to obtain a licence and provided a means of transport for her mother's many interests as she took the wheel of the new Vanguard car. This brought her into the circuit of meetings, fetes, cooking and needlework competitions and to a leadership role in the Younger Set of the QCWA in Dayboro.

While I was flat out finishing the house by the wedding date, Glenda was at full power making plans and preparations for our big day. There was the usual long list of arrangements for frocks, flowers, guest lists, photographer, reception, "going away" wardrobe, pre-wedding parties and so on. While this was a hectic time it was also very exciting for us both. We decided to be married in St Paul's Presbyterian Church, Spring Hill. This is where Glenda's mother and father had been married. The city location also simplified preparations for the reception. "Fairview" at Bowen Hills was chosen for the celebrations, with two grandmothers, uncles and aunts from all branches of the family along with a number of close friends.

Our big day on 19th November 1955 went entirely to plan. We were married by our local Presbyterian student minister, Jim Kinniburgh. A choir from my old school, BBC, sang two anthems and the sun shone brightly. Indeed, it shone somewhat too brightly. With everyone dressed in suits and their best frocks the temperature soared to 104 degrees F (40°C). Glenda was dressed in satin and several underlayers of clothing that became quite damp with perspiration. When confetti was ceremonially showered on us outside the church its colours were dissolved into the satin to leave permanent stains on the beautiful gown.

*The newly wed Ken and Glenda*

After food, speeches and photos we departed in a Ford Consul car borrowed from Glenda's brother to the rattle of tin cans and fluttering of streamers. Like so many young couples of the time we began married life with a stay at the Canberra Temperance Hotel on the corner of Ann and Edward streets. The subsequent honeymoon was spent economically with a tour to Yamba in NSW and a return trip via Glen Innes and Toowoomba.

When we arrived home we discovered that our custom-made bed had not been delivered and that we had no kitchen chairs. We slept for a while on the floor and sat on packing cases at meal times. Lounge chairs were a long way down the track.

Our new life settled down and it was not long before Glenda was turning out her delicious cakes and roast dinners in the slow combustion stove. Managing a slow- combustion stove was a new challenge that she soon mastered and we revelled in its efficiency, effectiveness and convenience. Various fruits were turned to jam and before long we bought a Fowler "Vacola" preserving kit to put up batches of various fresh fruits in season for later use. Hens provided fresh eggs and the occasional home-killed and dressed poultry meal.

At first the weekly washing (always on Monday) was done in a wood-fired copper boiler beside the laundry. This consisted of a cube shaped brick enclosure with a chimney, into which was built a 16 gallon (70 litre) copper cauldron. On Sunday evening the week's accumulated white clothes and sheets would be placed in the copper boiler with shredded "Velvet" soap or washing powder, covered with water and left to soak overnight. On Monday morning a wood fire would be started under the copper and the first batch brought to boil for half an hour or so. The clothes would then be removed with wooden tongs or short wooden poles and dumped into wash tubs, to be hand rinsed and partly dried by wringing or twisting each item by hand. A hand-turned wringer was later added to the primitive laundry equipment and this greatly eased the task of removing excess water. It would then be placed in a second tub containing a small amount of Reckitt's blue compound. This mild blueing of the white cotton items made them appear whiter when dry. A second and possibly third batch of clothes would follow in the boiler, with care being taken to keep the dirtiest working clothes till last. It was not over yet for the washerwoman. The blued items would be wrung out again and taken to a clothesline consisting of a single wire, perhaps thirty yards (27 metres) long, strung between two trees or posts. After the clothes were attached with wooden pegs the line would be hoisted well above the ground with one or two forked sticks about two and a half metres long known as "clothes props". Then the Hills Hoist became the fashion and we were proud to move up to this modernisation of the laundry process.

A few years later we gloated over a second-hand Simpson washing machine with power-driven wringer. What changes and advances we were experiencing in the brave new world of the 1950s.

After we graded up to a endless supply of laid-on water from the well we decided to upgrade to a home septic system. The installation was not without its moment of drama. As usual I did most of the donkey work myself. This involved digging a hole about two metres long by one metre wide and two metres deep close beside the house to form the underground tank when lined with concrete. The digging became almost impossible when I got down about a metre due to a hard strata of granite rock. I decided to buy a few sticks of gelignite to shatter the hard strata. Holes were duly bored, the explosives placed, the fuse lit and the location vacated at high speed. I turned and waited for the bang. Soon there was a dull thud and a heavy cloud of shattered granite ejected from the pit. Damn! The charge was a bit excessive and I now had several barrow loads of dirt to shovel off the roof of the house.

We had the phone connected and operated on a party line with my parents. The manual exchange operator would turn the generator handle in such a way that it rang at our end in the Morse Code signal for "U". When calling my parents the code "D" would be sent. We always had to keep an ear cocked for the code being rung to know who was being called. When we wished to make a call we first lifted the receiver to check that the other party was not using the line. If it was free we then simply turned the handle a few times to call the manual exchange and talk to the operator. We would ask to be connected to a family in the district by name. Any member of the Hedge family who worked the exchange at that time would know the subscriber number; plug into the appropriate socket and turn the ringing handle to raise the called party. When they answered there might be a few friendly words between all parties and then the connection would be free to continue. When the conversation was finished both parties would hang up and turn the generator handle a few times to alert the exchange that the conversation was finished. All connecting plugs would be pulled and the call would be registered on a docket for charging purposes.

About 1960 the Postmaster-General's Phone Department bought a plot of land from us near the Samsonvale Hall and delivered a ready-made Rural Automatic Telephone Exchange to the site by truck. This little shed with its modern equipment ushered in a new dimension in communications for us. In many ways it was more efficient but we missed the local news and gossip that was a valuable part of the old system. The loss of work and income for the operator was also a negative. Eventually Max Hedge had to find other means of income. Progress usually comes at a cost to someone.

My cousin, John Barke, suffered a near-fatal kidney complication soon after he entered high school and began a long recovery. He came to work with us in his mid teens and quickly picked up farmer skills and joined in the life of the district through the Junior Farmer Club and other social activities. He was part of our family and community life for about eight years and was a very good companion and offsider in everyday farm work.

My mother suffered severe depression for a number of years and Dad found that travel and holidays at our fibro cottage at Shelly Beach, Caloundra helped her condition. This meant that before I was married John and I had to "batch" quite frequently. Housekeeping and meals were seldom up to the standard we enjoyed when Mum and Dad were home. Washing and ironing were also not very popular, although my aunts, living nearby, often rendered valuable assistance. Getting married certainly improved life remarkably in the food and housekeeping department for John and me.

Glenda set about making our house into a home with interior painting, curtains, carpets and the like. We were very conscious of the overdraft and our share of fairly meagre farm profits. We often delayed our desire for new things and really appreciated each additional improvement to the house or furnishings when they eventuated. As an economy measure Glenda made all her own clothes and also made work clothes for me on her Singer 201K electric sewing machine. Eventually there was a quarter acre (0.2 ha) garden and the joy of the first crop of blooms and fresh vegetables. There was quite an area of lawn to mow and the old push mower seemed just too much hard work at a time when the Victa mower was quickly gaining popularity. I managed to buy one of the original models for about £25 ($50) and moved up one more notch in the "modern living" journey.

Almost two years after our wedding our son Paul was born after a prolonged and difficult delivery. There was great joy for grandparents and near relatives. Life took on new dimensions as the normal routine was turned upside-down with two- hourly feeds, nappy changing and washing and the new baby demanding constant attention. It was decided that I should prepare and deliver a midnight feed to allow Glenda a better night's sleep. Paul slept in a large basket and I would place it on the floor beside our bed so I could lay on my side and with one outstretched arm hold the bottle in place as he drank. Alas! Many a time I would receive a lecture on paying attention to my work. I would doze off and so would Paul after a few gulps of milk. The bottle would slip only to be discovered some hours later, cold and only partly consumed.

The large cane basket was most convenient when we went visiting or attending Junior Farmer meetings around the Brisbane Zone. On such outings Paul would be thoroughly spoilt by all the girl members. When he was old enough to walk he became my father's shadow and they had a special relationship that only living so close-by could enable. Years later as I travelled in Asia, I frequently saw that grandparents were a normal part of the family household and I came to realise that there is something very beneficial about grandparent and grandchild relationships where they live nearby every day.

Eighteen months later Jennifer was added to our family. She arrived a little early and in a hurry. Our doctor when contacted about the arrival signs told us to get to the Royal Women's Hospital at Bowen Hills as quickly as possible. When we got to Aspley we reached the tail-end of a queue of cars travelling at a very sedate speed and in my anxiety I decided to pass them all. Oops! When I reached the head of the line I realised why the procession was travelling so slowly. It was led by a police car. I sped on towards the hospital and of course the cop took chase with flashing light. We soon stopped and the officer came to my window with measured step and his notebook and pen drawn ready to write a ticket. I explained my mission and the doctor's instructions. He shone his torch in the back seat where Glenda was lying (pre-seatbelt days) and being satisfied with my explanation, told me to proceed, but to "do it carefully and don't kill anyone on the way".

At the hospital reception the middle-aged matron quickly took Glenda and her suitcase in hand, glared at me and said that I could leave. Fathers were not welcome in the labour wards in 1958. In a kind of semi-shock I did not think to hang around for further developments and perhaps rely on our friendly doctor to open a few doors after the imminent delivery. I went back home and got news of the addition of a girl to our family six hours later when the telephone exchange opened for a new day.

*Glenda and Paul*                    *Glenda and Jennifer*

As memory fades with time I am pleased that we have many photos of the children in those early days. We realise, like other couples we have talked to, that the first child features in far more snaps than the second child. Perhaps by the time the second child arrives some of the excitement and novelty of having offspring has worn off. In some respects Jennifer seemed to be easier to rear than Paul. Some older and wiser people observed that she had more competent parents the second time round. Apparently first children are the learner version.

Brother and sister played well together most of the time. Like most kids they enjoyed games involving sand and mud. When Paul was given a large toy truck it seemed natural to buy Jennifer a matching earth loader when it might have been expected that her birthday warranted a doll.

A significant discovery happened during the early childhood of our kids. Dr Salk discovered how to immunise people against the dreaded disease poliomyelitis. Up to that time there would be spasmodic epidemics of the viral disease that would take some lives, especially among children. The dead disease left many victims crippled with unusable legs or arms. The Pine Shire Council provided a vaccination service free of charge and it was good to feel that our kids would not run the risk of being ravaged by this terrible menace. Of course before this time common childhood diseases such as diphtheria, whooping cough and measles had been all but eliminated by vaccination at a very early age. A few years before our children arrived a nationwide compulsory testing for tuberculosis had been successful in practically eliminating this scourge in Australia.

*Off to school barefooted*

We tend to take these advances in science for granted now. However, it should never be forgotten that parents of earlier generations suffered so much fear and foreboding when one of the little ones came down with a fever that could so easily lead to death.

It seemed no time before Paul was due to start school. By this time the Mt Samson State Primary School had grown to two-teacher status. Bernard Wepner, as head teacher, taught the upper classes and Edith Dowse the lower grades. It was basically the same school building that I attended, consisting of one large room, but desks and equipment had changed somewhat.

In the mid 1950s the Education Department agreed to the P & C request to fund a school transport run from Kobble Creek to Mt Samson School and return each school day. This scheme replaced a co-operative agreement between a few families in Kobble who would transport each others' children to school on a rostered basis in their own cars and utilities.

I think that Bob Kunde was the first contracted carrier using an old Chevrolet utility with slide-in bench seating, back-to-back down the centre of the tray. This service passed to Wilf Kriesch and his Bedford truck for a while. When Paul began school the service was being

*Fred's "school bus" 1964*

provided by Fred Huggins, who was a share farmer next-door. Before they finished at Mt Samson the service had passed to brothers Jack and Bob Greensill. Note that I have not been referring to the school transport as a bus service. For a period of about 20 years it consisted of a temporarily converted open truck that would be used for general farm and goods carrying work when the school run was not occupying it. The primitive hard wood seating would be loaded on board as required. If rain was likely a tarpaulin was drawn across the top and tied down with ropes. Fred's truck had a hinged trapdoor on the front left side of the truck body and a step to assist kids to crawl in and out. In these early days of the 21st century it is difficult to imagine such standards as acceptable. It is well to remember that today's services had humble beginnings and that they were approved and greatly appreciated by the people of that time.

P & C committees over the years had gradually managed to improve the facilities at the school and in our turn we raised money by holding dances and concerts to continue these improvements. From early days Mt Samson kids had played on the rounded crown of the hill in the private cow paddock just north of the school with the kind permission of the owner, Rex Southwell. It was decided that a much better field could be provided if we were to flatten the crown of the hill. Rex willingly allowed Ian Johnson to bring in his dozer and convert the cow paddock into a quite creditable level playground

175

where sports such as athletics and team ball games could be conducted seriously. This assisted our kids to put in a good showing at area sports days. Tennis had always been popular in our district and eventually the P & C was able to provide a court for our kids. A visiting coach attended on a regular basis.

In due course Neil McQuillan replaced Bernie Wepner and in a very familiar pattern associated with country schools our single female teacher, Edith, was married to a local boy, Peter Fogg. She continued to teach at Mt Samson.

A year after Paul started school Jennifer was due to begin. A typical situation in bush schools had developed. At the end of his first year there were only two pupils remaining in Paul's class. The headmaster felt that he could not justify such a small class and pleaded with parents of those two to let their children repeat grade one and constitute a larger, more practical class. Thus our two were now in the same class. After their normal happy time at Mount Samson where they absorbed the rather quiet and restrained atmosphere they were both due to pass on to secondary schooling at the same time.

In about 1971 there was a move by local parents to achieve bus transport to a State high school for local kids. It seems surprising that up to this time there was no convenient way for young people in Kobble and Samsonvale to get to high school even though we were relatively close to the capital city. Parents would make various arrangements for their children to get to Dayboro or Samford to connect with existing transport to Strathpine or Mitchelton high schools. These inevitably resulted in a very long day for the pupils and little opportunity to take part in school sport. In some cases secondary pupils would board privately in the city or enrol in boarding schools. There was some hot debate as to which of the two possible chools should be chosen. In the end the service offered by Mitchell's Brisbane Bus Lines connecting to Mitchelton High School won acceptance.

Glenda and I regarded our days at boarding school as some of the most exciting and enjoyable days of our young lives and resolved to send our two to boarding schools if possible. We had been saving for this eventuality for some years. The memorable day arrived when, at the customary Mt Samson breaking-up picnic, they were finished with an almost idyllic part of their lives and faced a very different life at Brisbane Boys' College and Clayfield College for girls.

When the big day arrived and we delivered them to their new "homes" everyone had very confused feelings. On returning home it seemed to be so quiet and empty. Glenda and I would meet each other wandering the house, much in the way that a mother cat searches for her lost litter of kittens. Time passed and times became more normal. We felt for our children in the knowledge that they would be going through the depths of

*Off to boarding schools*

homesickness and the trauma of finding their place in a very different world.

They had opportunity to come home every few weeks for a day or weekend and we could see the gradual change in them as they settled into school life with its sports and other activities and opportunities. They gained another life with confidence and maturing outlook and in a way they grew up to be their own, independent persons from that day on.

*Glenda's garden*

*Our home from 1955 to 1973*

# Chapter 10.

## The Dam

So, the good life continued. Our valley produced ever increasing quantities of milk for the city processors. Pineapple and banana production boomed. The once significant egg and small-crop industries dwindled. Winn's sawmill turned selected trees from local forestry reserves into timber for a hungry city building industry. Social life thrived through various sporting interests, dances, various clubs and committees. Two teachers plied their skills in the small primary school and high school students were bussed to Mitchelton or Strathpine.

Little did anyone realise that a tidal wave of change was silently building up within the halls of power that would sweep away this satisfying, useful existence and change Samsonvale and its neighbouring districts for ever. Without fanfare or a hint of publicity, plans were being drawn up to flood our valley with a dam that would supply the growing urban demand for water that government planners foresaw as inevitable in the northern parts of Brisbane and adjoining towns.

The story of this significant happening deserves to be documented by a competent historian with access to all the official records available in various archives. A relatively few districts have the misfortune to be swamped by a dam and there is a need to tell the story of this particular event in the Pine Rivers Shire. There are significant economic matters that should be recorded and analysed. Historians might reveal to the world the role of State and local government bodies in such a large undertaking and review the appropriateness of their methods and actions. There is also a human story concerning the people affected that might be told, although at this point in time, 40 years after the event, it may be too late to salvage much detailed information concerning how a rural community adjusts to the utter dislocation of their lives by such an event. The following paragraphs consist of my personal recollections and opinions of this development.

The story probably begins in 1950 when the Australian Paper Manufacturing Company elected to establish a mill just east of the Petrie railway station. These were the exciting post-war years of industrial development throughout the country. Shire councils and State Governments were highly motivated towards development of secondary industry. The proposed paper mill was estimated to require 750,000 gallons of fresh water per day and this would require a dam to assure supply.

Through co-operation between the State and the shire engineers a site on Sidling Creek, only a few miles west of the mill, was chosen for a storage dam. Construction began without delay. The effect of this dam on the residents on that creek has its own story that should also be researched some day.

This project heralded a new era for the area. For the first time local communities were able to discard their rain water tanks and access town water. This in turn made it possible to install sewerage. These facilities, along with an influx of mill workers, in turn fostered a spurt in growth of local urban settlement in an area that until then had been a dispersed rural community.

It was calculated that there would be enough surplus water from the Sidling Creek dam, which had been officially named Lake Kurwongbah, to supply a growing need for water in the developing town of Redcliffe.

It appears that the people within the Co-ordinator General's Department who had planned the dam on Sidling Creek foresaw a continuing growth in demand for water for Brisbane and its growing fringe of shires. It decided to survey the Pine River Valley upstream from Sidling Creek as another possible dam site.

A small gang of surveyors made camp on a reserve on the north-east corner of our farm and spent several months combing Kobble Creek and the North Pine River, Rush Creek, Samson Creek and Terrors Creek. It seems strange so many years later that this activity did not cause warning bells to ring. It might have been asked: "What are these people doing poking about in our valleys?" But no serious thought seems to have been given to the matter. There was some mention of a dam, but all thought that if that were the aim any wall would be in the upper reaches of the valley. It would be another four years before the truth dawned.

In 1957 an elderly farmer, S. (Mick) Sharry, downstream from Gordon's Crossing, decided, due to indifferent health, to retire and listed his farm for sale. The farm had been pioneered by the Prothero family. A company trading under the name "Alfred Grant" signed a contract with the intention of subdividing the land into 10 acre (4 ha) blocks for the booming closer settlement demand of the period. When the buyer's solicitors searched Sharry's deeds at the Titles Office they were surprised to find that a caveat had been attached to his title. It warned interested parties that his property was part of a future water-storage scheme. Grants were not impressed that someone had tried to sell them a farm with such threatened prospects and told Mick so. It was the first that he had heard of the scheme and contacted neighbours to determine if they knew anything of the intended scheme. No one had an inkling. The cat was out of the bag.

It transpired that about 100 landholders were to be affected and the Gair Labor Government of the day had not felt it necessary to extend to them the courtesy of a personal letter or even a media announcement concerning their assets and the certain disruption to their future lives. What a great start to dealings that were to be subsequently played out over a period of more than 17 years.

The news spread like wildfire and meetings were held in an effort to get more information. Residents wanted to know if their farm was included and to what extent their land would be affected and over what time scale. A host of other considerations began to surface in the minds of everyone in the valley. Would there be land-use limitations on land above the waterline? What was to happen to road access to properties? What effect would such an exodus have on local business enterprises? Suddenly our satisfying lives were thrown into chaos.

There had been an historic change of government just a few months before this discovery and our local Country Party Member, David Nicholson, took our concerns to the new Premier and former farmer, Frank Nicklin, who ordered the Co-ordinator General's Department to send a representative to a public meeting in the area to answer the many questions that had arisen.

It was decided to hold the meeting in the Samsonvale Hall and on the appointed night every seat was taken and many people had to stand. The air was electric. A map on the wall depicting the high-water mark of the proposed dam was the centre of attention as each family crowded around to learn for the first time how the new scheme would affect their farm.

Engineer Harrison from the Co-ordinator General's Department addressed the meeting and answered many questions. He was heard with respect and was frank with his answers. It was evident that planning had not extended into minute details of the scheme at that stage. The tone of the meeting was a mixture of emotions ranging through disbelief, anger, resignation, anxiety and bewilderment.

The gathering learnt that the site was selected by the Stanley River Works Board, which had selected and supervised the construction of Somerset Dam during the previous two decades. A Brisbane Water Supply Planning Committee had been charged with responsibility to foresee future demand for water in the Greater Brisbane and surrounding shires and towns and to investigate means of meeting this demand up to 50 years into the future. The Committee had formed a policy recommendation to build a dam on the North Pine River about 1970 and follow that with a larger dam at the Wivenhoe crossing of the Brisbane River about 1980. Another dam was to follow near Wolffdene on the Albert River about 1990.

Sometime after this meeting surveyors appeared to undertake pegging the actual high- water mark for the dam. At last we all learnt just where the boundary of the project was in relation to our hills, gullies, houses, roads and so on.

Our family which had occupied our farm in Samsonvale since 1868 could see from the map that we would lose about 60 or 70 acres

(24 or 28 ha) to the rising water but it appeared likely that we could acquire remnants of two neighbouring farms to add up to a holding of about 400 (160 ha) acres. We felt that we could only wait and cope with the disruption as best we could when it eventually happened 15 or more years into the future.

For many others the future looked much more threatening. Joe Skerman, in his mid 60s had three sons who might well make a future on the block that had been settled by his parents about 1870, but his farm was to be left with only a small area of hilltop above water. Should the boys hang about working and improving a farm, only to see it submerged just as the boys were reaching their 30s?

Homan O'Hara owned a large and very productive farm that was to be almost completely submerged. He was in his mid 70s and was considering retirement. All his life savings were tied up in this farmland asset. How was he to find a buyer for this doomed farm? He appeared to be trapped and possibly would never see the commencement of the project. Keith Moore, who was farming almost 1000 acres (400 ha) which was originally the centre of the old Samsonvale cattle station holding, dating back to 1844, was in the process of selling the property and now found that he had a business that was virtually unsaleable.

Similar dilemmas faced almost every affected family. What could now be done to alleviate the problems that suddenly confronted them? In particular the 13 or more years' lead-up time was cause for so much anguish. A committee was formed in June 1958 to seek some solutions to these problems. Our neighbour, Tom Mason, was elected Chairman and I became the Secretary of the group. Our Member of Parliament, David Nicholson, was sympathetic to the dilemma of his constituents. He was a member of the Country Party which, in Coalition with the Liberal Party, had won the 1957 election in Queensland after about 25 years of Labor Party dominance. It was the Gair Labor government that had overseen the secret planning of the dam and was mainly responsible for the anguish that was gripping the district at that time. David arranged for delegates from the committee to meet with Premier Frank Nicklin in order to acquaint him with the problems that had arisen. The Premier received the delegation with warm understanding and soon after it was made known that the Government would receive requests from landholders to be bought out at a time that seemed convenient for them to terminate farming in the valley and move on to a new phase of life.

### Early acquisitions

Mr Sharry's property was one of the first to be resumed. Since his health had improved somewhat he had followed the possibility that he might stay on for a few years and he was offered a lease of his land at a rate of 3% of the purchase price of the land and 6% of the value of improvements. It appears that he did not take up the offered lease, as an old newspaper cutting reported that he settled for $10,000 and bought a new car and caravan to tour Australia on the proceeds.

Several of the remaining farms were bought up by the Co-ordinator General's Department in the following four or five years. As they were vacated they were advertised for lease on terms which allowed termination at six months' notice. The Skerman property, "Rockangle", was leased by the CSIRO as a field station for the Cunningham Research Laboratory at St Lucia. It so happened that senior researcher, Dr Percy Skerman, a grandson of the original pioneer settlers of the block, was able to be involved in plant-breeding work there. Another Skerman relative, Bob Prothero, became the resident manager.

Other working farms resumed at that time included A.J. Clay, K. Moore, Mr Brady, G. Hinz, R & L. McKenzie, F. Austin and W. Wood. There were probably others whom I cannot recall these many years later.

Most of the properties were leased by people who carried on beef-cattle grazing. The farm formerly owned by pioneer Frank Austin was used for successful potato production until the lessee, Bill Lane, died tragically when the farmhouse accidentally burnt to the ground one night.

A feature of this early acquisition period was the circulation of a variety of snippets of information concerning the way that landholders were treated by the construction authority. Often these could not be confirmed as sellers had moved away or were reluctant to reveal too much of their private business. It can only be assumed that they were satisfied with the negotiated settlements that were reached with the Co-ordinator General's Department.

I well remember Mr Harry Gordon, whose farm was quite near the dam site, telling one meeting that he had received a resumption notice in 1959 and on the basis of this he had sold his herd of stud AIS dairy cattle, only to receive a letter in 1960 that cancelled the original resumption notice. Overall there was a growing unrest that the resumption process was not likely to be a smooth journey.

In the early 1960s Pine Shire Councillors began talking about a struggle that had developed in relation to which local government authority should control the new water- supply project. It seems that some officials regarded the Pine Rivers Council as too small and lacking in experience to handle such a large undertaking. The council, on the other hand, claimed that it was dealing quite well with an explosion of industrial and residential development within its boundaries. The archived records would make interesting reading today.

### Project Authority

The upshot of the struggle was that the Government passed the "City of Brisbane Water Supply Act of 1962". This appointed the Brisbane City Council, headed by Lord Mayor Clem Jones, as the controlling authority. Jones had a reputation for getting things done and getting his own way in political issues. He was famous for successfully driving through his plan to completely sewer Brisbane. It was often pointed out in media reports that he did not treat impediments to his plans very favourably. It was soon discovered that he had scrapped the courtesy arrangement whereby the building authority would buy out affected landholders at a time of their choosing. Under Clem they would have to just sit tight until it suited the council to proceed with the scheme at an undisclosed date.

Clem's council also dealt us a preliminary blow worth recording. When the Dayboro Railway was closed in 1955 the rails and stations were removed and the land allowed to lie idle. We naturally let our cattle graze the 20 acres (8 ha) of land that the railway had occupied. The Government had resumed that land when the railway was built in 1919, but refused to pay any compensation to us on the claim that the coming of the railway had so enhanced the value of our farm that no compensation was warranted. In effect the line had divided our farm in two with heavy double sets of gates for access by cattle from one side to the other. That was hardly an enhancement. As there was no future public use for the railway land we approached our Member of Parliament, David Nicholson MLA, with the aim of getting his assistance to have freehold title to that land returned to us. He asked the Minister for Lands for this to be granted to all affected land holders along the line and was told that the Government was prepared to sell it back to former owners for what the Government had paid for it. We were delighted at the news that we would recover our old twenty acres free of charge.

Alas, when the government gazetted its intention to dispose of the redundant land the Brisbane City Council noticed that the land would eventually be needed for the dam and lodged a successful appeal that killed our expectations dead. We had looked forward to the righting of an old injustice relating to surrendering land for no compensation only to see it killed off by the BCC which, no doubt, recognised that they would have to pay us more compensation when the whole farm was eventually resumed.

My father had bought the small general store business that had been established in conjunction with the construction camp for the Dayboro railway line in 1919. When the camp moved on he arranged for the shop to continue operation for the convenience of local residents for about 10 years and then leased the business to a succession of proprietors. When the news of the dam project broke and residents began to move out there was little future for a shopkeeper and the tenant at that time decided to join the exodus in 1959. Dad requested, under the circumstances, that the Co-ordinator General purchase the building as had been done for several farms in the valley, but was told this could not be accepted. Correspondence shows that he made this legitimate request to the Co-ordinator General and again at least three times to the Brisbane City Council after 1962. He was told that the BCC would not be buying any property until it was ready to build the dam in the early 1970s.

The weatherboard building that comprised the shop area, a store room and attached three-bedroom house on about half an acre (0.2 ha) of land was beside the Samford to Dayboro road. It was not long before vandals broke in and wrecked the asset. By January 1963 there were 49 panes of glass and most electrical fittings smashed as well as huge holes in fibro walls and ceilings. Through no fault of ours we had lost rental income and had the general store rendered almost worthless as a direct result of the announcement of the pending construction of the dam. Could we see this in any other way than as an indication that property owners were not to be treated with reasonable consideration as the scheme progressed?

As a last resort, Dad consulted lawyers Cannon and Peterson to try to get some fair dealing on the matter. Their letter to Dad, after various unsuccessful approaches, reveals that the BCC had decided to abandon the Co-ordinator General's practice of buying properties from affected owners as a friendly accommodation of their trapped situation until they were good and ready in five to ten years' time. The letter contains a paragraph that has puzzled me for many years. The writer said: *"The matter appears to be a political one and should you wish to carry the matter further we think it should be approached on a personal basis"*. Could it be that the Gold family name was blackballed because as Secretary of the Landholders' Committee I had been outspoken on several issues that had concerned residents and the treatment that they had received when seeking definitive information on which to plan their futures?

### Information Please

In August 1964 I directed by letter a series of questions to the BCC concerning the future of our farm and whether it would be a viable property following construction. I was keen to know how much land would be taken; whether I would be able to add remnants of adjoining farms to ours; whether I would be able to continue irrigation rights. The reply was almost useless in that the BCC claimed not to know answers to such important questions. They did, however, say one important thing. They put in writing that *"It has been decided to acquire only the ponded area of the reservoir except in special cases where it will be more economical for the Council to acquire larger area"*. I deduced from that that I would be left with about 300 acres (120 ha) and could plan to continue to farm on the land first selected by my grandfather almost 100 years earlier. Read on and see what actually happened.

The 1960s saw the early stirrings of the modern Green Movement and one of its advocates appears to have cast doubt on the quality of the ponded water, should farming be allowed to continue upstream in the catchment. Several other issues began to arise as the implications of the dam, close to urban development, were considered. The Government commissioned a wide-ranging study of these issues. By 1963 a variety of experts from the Department of Primary Industries, local government and University of Queensland worked their way through the North Pine catchment talking to landholders about their farming practices and generally gathering a mountain of detailed information concerning the area. We gathered from this investigation that there was concern that these practices would adversely affect the water quality in the dam and that there might well be a variety of restraints placed on farming practices. Rumours abounded. This uncertainty cast a shadow on farm sales for some time. When the official report titled *"North Pine Dam Catchment Area Land Summary"*, which amounted to five thick volumes, was published it became known that some experts recommended the extreme measure of closing the whole North Pine catchment to human habitation. Others recommended the banning of the use of fertilisers rich in phosphorus and nitrogen because these might leach into the storage and encourage the growth of water weed and algae.

A new concern arose. The original maps showed the dam holding height as RL130 feet (40 metres) above sea level. The limit of the planners' original interest in land acquisition ended at RL 140 feet (43 metres). This provided a buffer of 10 vertical feet (3 metres) and was assessed to be more than any flood surge would exceed. If the stated views in the report were to have sway where would the boundaries be set now? Various enquiries to authorities who should have known the answers drew no useful information on which to plan our futures. Once again we felt that we were being treated poorly. More importantly there was an air of caution in the whole valley in relation to normal sales. Who in their right minds would buy into a farm in the valley while an official report was recommending that all farming be abandoned or at least be restricted in some important ways? There was a slow-down in the number of sales and a downward moderation in prices at a time when demand for land near the city was escalating and Australia was entering a period of severe inflation. Values that would be important benchmarks in determining the compensation to those with resumed properties were being driven down by the substance of the land-use report. Since compensation for resumed land would be related to sales of equivalent land in the area immediately prior to resumption, we clearly recognised that the report had damaged our prospects considerably.

In October 1964 my father died of a heart attack. In 1962 he had taken a back seat in farming our land by handing the dairy business to me and Glenda. He retained half of the herd and made a retirement income from dealing in cattle. He was born in the original house on the farm in September 1890 and was struck down one morning 74 years later while feeding some calves on the land that was so dear to him. He was more than a mere farmer for he had a great interest in the trees and native fauna that were seen every day as he continued to do light work around the farm. He had quite a collection of photos of favourite trees on his land. He took particular pride in the three acres of hoop- pine scrub that had been set aside by his father when clearing his selection in the 1860s.

After he died I found on his calendar, notes concerning the arrival of koel cuckoos on their annual migration or the sighting of a particular bird species that he had not seen for a long time. In some respects I am pleased that he did not live to endure much of the humbug and heartache that eventually played out concerning the land which he was so attached to.

In the changed situation there was no other course than to continue dairying as though we were destined to remain in possession of the higher land after the dam was full. I planted additional areas of improved varieties of grass and continued a maintenance level of fertiliser application. I took the expensive step of buying into bulk handling of milk and the cost of constructing an all-weather road to the dairy suitable for heavy tankers. I continued to exercise weed control, building and fence maintenance and took every opportunity to seek any shred of information that might shed light on the future. Of this there was precious little, apart from the odd meaningless press reports that there was to be a dam built on the North Pine River in the early 1970s.

On October 2nd 1970 it all broke loose at long last. Affected landholders received a letter in the mail from the Brisbane City Council advising that our land was required for the dam. The devastating surprise was that after many years of assurance that only the water-affected land would be lost, the whole of our farm was to be taken. In phone calls to other farmers it was found that in most cases far more land was being taken than was originally stated. The letter went on to state:

> *"However, please be assured that the Council regrets the unavoidable disturbance of your interests in this cas and it is most anxious that all acquisitions should be settled on an amicable basis.*
>
> *The council therefore would like to negotiate with you or your representative in an endeavour to reach a satisfactory and amicable agreement.*
>
> *The Council has authorised Mr T. Kinivan, Commercial Bank Building, 239 Queen St, Brisbane, to negotiate on its behalf and it would be appreciated if you would notify him as soon as possible of details of the compensation which you propose to claim in this matter."*

When various landholders approached valuers to assist in the negotiations these professionals expressed surprise that power to both value and negotiate was vested on one person. They said that this was rather unusual and some said that it verged on unethical and speculated on the details of such a contract. Was there a budgeted target gross figure to be achieved? Were there financial rewards for the valuer/negotiator for acquiring the area under that budget figure? I understand that one interested party tried to discover these details years later, but was prevented by the BCC from discovering the facts.

On 28th October we were served with a Notice of Intention to Resume the farm "for the purpose of the Pine River Dam". We were advised that under the Acquisition of Land Act we could object to the proposed action. We instructed our lawyers to object to taking of the whole farm of land on the grounds that only a quarter was below the surveyed high water level. We added that if the extra land was required as a buffer zone the notice should state that fact and support the decision with scientific data. We claimed that in comparison with other successful water sources such a buffer zone was excessive. We further claimed that the unnecessary resumption would adversely affect the life of my 75-year-old mother and take from our control the care of a private grave of my father's brother as well as the area of original hoop pine scrub that had been carefully preserved by our family for one hundred years.

The objection was put to council officers who were bound to bring the objection before the Governor-in-Council. I suppose that the matter was of small concern to the Governor and three Cabinet Ministers when they considered it because the appeal was overturned. Over six months later the *Government Gazette* of June 24th 1971 declared that the whole of our property, "The Pines", had been resumed by the Crown. This meant that any rights we previously held in the land under freehold title were extinguished and now simply converted to a claim for cash compensation. The axe had fallen and our future was not at all what we had been led to believe and henceforth was very uncertain.

A provision of the Acquisition of Land Act of 1967-69 was that a resumed party could deliver a claim for compensation any time after this resumption and that the resuming authority must pay its own assessed valuation to the resumed party within 90 days, without prejudice to referring the matter to the Land Court for adjudication if the dispossessed owner considered the council's offer was inadequate. Our next step was to seek professional help in assessing a claim. Essentially, someone in our position would expect to receive enough to re-establish on a farm of similar quality and location plus the reasonable costs of transferring to that property.

We were soon to learn that the Council had another view of the situation. It became obvious that it wished to get the land at the lowest possible valuation at the date of resumption. Several farms changed hands as Mr T. Kinivan, acting for the Council, swung into action. It proved difficult to learn the details of these settlements, but what we did hear seemed to indicate that owners would have difficulty in purchasing replacement farms of equal quality with the compensation reported to have been agreed. It was a fact of life that obtaining a valuation and going through solicitors took valuable time and during this time inflation at that period was rapidly pushing prices of replacement farms higher.

Many victims agreed that it would be desirable if one expert valuer were to work for most of us in determining an asking price and to assist with negotiations and perhaps Land Court appeals if satisfactory compensation could not be agreed. Our search led us to the firm of Taylor and Carter who were reported to specialise on rural valuations. The partners owned grazing properties of their own and Harry Carter grew up on the family dairy farm at Carter's Ridge west of Cooroy.

Harry made a detailed assessment of our farm. He advised that there is usually not much dispute regarding the value of improvements since the Land Court has established a formula over the years based on the estimated present-day new cost of buildings, fencing and the like, less a depreciation based on age of the asset. For instance, timber housing at that time was calculated to cost $650 to $750 per hundred square feet (9.3 square-metres) and the depreciation discount rate applied was 1% per year.

The house built by my grandfather in 1900, surrounded by a large garden with trees such as mangos, macadamias, palms and numerous shrubs was constructed in pine, beech and some hand-sawn and hand-planed red cedar walls produced by my great-grandfather, John McKenzie, in his pit-saw business at Terrors Creek about 1870. It had 14 foot (4.25 metre) ceilings with fanlights, contained four bedrooms, large lounge and dining rooms and covered 2100 square-feet (195 square-metres). It had wide verandas surrounding three sides and had been kept in quite good condition for its age. If it existed today it would be a heritage-listed building. Under the formula Harry Carter made a valuation of $4334.

The large, well-maintained, 1625 square-foot (495 square-metres), high-set house that my mother and father built 45 years previous to the resumption, also standing in large well-tended gardens along with a garage, hen-house and small shed, was calculated to be worth $5954.

The 16-year-old, 1250-square-foot (381-square-metre), three bedroom house that Glenda and I lived in, also standing in enclosed gardens, was reckoned to be worth $7875. The former general store, which in latter days had been repaired from its vandalised condition and used as the Samsonvale Post Office, rated a value of $3900. While the Land Court may have been happy that these were realistic values, I would defy anyone to buy equivalent houses for twice these values at that time.

Other improvements such as farm sheds, dairy building, almost seven miles(11.25 km) of barbed wire fencing, two irrigation wells, reticulation piping, tanks, cattle dip, electricity mains, dams and roads brought the total claim for improvements to $33,054. I employed a second valuer, Mr Vince Brett, to assess the claim for compensation for the whole property on the basis of a possible subdivision rather than a farm enterprise. This exercise failed to produce an attractive proposition. However, in valuing the improvements it is interesting that he independently came up with a total of $33,822. It was pleasing to see the closeness of these two figures. We were later to learn that the BCC valuer found the same improvements to be worth only $29,235, or 13% less than his experienced counterpart valuers, even though there was supposed to be an established Land Court guiding formula.

It had become clear that our main battle for just compensation was going to be the value of the land. Factors to be considered were the various types of soil and terrain, the degree of clearing and regrowth control, degree of pasture improvement and fertility improvement with regular fertiliser application, as well as the general productivity of the land. It was also vitally important to recognise that the property was only 22 miles (35 km) from the Brisbane GPO and was in the restricted area that had direct supply privileges to sell milk to Paul's Milk factory in West End under the guarantee of a weekly quota allocated by the Brisbane Milk Board at a premium fixed price. After considering a range of sales in the local area and some more distant sales that were deemed to be not tainted by the possibility that land in the valley might be affected by controls suggested in the land-use study published by the Government, Carter calculated that land would be worth $71,183.

We were to find after lodging our claim for a total of $121,579 that Mr Kinivan, on behalf of the BCC, considered the land worth $36,500 and that the council should offer us only $71,635 in total. We obviously had a battle on our hands if we were to transfer our farming operation to another property of equal quality and attractive location.

We duly submitted our claim to the BCC as required by the Acquisition of Land Act and expected, in accordance with the requirements of that Act, that we would receive from the council their payment of an amount equal to their assessment of a fair degree of compensation, within a period of 90 days. Acceptance of this payment would not prevent us from applying to the Land Court for a determination of a higher figure. It would, however, provide us with cash to begin negotiations for a replacement property and in our case find a new home for my 76-year-old mother.

To get her relocation under way we bought a vacant block of land at Caloundra near to where she had a sister and other relatives for $8750 and signed a contract with a builder to construct a brick-veneer house for $14,000. At the time of signing there was no sign of the statutory advance money from the BCC and we resorted to borrowing from our bank to get the project started, with the condition that we would repay the loan when the money arrived.

At the expiration of the statutory 90 days there was no sign of the payment required under the law. Our solicitors could not get meaningful answers from the BCC. There were repeated requests until our lawyer recommended that I personally knock on doors to discover what was happening. Finally, I was told that our papers had been farmed out to a firm of private solicitors and that they had been lost. So we waited. On reading the Acquisition of Land Act, I discovered that there were several grounds on which resumed landholders could be fined for breaching the Act, but there were no penalties for a government authority for breaching the same Act. They could fail to pay us on time without penalty. Nor was there provision for interest on a delayed payment. In the meantime we had the embarrassment of explaining to the bank why we had not honoured our undertaking to repay bridging finance by the agreed date. We eventually received our advance nine months after lodging our claim.

## *The Land Court*

At this point relations between the BCC and a core of landholders who were holding out for compensation that would fully cover costs of re-establishing themselves were at a very low ebb. Our only course was to list our cases for appeal to the Land Court for higher compensation and to await our turn for a hearing.

Newspaper clippings from the early days of the project state that there were about 100 landowners affected. I recall counting the active dairy farms at just under 50. There were a few people running beef cattle and about 10 pineapple growers. It seemed that there were then about 35 other landholders with non-farming or hobby-farming residential blocks. By the time the scheme fell under BCC control there had been about 10 acquisitions by the Co-ordinator General.

A perusal of the register at the Land Court reveals that about 20 of approximately 90 landholders at the time the BCC issued resumption notices eventually filed for hearing of their claim for fair compensation with the court. That represents 22% who genuinely believed that compensation was inadequate. Subsequently four of these did not proceed to a hearing. Presumably an improved offer was made by the BCC under threat of court action. By comparison, the court register lists that there were only about four court appeals in the much larger Wivenhoe Dam scheme, which was overseen by the Co-ordinator General's Department. These figures seem to confirm the assertion by Pine River landholders that they were treated in a miserly fashion where compensation offers were concerned. Searches for exact statistics are fraught with difficulty 35 years after the events. In some cases records have been destroyed. Perhaps a trained researcher might someday search out from several sources the exact position and list the many people who were caught up in the surrender of their land. It is a pity that the several human stories were not recorded accurately at the time

Eventually the first appeal came before Mr Walter Smith, President of the Land Court, for determination. There was much interest among affected landholders to see what the process involved and how the matter would proceed. We were astonished to say the least when Mr J. Kimmins QC, acting on instructions from the BCC, pointed out to the court that the subject land was, under the Town Plan of the Pine Rivers Shire Council, zoned "Special Purpose – Future Dam" and that such a zoning devalues the affected land.

We discovered that after the BCC became the designated building authority for the scheme it had persuaded the Pine Rivers Shire Council to create a special zoning to prevent any subdivision, control other developments and warn off possible buyers who might become interested in land within the designated zone. This measure was now being used to claim that the zoned land was inferior to other nearby land and the council should not pay equivalent market prices for it. We could not believe our ears. If there was ever any doubt that the BCC was playing a dirty game, here it was. If some future historian should write the story of the dam saga they should publish the court records of this case to the eternal shame of the council.

The Land Court was not impressed with the argument and set a benchmark for the several subsequent appeals based on local sales of equivalent land in the months or years before the resumption. Of course the many uncertainties surrounding the whole dam scheme had depressed these sales also and they were a poor benchmark for compensation.

Problems also arose for a few landholders due to another aspect of resumptions. There is provision within the Act, where only part of a parcel of land is required, to assess the value of the land taken and to then offset the assessed compensation by an amount considered to be equal to any enhancement to the remaining land that might flow from the project.

The council in a few cases decided that it might take only the flooded lower land and leave the owner with hilltops. These would then enjoy a view of the water and would thus be rendered more valuable. They calculated a notional enhancement value and deducted the amount from the compensation offered for the lower land. If a farmer wished to move on and re-establish himself on another farm he would then have the messy and very uncertain task of selling this remnant land before he had sufficient money in hand to make the transition. In the Gordon Kenman case the court rejected the play and ordered that the whole farm be taken. The irony for this family was that they moved to a farm on the Mary River only to be resumed again when plans for the Traveston Dam were announced 35 years later.

In another case my neighbour, Paul Zoeller, lost 10 acres (4 ha) from a hobby farm and was offered no compensation under the enhancement clause. He lost his claim in the Land Court. He took his case to the Appeal Court and lost again. When the dam eventually filled his view of the water was almost non-existent and in most seasons when the water level is less than brimful he has no view of the water at all. So much for justice. Ten acres taken, no pay and no view.

Meanwhile the project's time had come. In 1970 a contractor began the task of excavating the huge slot in the rocky terrain that would form the foundations of the dam wall.

The construction firm, Transfields, began erecting a concrete batching plant and skyway cables to mix and place concrete. An engineer searched the upper reaches of the

*The excavations for the dam wall*

197

river for gravel suitable for the kind of concrete needed for the structure. It transpired that the type and grade of gravel they were looking for was found under a few feet of topsoil on the creek flats of our farm and our neighbour Lyle Bennett's holding. Before long a huge dragline appeared and began to excavate the seam of gravel which was found to be about 16 feet (5 metres) deep in places. A bulldozer swiftly constructed a special dedicated five-mile (8 km) road from Bennetts' farm to the concrete batching plant. Things were really moving now.

Eventually more than a quarter of a million cubic yards (225,000 cubic metres) of gravel were excavated from our two farms. We at first thought that this would be fortunate for us and that we might expect some payment for the valuable resource. Since the operation tore up fences and caused our cattle to stray all over the surrounding lands we felt that we might also warrant some compensation for the extra trouble we were caused by the disruption.

Alas, since the farm had been officially resumed by this time and it belonged to the City Council we had no claim and had to "cop it sweet". How much would the construction authority have had to pay if they were to buy such a quantity of gravel commercially? Why then, in resuming the farm, should they not include in the compensation an equivalent amount?

In view of this situation I decided to be a bit cheeky and offered an unlimited supply of very good quality decomposed granite that existed in a steep hillside beside the excavation area to a local landscape supplier. He worked the site with trucks for many months and supplied me with pocket money that seemed to be ignored or overlooked by the BCC. By delaying payment of compensation they were hardly playing the game fairly anyway.

Our family had always been tree lovers. My grandfather in clearing his block in the years following his selection in 1868 had preserved a three acre (1.2 ha) clump of hoop- pine scrub that abounded in the north-east corner of the block. It had been fenced and cared for by three generations as a special legacy. It seemed that to have it pushed over by bulldozers in the clearing process would be sacrilege. I was determined to save it if at all possible and the Council agreed to pay whatever the Forestry Department determined to be the commercial value of the pine trees in that area. This turned out to be $2500. However, there were many dozens of other hoop pine and silky oak trees scattered about the creek flats and cattle shelter belts adjacent to the farm buildings that did not seem to rate preservation efforts. I contacted MD & JE Jeremy who ran a saw-mill at Aspley that specialised in this kind of timber. After agreeing a price a timber-cutter arrived to harvest these scattered trees, many of which would be in the ponded area. I was surprised when the harvest was completed to total up a yield of 20,000 superficial feet of silky oak and 30,000 super feet of hoop-pine which had been gracing our surroundings and enhancing the appeal of our farm. A superficial foot of timber was

*Gravel for the dam wall taken from our farm*

deemed to be a board one inch thick and one foot square. In metric terms the quantities were 47 cubic metres of silky oak and 71 cubic metres of hoop pine. Again I pocketed the money without any objection from the council since commercial timber would have been an aspect for compensation in the final argument.

My father had planted 200 radiata pine trees in a small plot in 1944 in response to some

*Gold's Hoop Pine Scrub (centre) fortunately saved*

199

newspaper article, in the hope that it would meet some future need for softwood timber. Unfortunately I could not find any miller who would consider that kind of log in those days even though they were over 16 inches (400 mm) in diameter. They were prolific seed producers in their old age and wind-blown seed germinated in large numbers in adjacent paddocks. Thirty years later the Water Board harvested hundreds of logs, which by that time were in commercial demand.

## Time to Go

Our need to make plans to move out were now becoming ever more pressing. The council had advised that we should vacate by December 1972 and I needed to find another farm to move our cattle and plant to. Preferably it should be in the direct supply zone where my quota would be useable. It was desirable that the new place be equal to the place that we were being forced to leave. Farmer friends in Beaudesert suggested that I might find a place in that district and guided me to three possible places. On inspection it was immediately obvious that we would need more money than was to date offered by the council if we were to follow those leads. I inspected Muriel Drynan's "Cryna Meadows" block of 120 acres (48.5 ha) and found that the asking price was $100,000. The Farren-Price property was on market at $90,000 and Steve Brimblecombe's place was listed at $130,000. All had about the same or slightly better productive capacity as our own place, were in the direct supply zone with milk quotas, but were further from Brisbane.

If we were to follow these leads we would have to borrow money to achieve an equivalent place. At this stage we had not received any compensation at all that would allow a deposit to be paid on a purchase contract.

Nearer to home I looked at a few places in Dayboro. One looked to be a possibility because the vendors, Henry and Des Bradley, were not in a hurry to settle. The place stretched along the western side of Samford Road from opposite the bowling green to the river south of Dayboro. It had a fair frontage to the Pine River with good irrigation prospects. It was not operating as a dairy and the house and dairy required considerable renovation. It was similar in soil type to our own place, but at 280 acres (113.3 ha) was considerably smaller. Their asking price was $70,000 and I estimated that I would have to spend up to $30,000 to bring it up to working condition with improved pastures, irrigation, building improvements and fencing. The council's offer was just over $71,000 and out of that I needed to spend about $25,000 to provide a house for my mother. Even so I took an option to buy from the Bradleys.

As days passed and I did the sums again and again I got less enthusiastic about the prospect. Why should I be going into a debt equal to 50% of the equity for the privilege of milking cows twice a day for seven days a week? In gearing up the property there was a distinct possibility of losing quota entitlement if production fell in the initial year and that would affect the budget considerably. Why should this dam business put me in such an undesirable position? I withdrew from the option. Henry and Des were understanding and generous to return my holding deposit.

As I struggled to find the way to a life after Samsonvale, I applied for two advertised positions for which I thought my experience might be an asset. One was as a Technical Assistant at the Samford Pasture Research Station of the CSIRO. I learnt that the classification for this job was tailored to school leavers and at 40 years of age I was considered too old. The second was as a Field Officer with the Queensland Agricultural Bank, but even though I made the interview short list it seemed such work was out of my reach.

Time was bearing down on us and reality dictated that we must consider selling our stock and farm machinery, turn our back on dairying and buy into some off-farm business such as the motor-mower and motorcycle retail shop that was offered by an elderly friend at Strathpine. Amid much mental turmoil and anxiety we listed our cattle and farm chattels for a clearing-out sale just as several other farm families in the affected area had done before us. It had finally come to this and it was one of the most awful moments in our lives.

The sale was set down for 14th February 1973. Clearing-out sales were most popular in the autumn months because farmers who needed to produce high quantities of milk in winter to achieve higher supply quotas were looking for extra producing cows at this season and thus competition at auctions was higher. One disadvantage in selling at this relatively late date was that there had been many similar clearing-out sales in the area in recent months and this reduced demand for much of the stock and equipment to be offered.

As the date approached days were spent on sorting out what equipment should be sold and what might be kept and stored for life after dairy farming. The accumulated stuff of over 100 years of occupation was considerable and there was a need to lay it all out on display and to have it looking its best for the big day. Cattle had to be sorted into appropriate groups to assist smooth conduct of the auction by the chosen agents, Fitzsimmonds & Co.

It was common practice for sellers to miss the milking on the evening before the sale in order that the udders of milkers would be swollen and give the impression that they were producing more milk than they really were. We avoided that ruse and announced on the day that the herd had been milked at the normal time of 4pm on the previous day. Perhaps that cost us some cash, but it is good to sleep well at night without a guilty conscience.

On the preceding morning it began to rain heavily and continued at an alarming rate. By evening we found that the rain gauge was holding six inches (150 mm) and creeks on all the roads to "The Pines" were flooded. We were in a panic. Could the sale proceed? If it did would it attract a crowd of competing buyers? We spent a long and anxious night.

At first light we saw that the sky had cleared somewhat and creeks and gullies had fallen. The sale could proceed and we hoped that buyers would be brave enough to turn up. The auctioneers set up their "office" in the milk room ready to accept buyers' cheques and issue receipts. The local CWA set up tables, made sandwiches, unpacked cakes and got their hot-water urns boiling in the hay shed to cater for hungry visitors.

By the advertised starting time quite a large crowd had gathered around the concrete holding yard and every available vantage point to take part in the auction of cattle. As usual livestock were to be auctioned first in order to allow new owners to truck them home for the evening milking. There were occasional showers of rain, so most people tried to find a place in the milking shed while others relied on raincoats or umbrellas as required. Keen buyers arrived early and walked among the yarded cattle to pick out their preferred animals. Those who had an interest in machinery and tools did the rounds of the assembled lines of stuff on offer and others simply talked to friends and neighbours because sale days are a popular entertainment and social outing for farm folk. For many, this was just one more of a series of closing-down sales due to the construction of the dam as history unfolded. I distributed a printed sheet welcoming visitors to "The Pines" for this significant day when after 106 years in continuous occupation the Gold family was reluctantly calling it quits. The sheet described the history of the herd as it progressed by cross-breeding from predominantly Australian Illawarra Shorthorn cattle to Friesian. It stated that the herd had been bred by using superior bulls through artificial insemination for the past 12 years and that breeding females were selected on the results of the DPI Herd Recording Scheme for almost 20 years.

"SALE-OH" was called and the process began. I must say that that was an overwhelming moment. Our lives had come to this. It was so final. The next few hours were something of a blur as cow after cow went under the hammer. Cattle that had been reared on a bucket by Glenda and had a name and personality just like friends were passing to another owner. We wondered what their lives would be like in future on another farm under different management. All the concerns and tentative plans made during the drawn-out North Pine Dam saga were now brutally real and so final.

During the previous week beef-cattle sales at Cannon Hill sale-yards had reached record prices. This appeared to be extending to the prices being bid for dairy cattle and we were quite satisfied with the average realised price of $146 per head for our herd, which ranged from calves through heifers to milking and dry cows.

An unexpected sequel to this favourable disposal came as a surprise when the annual income tax return was being prepared. I had followed my father's lead in valuing natural herd increase in the tax schedule by using the allowed option of $2 per head. This was standard practice with most farmers because it avoided the annual tedium of estimating the debatable market value of every individual animal on hand. The practice was fine for people who were not cattle dealers and planned to continue farming way into the future. However, we had completely overlooked the tax problem that arises if the whole herd is sold at a relatively high price. Tax is payable on the difference between annual carrying "cost" valuation and the actually realised value. We now had an abnormal income boosted by the sale of 156 head at a profit of $144 per head. There was at that time a provision within the Tax Act to mitigate tax because of a forced sale such as ours due to resumption. Also the rate of tax for each dollar was in those days based on a five-year rolling average for farmers. Even so it appears that by the time all these factors were worked through we lost almost half the cattle-sale income to the Tax Department.

With the cattle and two riding horses disposed of, the auctioneer moved on to the chattels and item by item our farming lives drew to a close. Cattle buyers were keen to load their trucks and head for home with their new cattle. The usual livestock carriers compiled their lists and lined up to collect their load. Each beast was marked with a paint number indicating the buyer and there was much sorting and drafting for this process. Meanwhile

*The last of our herd leaving their home farm.*

rain began to fall seriously again and darkness closed in before all the stock could be loaded. The approach to the loading ramp became boggy. There was nothing for it but to yard the remaining stock and milk them. Luckily the milking machines and the bulk-milk vat had not been sold. Overnight we had a renewed deluge and the next morning saw flooded creeks again. It was three days before the last of the stock were gone. It seemed that some power was drawing out the painful process.

I will never forget the forlorn feeling that settled over the dairy shed where we had toiled twice per day for three generations. The silence, the smell, the sight of everything my eye rested on shouted "It is over for ever". The site of such a long sequence of useful, productive activity was about to be bulldozed and returned to nature. I recalled the old philosopher who wrote the Book of Ecclesiastes saying "All is vanity and vexation of spirit". He was so correct. I wondered who would know or care, in years to come, what activity had gone on here, how it filled the lives of a few people and what part it played in building the nation?

In the following weeks I dispatched some items such as the milking machines and the bulk-milk vat that had been sold by treaty before the auction sale. Since I still had two other small blocks of second-class forest land in the district I retained a few items of farm equipment such as the tractor, plough, harrows, etc, in a shed on one of these blocks with the intention of possibly doing some hobby farming someday. Since these items had been written down by depreciation in my tax schedules any realisation would be highly taxable anyhow.

### A new direction

Late in 1972 an aunt showed me a newspaper advertisement in which the Australian Department of Foreign Affairs was seeking someone to establish a dairy project in Assam, India under the "Colombo Plan" Foreign Aid Scheme. She said I should have a go. Since plans for our new phase of life were not going well I decided to lodge an application and eventually Glenda and I were interviewed regarding the application. Some months passed without result. We pressed on with our search for our next move.

Being now out of dairying and still inclined to remain in primary production I examined the prospect of engaging in beef production. It seemed to be wise to seek a place south of the cattle-tick area yet in the higher, reliable, coastal rainfall zone. This led us to visit the

Lismore district and canvass various agents to find out asking prices and carrying capacities of possible properties in that area.

While we were in Lismore we received a telegram from home to advise that we had been selected for the Foreign Aid position and we hurried home to take the matter further. There were further interviews in Canberra and some educational sessions to bring us up to speed with the project and our two-year contract.

Life took on a new urgency to finalise our Samsonvale affairs and be ready to fly to India early in May. Our children, Paul and Jennifer, at this time were in boarding schools in Brisbane so the Government offered to pay their school fees and fly them to India twice a year for holidays. We had to sort our household effects into those that would be stored by the Government for us in Brisbane and those that we elected to have sent to India by sea. There was yet another pile which we would take with us by plane. There were also many items that were to be left with relatives for future use. These were busy days indeed.

Preparations were clouded by the fact that construction of the house being built for my mother at Caloundra had bogged down and we could not get reasonable progress with the builder. It was evident that she would be left alone in her house on the farm after our departure and that others

*A very sad day - preparing to leave*

would be left with the responsibility of caring for her in her 77th year and to also organise her move to Caloundra when the time eventually came. My sister had taken a dedicated hand in caring for Mum's many needs by visiting from Brisbane once per week. We reluctantly loaded her with much additional responsibility. Mum's isolation on the farm was solved to some extent by the kind dedication of David Barke, grandson of Mum's sister, who lived with his parents, John and

Shirley, in the converted old general store where Shirley conducted the soon to be doomed Samsonvale Post Office, originally began by my grandfather, Henry Gold, in his house on the farm in 1870. David, who attended Mt Samson Primary School at the time, would faithfully walk almost a mile (1.6 km) every evening to sleep in the house as company for Mum until the Caloundra house was habitable six months later.

Eventually, packing day arrived for Glenda and me. Part of the contract was that the Government would send professional packers to our house to place our belongings in shipping crates for sea freighting to Calcutta or for storage in Brisbane until our return. After the packing was finished the sound of the empty house, without carpets, furniture or curtains, was haunting and heart-rending. This was the house that I had helped to build with my own hands and which Glenda had lovingly decorated and turned into a happy home that raised two children over the past 18 years.

Time passed relentlessly and the morning arrived when we must load a borrowed car with suitcases, drive to the airport and begin a new life as foreign-aid workers. We drove out of the farm gate with minds that were almost numb and with not a backward glance, closed a proud and satisfying chapter of our lives and faced the uncertain unknown future.

Armed with our special official passports we flew first class to Sydney and transferred to a jumbo jet bound for Singapore. If we had been superstitious we might have been daunted by the fact that the plane struck a flock of seagulls on take-off and with one engine disabled we were taken out to sea where many tons of fuel were dumped until the craft was light enough to land back in Sydney. Everything was transferred to another plane and we took off again a few hours later. After we had a day shopping in Singapore we took off in first-class luxury for Bangkok where on landing the plane sucked some gravel into one engine and we had to languish all night in a transit lounge watched over by soldiers with guns. With a new engine fitted, we flew on to New Delhi where we were met by other agricultural aid workers attached to the Australian High Commission and welcomed into the circle of the Foreign Affairs community.

Our attempt to execute a meaningful foreign-aid project in Assam ended in disappointment and I will outline our experiences in India and the reason for our return to Australia after 14 weeks in a later chapter.

Over at least two generations there had been a relentless drift to the cities from Australian rural areas. This drift must have numbered several hundred thousand people and the story of their relocation and re-establishment should be told some day. My purpose in this work is to tell mainly the story of Samsonvale. Perhaps some details of my resettlement will be recorded later, along with many observations on the change and its effect on the character of the nation. For the time being it can be recorded that after a deal of trauma I found a place after farming and settled down to a very different new life.

However, at this stage our dealings with the BCC were far from over. We had made our claim for compensation. The council had made a much lower offer. We had asked for an advance, payable within 90 days under a clause of the Acquisition of Land Act. We also advised that we would be applying to the Land Court for adjudication. We eventually received our advance after nine months and awaited a court-hearing date.

I was to learn that the wheels of the legal world grind slowly. Through a series of delays a hearing date was set for 28th November 1973, a date that was almost two and a half years subsequent to the original resumption. Records show that the date was altered three times and that the actual court hearing took place on 7th May 1974, almost three years after resumption and 15 months after our clearing-out sale.

The president of the Land Court, Mr Walter Smith, who had heard all of the foregoing North Pine cases, was distantly related to me and declined to hear our appeal. A relatively newcomer to the court in Queensland, Mr S. Dodds, was appointed to the task. This was unfortunate in a sense that Smith had a detailed overall knowledge of the whole situation and could be relied upon to sense all the undercurrents that were at play.

My first impression of the courtroom scene was one of unease due to the body language of our opponents' barrister, Mr J. Kimmins QC, in conjunction with valuer, Mr T. Kinnivan, for the BCC. We were represented by barrister Mr B. Ambrose QC and valuer Mr. H. Carter. The proceedings were recorded in almost 150 pages of transcript, which tell of the thrust and parry of argument and counter-argument concerning valuation.

I was cross-examined on many details relating to sales, negotiated settlements of many resumed properties with the intent to show that our claim was unreasonable. I was not prepared for this tack because I had been assured that negotiated settlements were not acceptable to the court as evidence of valuation. Valuation must be based on genuine sales were not over keen sellers and buyers settle. I was also disappointed with some of the BCC valuers' disparaging descriptions of our farm such as improved pasture being run-down and reverting to the old grasses. The 70 acres (28.4 ha) of improved pasture on our farm was rather unique for the land taken in the valley in that it had been ploughed, laboriously planted from green cuttings of Pangola Grass rather than seeded varieties and the soil chemistry had been improved through having been fertilised for several years. The pasture that was claimed to be on its way out is still there to be seen growing vigorously today.

After the courtroom hearing the court visited the area to inspect and compare various properties which had sold in the general area. When we reached our farm I was shocked to view the run-down state of the place. In the 15 months since we had left the grass was waist high and unattractive because it had not been grazed or cared for. Several buildings had been removed or wrecked by invaders who had salvaged building materials. Fences had been cut or demolished. Weeds abounded. This looked nothing like the place we once took pride in owning.

The Court award was handed down on 24th July 1974 and in total the BCC was ordered to pay us $88,350 as compared to the BCC offer of $71,635. In addition the court ordered that we be paid interest of $14,284 on the awarded compensation to cover the period from resumption date to date of settlement. In the final analysis we received a total compensation of $102,634 and felt justified in our stand and our referral of the matter to the court. In the final analysis we received 43.27% more than the BCC originally offered us. After deducting the legal costs associated with the case we were 35.38% better off than accepting the offered compensation. During the court hearing the main point of contention was the value of land. In that detail the court awarded 42.6% more than was offered.

We breathed a sigh of relief that it was all over and that we could get on with a new life after farming. However, there was one more sting in the tail of the affair. When lodging an income tax return for the year, the interest that was awarded by the court and calculated over a period of four separate tax years was regarded as a single windfall receipt in the final tax year. Also, the Tax Department has made no allowance to cover the proportionate legal costs associated with gaining that interest via the court system. We had to resort to an appeal, which was eventually resolved partly in our favour through allowance of the legal costs, but by treating four years' interest in one year the tax bracket rose to 55 cents in the $1 instead of 32 cents that would normally be applied. So in the end Big Brother got his chop.

By early 1974 almost all properties had been vacated; the dam-wall construction was well advanced; bulldozers were clearing trees and demolishing any structures that remained; new roads of a quality never dreamt of in former years were under construction; houses and barns were being sold for salvage or removal at giveaway prices and our beautiful, productive happy valley was in its death throes.

*Our bulk milk vat on its way to a new owner*

# Chapter 11.

## Transition

By the time we vacated our farm the dam wall had been built by Transfield Constructions to perhaps two-thirds of its designed height and work progressed on schedule. The design included three earth walls across low saddles in adjacent ridges to maximise crest height. These were nearing completion and bulldozers had begun clearing the land to be inundated. All trees were felled and burnt, fences flattened and any buildings that had not been sold and removed were dozed into heaps and burnt.

The house that Glenda and I had built and occupied in 1955 was relatively new at the time of the exodus. It was put to tender and my cousin John Barke was the successful tenderer. He paid $1200 for it and had it moved in one piece to his block of land at Kobble Creek.

Fortunately two old significant buildings in the resumed area were preserved. About 1972 the fledgling Pine Rivers Historical Society had arranged to have the old slab barn that stood on Steve Kriesch's farm moved to a site near the Petrie Court House, where it was hoped a museum complex might eventually be developed. The Society's preferred site for this proposed development was Hyde's farm on Sidling Creek, but at that time legal proceedings in relation to the Pine Rivers Shire compulsory acquisition of the property were in progress. It was some years later that the issue was resolved and the barn with of its split blue gum slabs measuring almost a metre in width was relocated again.

The other significant building that was relocated stood on the property pioneered by Charlie Hay a few miles from Dayboro. It now stands in Williams Street, Dayboro and serves as a tourist centre under the name Hay's Cottage.

Since old surveys placed roads mainly in the valleys to be flooded, a complete new system of roads extending 27 kilometres was required on higher land. The Petrie to Dayboro road required relatively minor realignment, but the Strathpine to Samsonvale road had to traverse many deep gullies and high ridges almost all the way from Bullockies Rest to Mount Samson. It was appropriate that this road was renamed "Winn Road" in honour of the pioneering family who over three generations had harvested and sawn timber from this area. The road passed through kilometres of land that had been used for gunnery training during WWII by the US 1st Cavalry Division camped near-by. This made the earthworks somewhat dangerous due to unexploded ordnance. Fortunately, over the years after the war, bushfires in the area had already caused many dangerous unexploded shells and mortar bombs to self-destruct.

The Samford to Dayboro road was to be flooded for a distance of about two miles (3.2kms) and planners decided on a radical realignment of the route between Closeburn and Armstrong Creek. It was decided to follow the old disused railway line route to eliminate the hilly section of the old road north from Closeburn. To do the same from Kobble to the junction with the Postman's Track. The intermediate section through old Samsonvale was moved west to cut through land already acquired by the construction authority. It cut through the Gold farm from its southern to its northern boundaries and provided a branch road through our old territory to the Samsonvale Cemetery. Sometime later some local people agitated for that branch road to be named in recognition of our family which had farmed that land for 106 years. The road to the cemetery was named "Golds Scrub Lane".

The district had never enjoyed the luxury of sealed roads. Every journey entailed travel over mostly dusty, corrugated roads that were usually graded two or three times a year. Moreover, they were quite narrow in places, which made passing oncoming vehicles a matter for considerable care. Overtaking other cars was frowned on because of the disrespect of giving someone else your dust. It was manners to hold back at a respectable distance where the dust had cleared and to be patient. Passing slow trucks was regarded as OK.

One of the disadvantages of dirt roads was that cars were always dusty or muddy. In earlier years when car design was not advanced the interior and the passengers suffered a fair dusting as well. For those who remained in the district and for tourists in general the introduction of sealed roads was a great advancement and many observed that it was unfortunate that it took a dam and the exodus of hundreds of people to bring about these improved roads.

One significant feature of the district became a casualty to progress. A well-preserved Aboriginal Bora Ring system existed on adjoining properties once owned by two branches of the Kriesch family on Basin Road. Whether engineers who planned the new road in this area were aware of the existence of this historic feature is not known. However, the new road cut through the connecting pathway between the two rings of the Aboriginal feature, leaving one ring west of the road and the other on the east side. Thanks to the efforts of Ian Kent who had taken a keen interest in Aboriginal history on the property that adjoined his home block, these remaining rings have been fenced to better preserve them. It is unthinkable that such a development could happen in these later times.

Other services required reorganisation. The telephone exchange and phone lines were moved away from the water, but it kept its reduced number of subscribers and gained the advantage of underground cables to reduce the risk of damage by electrical storms. High-voltage power lines underwent a major redesign to serve a very different mix of users.

*Ian Johnson's bulldozer relocates the Samsonvale hall*

Ten thousand acres (4000 ha) had been resumed for the storage, although only 5000 thousand acres (2000 ha) would be covered when the dam was full. There was a need to securely fence the acquired area. This work was let to tender and a Samsonvale father and son, Clarry and Ian Kent, won a considerable amount of this work. Ian was later to become the ranger for the area and his considerable knowledge of the area was an asset in caring for the dam and its surrounds for over 30 years.

The remaining community insisted on retaining its meeting place and the council agreed to the removal of the very functional community hall to a new site on land that was once the site of the Mt Samson railway goods shed. Photos of this large building being moved in one piece are remarkable. It seems that Ian Johnson, the local bulldozer owner, smoothed the path for the two km shift. First the Samford road was used. When the railings of the Samson Creek bridge became a problem they were simply sawn off. Then the track of the old railway formed an excellent path for the juggernaut. The old hall, which had seen three locations over many years, suited the new site well and regular dances and community meetings continued. In later years the shire council took over responsibility for the hall from the local volunteer committee that had maintained it for so many years. In 1999, with the backing of ratepayer funds, the hall received a makeover that enlarged its floor space added verandas and flush toilets and an enhanced entrance. After an opening ceremony the old building that had seen so many community functions dating back to 1938 took on a renewed life.

The Presbyterian Church, erected in 1886, was situated beside the Samsonvale Cemetery. It had closed its doors in the mid 1960s as the population of the district diminished. It stood beside the Samford to Dayboro

*Our house on the move to Kobble*

road and although it was locked, a year or so after it was closed I noticed that a door had been forced. On closer inspection I discovered that the pedal organ, baptismal font, communion table and elders' chairs had been stolen. The building and land were sold to the council for $3000 and the old, well-kept building was eventually sold and demolished for second-hand building materials. The remaining furniture was relocated to the Dayboro Presbyterian Church, where some is still in use today.

There was speculation that the cemetery would also be closed, but commonsense prevailed and burials were allowed to continue. A check of the names on various tombstones reveals that many of the recent burials are of people who have no historical connection to Samsonvale, but rather share a very peaceful site overlooking the expanse of the dam water. Under council care the cemetery, which was once part of my grandfather's selection, took on a much improved appearance with regularly mowed lawns and appropriate fencing. I am sure that my ancestors who lie in peace there would be pleased with the present situation. Unfortunately this sacred ground is now at the end of a lonely access road and vandals have, on occasion, desecrated several graves and tombstones.

There were some graves dating back to the very early days of settlement on the Skerman property at "Rockangle". The council arranged for the remains of these pioneers to be relocated to Toowong Cemetery before the water covered the site. On our property the grave of my father's brother, who died in infancy before the cemetery was established, was above the waterline and marked with a stone and plaque. I was pleased to notice that the Water Board erected a fence around his grave site.

*Bulldozed and burnt - the general store and P.O.*

Soon after completion of the dam a weekly flea market was established at the Closeburn Hall. It proved to a great attraction and became so successful that the site was quite inadequate for the crowds that gathered weekly. Adjacent roads could not accommodate the influx of traffic. Someone decided that the land directly south of the Samsonvale Cemetery would be an ideal alternative site. It had virtually unlimited space on relatively level ground on a dead-end road. This proposal caused great consternation among the remaining residents living nearby because they visualised an end to their quiet existence. I gave my support to the protest on the claim that the land had been forcibly taken from me by the Brisbane City Council on the pretext that it would not be safe, for water-quality reasons, for me to continue to graze cattle there, yet the shire council was considering a permit for a gathering of many hundreds of people on the same land every weekend. Our arguments prevailed and the markets were moved to the site of the current Historical Village near Petrie.

In view of the council's insistence, for wate-quality safety reasons, on resuming so much land in excess of the actual ponded area, it also seemed somewhat inconsistent that the dam should be stocked with fish such as Perch, Freshwater cod, Saratoga and Bass for recreational fishing. Four picnic areas were established on water's edge and a Sailing Club was permitted to erect a club house on the water's edge and conduct recreational sports on the water.

The North Pine River had naturally abounded in mullet and catfish and in its lower reaches the famous lungfish were occasionally caught. In view of the action of the Federal Government in 2009 to ban the construction of the Traviston Crossing Dam on the Mary River, on the pretext that a dam would endanger lungfish, it is interesting to note that fishermen report that the lungfish population in the North Pine Dam is flourishing 36 years after the dam was filled. They are so plentiful that many are washed over the spillway of the dam when it floods.

While all the road- works, clearing and relocation of services proceeded, the last of the residents were forced, even so reluctantly, to move out. One of the last to give up was the Winn family, who owned and operated the family sawmilling business begun by their grandfather in the mid 1860s. Their claim for compensation had dragged on like some others and they resolved not to move until they received compensation. The mill was the only non-farming business in the dam area and employed twelve local men, some of whom were not affected by the resumptions, but nonetheless were due to lose their jobs. Eventually the electric power was cut off to the mill and that would seem to be the final blow. However, the inventive brothers brought in a generator and powered the mill and residential houses with that and with their tractor. On one occasion the Court Sheriff turned up with an eviction notice and some quick thinking by Alice and Richard Winn aborted his attempt to serve the notice. Eventually rising water ended their occupancy. The details of this saga are more lucidly set out in Rhylle Winn's book *When a tree falls.*

It is interesting to note that in the end the four brothers received no goodwill for the destruction of their sawmilling business. Compensation for the 400 acres (162 ha) of good farming land, watered by Samson Creek and including the mill along with four homes and three workers cottages, farm buildings and various improvements, was not sufficient to buy an average suburban home for each of the four brothers.

One of the last services to close was the Samsonvale Post Office. The enterprise had been started by my grandfather Henry Gold in 1870 and run by the Gold family until 1949 and continued for 20 years thereafter by Max Hedge. For the last five years prior to the time of the big exodus the post office was run by my cousin, Shirley Barke, out of the old general store. Henceforth, residents would rely on road delivery of mail and attend a PO in Samford, Dayboro or Strathpine to transact business.

The two-teacher state primary school at Mt Samson, which usually served about forty children diminished in enrolment due to reduced population and soon dropped to one- teacher status. Thankfully the tenuous situation held on for some years until the district began to take on a new profile due to subdivision of farms into residential blocks. Population of the district increased and the little school enlarged dramatically.

A well-remembered event during all these transitional activities was the visit of Cyclone "Wanda", which caused extreme flooding in South-East Queensland. The concrete wall of the North Pine Dam was still in the process of construction although the three earth walls across low saddles in the ridges to the south of the wall were complete. The dam, which was holding water at a relatively low level, filled virtually overnight to everyone's surprise and was pouring over the incomplete wall in a tremendous cascade. Much of the construction equipment such as formwork and tools were washed downstream. A bulldozer that was engaged in the forest-clearing contract near Sandy Creek was left parked for the fateful weekend. The owners returned after the flood to discover that the machine had been under water for some days. The Winn brothers had moved from their houses, but had not concluded salvaging whatever machinery and remaining timber stock piles were on site. The flood drenched the machinery included valuable electric motor. These were later retrieved and repaired. The heavier hardwood sawn-timber cuts were not moved by the rising waters. but cuts from some lighter varieties began to float away before the owners' eyes. Monica Winn was a strong swimmer and she took to the water and dragged the wayward planks back to dry land for future sale.

Much of the unwelcome flood-water was released and the finishing touches progressed without event until completion of all works in 1976 at a cost of $20 million. Substantial rains filled the dam in 1975. One of the surprising features of the creation of this new body of water was the influx of water-birds of many species ranging from black swans, pelicans to several kinds of ducks. There were literally thousands of these. Where they came from and how they knew that the new lake abounded in food remains a mystery.

After all the disruption caused by the construction of the dam the district was ready to settle down to a quietly adjusted existence. However, a subtle phenomenon had been at work for several years. A district that had, for three generations, been exclusively farming country merely 20 miles (32 km) from the heart of Brisbane became one that was destined to be used for residential purposes by city workers.

In those days the declining financial viability of smaller farms, linked with the increasing age of farmers whose children had chosen to not follow their parents on to the land, saw a gradually increasing number of farm sales to so-called developers. The profit margins that developers could make on this rising market for spacious blocks in the near city fringes of Brisbane guaranteed that they could outbid ordinary farmers when a farm was offered for sale. Gradually milk and fruit production declined and more and more land was subdivided into mainly 40 acre (16 ha) or10 acre (4 ha) blocks, which soon saw the erection of rather expensive modern houses where once cows grazed. The district gradually lost its farming character and with that its rural community spirit to some extent.

The greatly improved roads that the dam caused to be built accelerated this trend greatly in the mid 1970s. A few younger dairymen and banana growers persisted, but by 1995 there was not one active dairy farm left in the district. Pineapple production had greatly declined as well as banana production.

A drive through the districts surrounding the dam today reveals little of the activities of the past 150 years and the toil and persistence that carved a productive farming area from virgin bush. I have not been able to obtain reliable primary production figures for the district in its heydays. A rough estimate of the milk production from our farm over the years since it was pioneered would be more than eight million litres. And that figure could be multiplied more than 50 times when estimating total production from other farms in the district.

I find it beyond reason when travelling through the area these days to see contractors on tractors, laboriously slashing surplus grass on the subdivisions where cows once grazed and turned that troublesome grass into thousands of gallons of milk each day.

For those with a long association with the area there is another

*Our Farm (centre) - cleared grazing land*

notable feature that has changed in this urbanisation of the general landscape. As well as long grass and an increase of various untreated weeds, the scenery has changed remarkably due to a great increase in trees. When cattle were removed, particularly from the land within the bounds of the dam reserve, native trees began to reclaim the land that had been laboriously cleared by the pioneers' ringbarking axe and cross-cut saw. There was no need to replant these native forests. They simply happened by wind-blown and bird carried seed. At first wattle appeared to dominate but then other varieties such as iron bark, blue gum, spotted gum, grey gum, bloodwood and other species that originally covered the valley seem to be reclaiming their former domain. The "greens" do not need to worry that nature cannot look after itself. The land that is now returning to bush had been cleared for grassland. With much hard work, it had been kept clear for over a 100 years. It is well on its way to its former state.

Most blocks have a few grazing animals such as horses and natural reforestation on these lands is progressing at a slower pace. This phenomenon is most strikingly recognised if the aerial photos of the area taken in 1950 are compared with the most recent photos of the same area on the Google Earth website.

I was surprised therefore to note that considerable money and effort has been expended in planting trees on our old farm. As well, many of the species planted did not grow naturally at that location previously. I would have thought that a preponderance of hoop- pine, which gave the shire and our farm, "The Pines", their names and which originally covered that land, would have been more appropriate. To a large extent there has been an increase of weeds such as lantana on the dam lands. When we vacated our farm we had hoped that the water board would ensure that the patch of native hoop pine scrub preserved by my grandfather would be cared for by controlling fire and weeds. Unfortunately a persistent climbing garden plant, "Cats Claw", had escaped into this area from grandmother's garden many years previously and after we left this weed spread wildly among the trees. After several complaints about this degradation, $75,000 (more than the council offered us for the whole farm) was allocated out of the Commonwealth Government's Natural Heritage Trust to a band of volunteers from the "Men of the Trees" and "Greening Australia" to clean up this pest. The task was considerable and the group must be congratulated on their super effort. At time of writing the problem appears to be returning.

The dam was built specifically for city water supply and the project included a treatment plant. There was a big surprise when this plant began processing its first water. Filters clogged up with a troublesome flocculant. It was found that the water contained an unexpected trace of manganese. The treatment process had to be modified to eliminate this unwanted element.

And so we can sum up this North Pine project as having a profound effect on a large area of land and the people who lived and worked on it. City people can bathe, wash clothes and cars, drink and cook, water their gardens and fill their swimming pools because a community profoundly disturbed and made a significant sacrifice.

In these later times we have witnessed great orchestrated demonstrations and political activism at any proposal to build additional dams to meet the water needs the burgeoning population in South-East Queensland. In the 1800s Enoggera Reservoir was built to supply the small growing city of Brisbane. It involved the removal of several market gardeners. Then the Gold Creek Reservoir was built to add to the supply at Enoggera and to service the water needs of the growing city. More farms were eliminated. This was followed by pumping and treatment of water from the Brisbane River at Mount Crosby. Lake Manchester was built to augment supply to that facility. In the 1930's a large number of farmers lost their livelihoods as the Somerset Dam was built. Increasing demand for water seemed to know no bounds. In a way the construction of the North Pine Dam was inevitable. While very many people had their lives disrupted in an agonising and profound way, it seemed to most rational people that this was a logical and necessary trend.

The construction of the really large Wivenhoe Dam followed with more displacement of farmers and graziers. It had the planned additional function of considerable flood mitigation as a benefit of down-stream communities. At Wivenhoe the building authority is seen to have acted generously towards those disposed landowners. As with all the foregoing projects, there was an absence of the "not in my backyard" sentiment that has been a feature of more recent proposals. I wonder at the change in public spiritedness or sentiment that has arisen in recent times. There is no doubt about the need for ever more supply of water. Dams are by a long, long factor the most effective means of providing it. Alternatives such as recycling and desalination of sea water are greatly more expensive and environmentally destructive in the long term. It seems to me that provided affected parties are adequately compensated, governments should do the rational thing and get on with it. The people of the south-east region will pay dearly in time for political cowardice in not building the Wolfdene and Traviston Crossing dams or dams on other suitable sites in South-East Queensland or Northern New South Wales

Far too often governments are found to be mean and stingy towards the people who must inevitably suffer as a consequence of public works. Politicians and their advisors appear to take pious pride in declaring that they dispense justice when offering "Market Value" for land taken for the infrastructure that must be built to cope with unstoppable growth in population and commerce. They seem not to comprehend or will not open their eyes and hearts to the fact that property dispossession is only part of the story. Why not consider payment for disruption to the lives of affected parties? Some enlightened governments in other States have been paying a margin above "Market Value" to affected parties. In some cases this premium is as much as 15%. When one considers the huge amounts that courts award in personal defamation cases for what amounts to nothing more than hurt feelings and damaged reputations, some award for great disruption to the lives of people involved in public works seems equally reasonable.

So, here I must leave my account of my life at Samsonvale. For many years I would find it difficult to drive the new road through my old farm without welling up with a mixture of pleasant nostalgia but bitter memories. Occasionally I would take a walk across my once familiar ridges and gullies and conclude that such is life with its twists and turns. So many years, so many lives, so much toil across the generations in a beautiful valley have come to this silent end.

*Lake Samsonvale – our farm in the centre foreground*

# Chapter 12.

# Life After Farming

Since the Industrial Revolution there has been a worldwide movement of people from farms to cities and towns. This trend continues at an accelerated pace. This relocation of people was mainly an economic one as factories and commerce required ever more workers and because advances in mechanisation and more efficient farming methods required less physical labour on the land. No doubt there was a lifestyle factor involved as well, because town living often provided shorter working hours and more prosperity. Market forces and the vagaries of the climate for many years resulted in poverty for less viable farming businesses. The phenomenon of people movement was often referred to as "The Drift to the City" and was looked upon by country folk as a disgraceful thing. Little did I imagine that I would join that drift because my farm was resumed by the Brisbane City Council for a dam. It may be of interest to record our experiences as just one of those families who made the move.

As described before, my preference to continue farming seemed beyond my grasp due to the low initial compensation offer by the council; the fact that the amount offered was not nearly enough to buy an equivalent farm and its long delay in delivering initial cash payment.

As mentioned earlier I was successful in my application for a posting with the Foreign Affairs Department to a foreign-aid dairy project in India. After a sad farewell to our farm we were on our way with our official government worker passports, flying first- class to India.

In New Delhi we were housed in the premium Ashoka Hotel near the Australian High Commission and proceeded to be inducted into the life of our government's overseas service. This process was a steep learning curve indeed as we adapted to a very different life to that which we enjoyed at quiet Samsonvale. There was some cultural shock as we came to grips with a very different Asian culture. The social life at the High Commission was most enjoyable as everyone tried to make us welcome and teach us the "drill".

As days and weeks passed I tried to learn more about the Assam project but found some vagueness about arrangements and details. I later found that I was to be a joint manager with an Indian official and that he had a PhD. in Agriculture while I had no matching university degree. How could anyone run a thirty cow dairy herd without a PhD? It was proposed that I accept a matching honorary degree. That troubled me somewhat and I squashed that idea. This detail appears to have been solved during a visit by Gough Whitlam so we prepared to fly to Assam. Alas, on the night before departure Glenda and I both developed yet another serious attack of diarrhoea. Subsequently it was found that we had contracted the dreaded amoebic dysentery and a course of rather unpleasant treatment followed. Again recovered and judged fit to travel we were ready to fly when Assam was deluged by monsoon rains and very severe flooding, so we waited and tried a few weeks later. The flight to Calcutta and Guwahati through numerous thunderstorms, mixing with the teeming millions in crowded places and being very much out of our comfort zone, was a big challenge.

The slow four-hour drive to the project farm at Barapetta was an eye-opener as our driver wended his way past working elephants, drays drawn by buffalo, the odd rickshaw, many bicycles and hundreds of travellers on foot. Houses were mostly primitive timber or even arrangements of palm fronds. The scenery and the climate reminded us of Innisfail in Queensland and seemed to be unsuited to dairy cattle. We were greeted at the 220 acre (90 ha) farm by a workforce of 28 people in a tropical garden surrounding a timber office block. Pleasantries were exchanged and eventually details of the farm operation were discussed.

The Australian Government had air-freighted 30 pure bred Jersey heifers and two bulls to the project at great expense some eight or nine months previously. These were to be the nucleus of the breeding herd from which the highest producers under tropical conditions would be identified and their male calves used in a local artificial insemination scheme. Pilot tests had shown that cross breeding the stunted local Asian cattle with the Jersey breed could lift milk production from one pint per day to as much as eight pints per day and that was the aim of this ambitious foreign aid effort.

When I asked how the gift cattle were progressing there was an embarrassing silence and eventually someone confessed that they had all contracted foot and mouth disease and had been removed from the farm, some dead and others so affected by the disease that they would be useless for the project. Suddenly, I found that I was co-manager of a modestly sized farm with 28 workers, two working buffalos but no stud cattle so essential for the specific aims of the project.

It was suggested that we should press on by ordering a replacement batch of cattle from Australia. I should settle in somewhere until our partly constructed house was finished and wait for results. More enquiries revealed that several other essentials for the project were also well behind schedule and the whole project appeared to be in a state of hopeless disorganisation. The promised house on the farm was nowhere near completion and the alternative accommodation on offer was a two-room circuit house that visiting officials sometimes used. It had no toilet and the cook prepared meals on an open fire on the floor of a lean-to at one end. He drew water from a hole in the ground nearby.

It was suggested that we might find better accommodation if we prevailed on the generosity of an old Italian priest who ran a Roman Catholic convent a few miles away, but the more we assessed the project the more it appeared to be hopeless. Before it could progress there would need to be a second shipment of cattle from Australia and we knew that advertising, selection, vaccination and air transport of 32 replacement stock would take almost a year. We heard also that the Australian technician who was to establish the Artificial Insemination branch of the proposed project had declined to move to India. Graham Calley, an Australian Vetinary professional who had assisted such projects in India for several years, commented that such bungles were not uncommon and that extreme patience was often required. I understand that the project was revived some time later and was working reasonably well.

It seemed wise to return to New Delhi and tell the High Commissioner that we had no faith in the scheme in its present state. It was agreed that we should return to Australia. It was a sad journey home to an uncertain future.

Fortunately, my mother was still in her house on the farm and we were able to stay with her while readjusting our lives. I was able to get some carpentry work on a friend's house while reorganising our affairs. We decided to buy a house in Brisbane and aim to find work in the city. I determined to take any kind of work to keep cash coming in. We looked at houses near Clayfield where our daughter, Jennifer, was doing her secondary schooling as a bparder, but decided that prices were too high in that area. The following week another agent showed us several houses in the Toowong area where our son, Paul, was doing his schooling. We found prices in Toowong also above our expectations and our agent worked outwards to Kenmore where we found a just-listed three-bedroom brick house to our liking. Within 15 minutes we decided to buy it for a reasonable price, partly furnished. We paid cash the following week and moved in to become city "slickers". Another family of "bushies" had drifted to the city.

A city friend told me of a landscaping firm that was looking for a foreman to lead the development of the display village and community centre at Bellbowrie. My application was successful and without much fuss I had found work that I felt could satisfy me. It was after all rather related to farming, including some hard physical labour at times. On the job our freshly laid turf was wilting under the summer sun, so Glenda was able to also find work as a member of the gang which kept the lawns and freshly planted greenery watered and growing well. Our children became day pupils at their respective boarding schools and there was a feeling that the turmoil in our lives was over.

It was a surprise, a few days after moving into our new home, to meet our new neighbour over the back fence. John Armit happened to have been our dairy inspector in years past. We found that Jim and Betty Roberts across the road had been dairy farmers at Gympie and Jim was working at the DPI Artificial Breeding Centre at Wacol. Our next-door neighbours, George and Lil Coxon, were retirees from a sheep station near Isisford. Quite by chance we had bought into a cluster of neighbours with a common rural background and this made such a difference in our time of transition. We had all left communities where neighbourliness was an important feature of life. We observed that this characteristic is very often lacking in city living. Our other neighbours, Col and Zelda Williamson were already part of this friendly cluster and we were pleasantly surprised that we had bought into such a location. We discovered that neighbours in the city often do not know each other or even talk across the dividing fence.

In keeping with the ways of our former life we sought out a local Presbyterian church and found that the Indooroopilly church minister, Rev. Doug Brandon, was one who had spent three years as a student in the Upper North Pine Charge (Dayboro Parish) several years earlier. Indeed, I first met Doug as a student at Brisbane Boys' College in 1949. We were quickly welcomed into the Indooroopilly congregation and I soon found myself (as at Dayboro) on the Management Committee with duties relating to property. This proved to be an appointment that lasted over 30 years.

Glenda was soon invited to join the small group of ladies who regularly did sewing and mending for the church's W.R. Black Home for disabled children. Upon the establishment of The Wesley Hospital at Auchenflower she joined the congregation's band of ladies who arranged flowers in the wards for a period that spanned more than 28ht years.

These were the Whitlam years when it appeared to most farmers that rural Australia was being badly neglected. As an active member of the Country Party while farming, I found that there was just one branch of the party meeting in Brisbane, comprised mainly of people like myself who had come from the land. I transferred membership to this branch and soon it was expanding into several cells in the suburbs. I found myself as Chairman of the Western Suburbs branch and active in raising funds, selecting candidates and conducting campaigns in the city. Our role was useful in harvesting votes for our Queensland Senate candidates. During the Coalition split of the 1980s we fielded a candidate, Ced Dowdle, who topped the primary poll in the Moggill electorate only to be beaten by 190 Democrat preferences directed toward the sitting Liberal candidate, Bill Lickiss. Through its ups and downs I stayed with the party which later changed its name to the National Party. After 50 years of service I was made a Life Member. Eventually I was pleased to be part of the amalgamation of the Liberal and National parties and to continue to support conservative politics within the Kenmore area.

Glenda was invited by an acquaintance to join a weekday tennis group and found great pleasure in the game and the fellowship. This morphed into a second tennis group which met on week-nights and included our whole family and multiple members of other families. Our children involved themselves in college sport and adapted to their new life situation.

We made fortnightly visits to my mother, who had resettled at Caloundra, as well as visits to Glenda's parents on the farm at Mt Pleasant. After a year of settling-in we were somewhat surprised at how satisfactorily our big life-changing relocation had worked out.

### A New Job

About a year after I began landscaping, a farmer friend contacted me to advise that there was a vacancy on the staff of the Queensland Dairymen's Organisation that might suit me and the farmer group to which I once belonged. After an interview with the then secretary, Bevan Whip, I began a new phase in my life. My task was to attend to the secretarial work of the Jersey Cattle Society, the Australian Illawarra Shorthorn Cattle Society, the Friesian Cattle Society, the Queensland Stud Pig Breeders' Society and the Queensland Industrial Pig Producers' Association, which in my time progressed to become a statutory grower organisation known as the Queensland Pork Producers' Organisation. As well I would be called on to prepare details of matters that were being taken up with various government departments concerning commercial enterprises relating to milk production and farming enterprises. In a sense I was working for a kind of farmers' union.

I really enjoyed this work even if the diversity of subject matter piling up on my desk could become daunting at times. I was especially pleased that I was back in my farm politics environment, working with good friends and for a cause that I keenly believed in. If I was to be deprived of being a farmer this was a rather good substitute, especially on cold, wet mornings and at weekends when a cosy bed was such a good place to be.

After all the country to city change and the finalisation of our compensation claim in the Land Court we had some surplus funds. Like most farmers we had no superannuation or other adequate provision for retirement and it became obvious that we should take steps to generate reserve funds. On the advice of a neighbour who had become a landlord we bought a small house in Paddington and were surprised that we were receiving a gross return of 10% on the investment with little effort apart from minor repairs. It was great to knock on the door every fortnight and be handed the then $60 rent without the physical effort that we were used to in the farm business. After rates and insurance the return seemed to be about 7.5%, so we plucked up the courage to borrow to buy a second house. By applying all the rent to repayments we were able to save deposits, allowing us to borrow for further property purchases that were encumbered with a considerable mortgage.

By this stage weekends were becoming rather stressful as the demands of many tenants had to be met. We found most tenants a pleasure to deal with and would be pleased to see them save until they could move to a house of their own.

However, there were about 10% who made the business miserable. It was common to have to spend days cleaning and repairing damage when they left or had to be asked to leave for failing to pay rent for several weeks. I sometimes muse about the man who absconded owing six weeks' rent and leaving a bitch with eight pups as well a truck-load of old motorcar parts for me to deal with. Another fellow took off owing a similar amount as well as taking a washing machine, refrigerator and kitchen furniture. Another couple just walked out, apparently leaving almost everything they owned, including family photos and baby clothes. What can I say about the tenant who was restoring an old Ford utility and who spray-painted a door in the middle of the lounge room carpet, leaving a perfect silhouette of the door as a reminder of his stay? This fellow left his female cattle dog behind in the house with all doors open. She was on heat and a dozen or so local dogs came to stay, fighting for favours and spraying the interior in their excitement. Fortunately a kindly neighbour phoned to alert us to the situation.

We decided to sell out of some domestic property and buy commercial property where tenant turnover and repairs were less demanding. The operation was a profitable one for a couple who had no superannuation and these dealings formed the basis for eventual comfortable retirement as we transferred completely from property into shares.

Seven years after my appointment to the Queensland Dairymens' Organisation The Queensland Pork Producers' Organisation, which had grown to be a major part of my work-load, decided to set up in a separate office with its own full-time secretary. I was passed over for that appointment and felt that it might be time to seek another field. At that time Ian Jones, the man who had been president of the QPPO for several years, approached me with an offer of a considerable salary increase to work as an organiser for Stockyard Industries, a company he and a friend had formed to construct modern piggeries. I took the plunge into this new world at the time when a new-concept 20,000-pig enterprise near Warwick was in its early stages of construction. This $2.5 million r project was being built for a consortium of farmers and industrial companies under the name of Glengallan Farmers Pty Ltd. The enterprise was later destined to be famous when the original owners sold out and Prime Minister Paul Keating became a shareholder in the new consortium.

My duties were to assist procurement of materials and to co-ordinate scores of logistics connected with the project. On completion of this Warwick contract one of the partners, builder David Clarry, withdrew and I found that Stockyard Industries was wholly owned by the well-known stud piggery group Cefn Pty Ltd., based in Clifton. As we moved on to other projects I found myself heavily involved in design, innovation, costing and co-ordination of Stockyard Industries projects from an office in Taringa. I found this work challenging and most enjoyable. It presented such variety and a significant amount of travel up country. Ian Jones was a dynamic boss who was continually trying new ideas in his own piggery and in the industry generally.

There were few dull moments. The whole piggery and construction team worked in friendly unison with Ian overseeing and with his wife, Shirley, managing accounting and general office activity.

Cefn Stud was well known internationally and I would often find myself at Brisbane Airport to collect incoming buyers of stud pigs and also in the air-freight terminal assisting the export of their purchases. On one memorable occasion I was involved with others in loading 300 squealing breeding stock into a freight plane bound for

*I was employed to co-ordinate piggery construction*

Singapore. Later, Cefn Stud piggery secured an important export contract to supply 6800 foundation breeding stock for a new piggery venture in Pontanak in Borneo. These were delivered by road train in batches of about 1300 young boars and sows to Darwin where they were loaded on a specially built 1000-tonne pig transport ship for the eight-day voyage to the piggery wharf in the Kapuas River. I was selected to accompany the last shipment and to take with me a consignment of electric shed-temperature control equipment that had been developed and manufactured for Stockyard Industries by my friend Mackenzie Brown. I was to train local staff to install and operate this system on arrival. I have often mused about the path that my life has taken since being forced from the family farm at Samsonvale. It could really be described as an exciting adventure beyond my imagining.

As technology played an increasing part in piggeries we moved to become agents for a Dutch system that used a computer to feed dry sows individually prescribed amounts of feed and to keep considerable record of each individual animal's life history. This system allowed sows to be housed in groups of 50 without the individual stalls so despised by animal welfare activists. It had been found that when pigs have random access to feed at any time of day or night they do not fight and wound each other as they do when they are fed all at the one time on a schedule. To enable installation and servicing of this equipment I travelled to Holland to undergo factory training on the new innovation.

During a tourist trip with Glenda through China in 1984 I was surprised to learn that China keeps about one-third of the world's pigs and I could see that their genetic quality and housing were way behind the Western world. I suggested to my boss. Ian Jones, that he take an interest in the opportunities that lay waiting to be exploited there. I joined a trade fair to a town near Beijing in an effort to make sales of breeding pigs but had no success. However, a Hong Kong agent whom I met was instrumental in introducing us to a branch of the City Council of Chokow, in central China, which was interested in building a modern piggery and stocking it with high-quality Australian pigs.

It transpired that they wanted Cefn Stud to form a joint venture which resulted in my travelling to Chokow twice in relation to project details. While I spent considerable time in design and costings, it eventually became obvious that the project was too risky and that dealing with China as it emerged from international isolation in 1987 was a most difficult task. The plan was abandoned. Another prospect for a piggery for the Chinese Navy on the island of Hainan faded out, like so many foreign prospects of those times, despite considerable effort

After 10 eventful years with Stockyard Industries I had almost reached the age of 60 years. Our rental properties were paid off and it appeared that I could retire in comfort on rents alone. The pig industry had entered a period of depressed prices due to cheap imports and farmers were reluctant to invest in new buildings. It appeared to be a good time to retire, but making the final decision was an anxious time. I was somewhat sad to resign, but as it turned out I continued to do some intermittent work for the old company. This proved to be an appropriate phasing out from a job that I really enjoyed. We still held several rental properties and this demanded a reasonable amount of maintenance work to occupy my days.

233

One concern in making the big decision was that I might get bored with no regular work load to address every day. I even made a list of projects that might keep me occupied. I need not have worried. Retirement has kept me extended and a few

*Retirees on tour with a rooftop camper*

projects on that now 20 year old list have still not been completed.

It might not be generally realised that owning a farm brings with it considerable ties, which limit the owner's ability to partake in activities that the general population take for granted. This is particularly so where animals are involved. They must be constantly checked and attended to for health and welfare issues. For a dairy farmer milking is a twice daily, seven days a week chore that binds the farmer to his farm. One unexpected benefit of being banished from my farm was that I found time and freedom to do many things that were formerly impossible.

My Junior Farmer exchange trip to Britain in 1953 had left me with a yearning to travel far and wide. As a city dweller, with fewer ties, I could indulge this desire. We had travelled Eastern Australia in our farming days during short-duration trips, but now we could take longer breaks. We bought a roof-top camper for our four-wheel-drive and reached Far North Queensland, Tasmania and the Flinders Ranges. We joined two camping coach tours organised by a group of friends from our church that took us to Central Australia, Northern Territory and the Kimberley area of Western Australia. Later we hired a campervan and explored South-Western corner of Australia.

With Glenda I was able to revisit my former hosts in Britain over a period of 12 weeks in 1980. We bought a VW Kombi camper van and explored much of Britain and Europe. We repeated that adventure in 1990 in a cheap Fiat sedan, using youth hostels and B&Bs where

234

necessary. There followed trips to Canada, USA, New Zealand, Pacific Islands, China and several Mediterranean countries.

Late one evening I received a phone call from Koh Seong Pek, the man who acted as agent in Asia for Cefn Stud Piggery, my former employers. We had become good friends and he had been asked by one of his pig industry clients in Thailand if he could obtain 20 camels for a new zoo that a piggery company was establishing at Chonburi, about three hours' drive from Bangkok. He thought that I might be able to form a joint venture with him if I could obtain the camels. I recalled that our camping tour a year earlier to Central Australia had spent a night at the Kings Canyon Pastoral Company camping ground and that while there I had discovered some camels in a nearby stockyard. A phone call to the owner, Ian Cameron, revealed that he often caught and sold wild camels, which abounded on his large pastoral holding. He required a deposit of $250 before he began the capture and the balance of $250 when he delivered them to Darwin. I made a verbal agreement with Koh and we decided to make a profit of $500 per head after all expenses in getting the animals to their destination.

I must say that deals like this require a lot of persistence. It took a year to get all the details in place. We had planned to transport the camels to Singapore as deck cargo on a regular shipping service and transfer them to another service between Singapore and Bangkok. However, all efforts to obtain permission to transfer the shipment in Singapore failed because it would involve a few days on land. Cameron suggested that he round up a batch of young, six-month-old camels and that we fly them to Thailand. We then found that we could not get appropriate air freight from Darwin to Bangkok. At this stage I suffered a heart attack and all plans appeared to be doomed.

In due course I made a good recovery and Koh Seong Pek was still keen to proceed, so the plan now turned to getting baby camels to Brisbane where they could be loaded on to the lower deck of a passenger plane to Bangkok. My old firm by chance was delivering a semi-trailer load of export breeder pigs to Darwin and would be pleased to bring the camels back, free of charge, as back loading. The pieces were falling into place and the mountain of paperwork began. I never imagined how much detail has to be transacted when exporting goods. Our only option was to employ a customs Agent who knows all the angles. I engaged the man who had handled the Cefn pig exports. He attended to procuring regulation wooden crates for the live cargo, veterinary health clearances, export permits, airline bookings and fee payments at every stage.

*One of twenty camels exported to Thailand*

At the Thai end a similar mountain of paper was accumulating as further permits were arranged. Thank goodness for the fax machine in 1994.

With all in place the camels duly arrived at the farm of my son-in-law and daughter at Moggill where the 20 animals were rested for a week after their two- day journey from Three Ways, NT. Here they received a final treatment for possible ticks and began their trip to the airport.

True to form there was yet another surprise. Ian Cameron could not catch 20 baby camels and he settled for at least four that were about 18 months old. These were MUCH bigger than expected. How would these fit into the crates and the low ceiling of the cargo bay of a DC10 plane, which has a door 72 inches (180cm) high? Ian said that the camels would sit down as soon as their crate was on the move. Famous last words. I can still feel my blood pressure rise when I think of the problems we had in getting these animals to squat and to stay on the floor until they were loaded into the aircraft.

Eventually, I was able to change into travel clothes and join my faithful aide and supporter, Glenda, for the eight-hour flight to Bangkok. Once there, we were taken from the plane exit door, down stairs to the tarmac to supervise the unloading among the furious activity that surrounds a newly arrived international flight. To my alarm some of the camels were standing up and there was some difficulty in extracting them through the low cargo door. More alarming was the sight of the damaged ceiling of the cargo deck. I felt that I would get a big bill to replace these panels and was relieved when no bill arrived.

With the efficient processing of the unusual cargo we were soon on our way to the zoo at the end of a very long day. In the following days we settled the camels into their new surroundings and enjoyed the generous hospitality of our buyers as they showed us around that part of Thailand for a week. The camels thrived under their excellent care and there followed more requests for kangaroos, emus, welsh ponies and miniature ponies. All efforts to finalise these prospective deals failed due to bureaucratic barriers and stumbling blocks. Well, we made a few thousand dollars for our efforts and had a lot of experience and fun in the process. I guess that it would not have happened if I had not been a farmer in my past life and if I had not been driven off my farm at the age of 41.

One more adventure followed my farming years that might be of interest. I had watched aeroplanes flying over our farm, which was on the light aircraft lane of entry to Archerfield aerodrome for many years. I had developed a strong desire to learn to fly. When our children were finished with schooling I determined to achieve that dream. On alternate weekends I usually visited my mother at Caloundra where there was a flight- training school run by Kevin and Margaret Henebery, who incidentally were also former farmers. I did the theory studies by correspondence and would fly for about an hour, once per month. It seemed an extravagance, but I felt that I had earnt the indulgence. The experience in middle age of formal study and

*Learning to fly a Cessna 172*

237

demanding tests was a novelty that I enjoyed. Pilots never forget that scary day when the instructor opens the door, steps out of the plane and says "OK, go and do a circuit on your own this time."

I held a private pilot's licence for about twenty years, mostly flying about with friends on board just for the fun of it. On occasion I would fly my boss to distant places in connection with piggery projects. A heart attack in 1994 put a pause to my licence qualification. Later, to avoid the complications of health tests associated with the private pilot licence, I took up flying ultra-light class planes where health requirements for a licence are the same as for a car driver's licence. That aspect of my post-farming life has given me much pleasure, including two visits to the biggest air show in the world at Oshkosh, USA, to the Kennedy Space Centre in Florida and to various aero museums over the years.

Just as there were many opportunities to join in the social life of Samsonvale through its many committees and leisure groups, we found that there were similar opportunities for city dwellers if they will but seek to mix and to volunteer for various worthy causes. The transition to the city for Glenda and me was made easier by getting involved in our new community. However, I feel that in moving to the city we missed the sense of community that we knew at Samsonvale in the pre-1970s era. It is always good to return and meet old friends and to relish discussion of old times. Even though our children were but teenagers during our relocation they retain a side to their personality that is rooted in the country. Indeed, our daughter Jennifer enjoys her life on a 10 hectare farm at Moggill where she works happily with cattle and alpacas. Our son Paul became an electrician and is pleased when his work takes him to country areas.

For some years we retained a connection with the district through ownership of two parcels of land that were not part of the main home farm that was resumed. The 34-hectare block, Portion 46V on the Postman's Track, had been useful to run a few beef cattle. I was pleased to put it to better use when Ken Heathwood and John Barke took out leases on parts of it to grow pineapples and bananas. Eventually I decided to sell this block and apply the proceeds to our mortgages on our city rental properties. The buyer, Michael Cruice, who at that time owned the Crown Hotel in Dayboro, expanded pineapple growing there. but eventually sold the place, which soon had two substantial houses on it for the first time in history.

My father became the owner of the 65hectare block, Portion 63V, when his uncle, ageing Ralph Farrow of Dayboro, urged him to take it over. It was the last freehold land on that branch of Kobble Creek. It had originally been pioneered by a Mr Frank Clark and adjoined the then State Forest on the northern slopes of Mount Samson. It had little value as farm land, but during the 55 years that we owned it we were able to selectively harvest three crops of the largest trees for milling. We found that when the largest trees were removed the surrounding trees seemed to accelerate their growth to replace the harvested trees. We were simply copying the successful, long-standing practice of the Forestry Department on its adjoining land. After we moved to the city this block became a much-valued place to "go bush" to at weekends. We built a shed and some camp facilities, including an old caravan to add comfort to our visits. We enjoyed having family and friends share the tranquillity and the scenic walks up the picturesque creek with its little waterfalls and swimming pools.

I thought that in my retirement I might establish a flower farm using the water that gravitates from the upstream pools of the creek. However, distance from home and other competing interests prevented this. Relentlessly

*Camping at our Kobble Creek block*

increasing council rates and State land taxes eventually persuaded me to sell the block. I offered it to the National Parks Department, which by this time controlled the land adjoining me on three sides. However, after much delay it transpired that the Department had no funds for the transaction and I offered it to my neighbours, who were pleased to add it to their holding. That sale ended the Gold family's landholding connection with the Pine Rivers Shire which extended back 140 years to 1868 when my grandfather, Henry Gold, selected his first block in Samsonvale as a 23year-old migrant from England.

When we bought the Kobble block our neighbour was Dave Pringle, a descendant of a pioneer family and one of my father's boyhood friends. We had a long and friendly relationship with him and on one occasion he asked me if I would assist him to make a farm trailer by cutting his old unused 1927 Chevrolet truck in half. He intended using the back axle and the truck tray for transport and adding a trailer hitch to the front end of the modified chassis. Something stirred in my brain and I said that it was a pity to destroy such an old truck. I offered to swap my farm trailer for the truck, which had not been used for 17 years. Dave had bought it new and had travelled only about 22,000 miles in it in 28 years. He agreed to the swap.

The vehicle was towed home to the farm a few years before we had to evacuate and with a new battery, some petrol and minor tinkering it was running well. Our kids had fun driving it around the farm, even though it did not look very presentable. When we left the farm it was stored in a friend's shed for future restoration. Out of sight and out of mind, the old veteran continued to deteriorate for 30 years before the urge to restore it took over. I enjoyed the challenge of completely stripping the "old girl" down to the bare bones, stripping off rust, repainting, finding replacement parts, having the wooden spoke wheels renewed, replacing the upholstery, getting advice from fellow vintage car restorers from the Queensland Vintage and Veteran Chevrolet Club and finally presenting it for a roadworthy certificate. When it is taken for a drive, curious heads turn to study this remarkably simple and primitive old machine. I get special pleasure in driving it at the roaring top speed of 55 kph to its old home town of Dayboro to join the annual street parade.

All things considered, my post-farming years have been quite eventful and satisfying. Thus ends my comments on the relentless drift of rural people from the country to the city. In our case our family seems to have survived the change and lived a very interesting and fulfilling life change.

Through all this life journey Glenda was my constant companion and support. She made the most of every situation during our 54 years of marriage. She was ractical and talented in so many fields. She had surmounted several health problems since childhood, but was not able to win her three year battle with bowel cancer, which involved two major operations and periods of chemotherapy. She passed away on 7th December 2009 at the age of 77 years surrounded by her family. She is greatly missed and so often remembered. Life can never be the same for me now.

*My restored 1927 Chevrolet truck*

# Chapter 13

# Conclusion

The recording of these recollections began 1995. My aim was to supplement the work that my father did in recording the district's history prior to 1962. I aimed to place on record my memories of the Samsonvale of the 1930s through to the 1970s. Typing has been an "on again-off again" process over almost 17 years and I notice that the work has ended up more as an autobiography than a history. I trust, in spite of that outcome, that the history of Samsonvale during my time will show through and be of interest and relevance.

I have been pleased to ensure that our family's many photos and other records of the district, which stretch back to 1868, have a place in the historical section of the library of the former Pine Rivers Shire. Some of our old possessions have found their way into the historical museums in the shire.

As I pass my 81st birthday I realise how much amazing change I have witnessed and been part of along the way. Thanks to modern science people are living much longer. Replacement joints, heart, brain and eye surgery, transplanted organs, antibiotics and other amazing drugs have all brought unimagined benefits to people in my lifetime and I have shared some of these benefits. The big telephone on the wall has developed into a tiny box that fits in my pocket and can send and receive calls and pictures wherever I may be. Its messages reach me via satellites far out in space. I am entertained by a great selection of sound and moving, full-colour, images on a picture box in my lounge room 24 hours each day. I witnessed by the magic of this television invention, man walking on the moon. Computers have replaced almost every process that was formerly achieved by pen and pencil. At the tap of a keyboard I can process my banking and pay my bills. I can search the world for information and have face-to-face conversation with someone on the other side of our planet. When I do need to write it is done with a ball-point pen rather than with inconvenient ink and nib. Almost every utility item in my house is made with numerous forms of plastic unknown in my boyhood days.

A flick of a switch brings light, room heating or cooling to my desired temperature. I can prepare food in a few minutes via the microwave oven. My digital camera records history in an instant, The image can be modified and printed on my computer in minutes and transmitted around the world. Should I wish to travel to some distant place I need not drive in an open canvass hood car over dirt roads or by slow ship, but rather use my computer to book a ticket on an aeroplane, pay by credit card and be transported at 1000 kilometres per hour to my destination. I have seen the devastation that an atomic bomb can bring to waring nations. Via the media I am graphically made aware of the desperate plight of so much of mankind.

When I drive out through Samsonvale along sealed roads that were once only dirt tracks and see so many houses on places that used to be well-known dairy farms I can only wonder what the next eighty years will bring to the area. I gaze at hillsides that once produced thousands of tons of bananas or pineapples but are now supporting only houses. I ask myself what our pioneers who laboriously cleared the forest by hand in order to produce food would think now of their past efforts. Have successive governments simply missed the point that our expanding world population needs productive land and that they have failed their obligation to manage land use just because there is a dollar to be made by some subdivider, or that the rewards for farming have become so small that farming is no longer an attractive occupation?

I have tried to obtain statistics relating to the quantity of milk, cream, eggs, fruit and vegetables that the Pine Rivers Shire produced at its zenith in the 1950s but unfortunately they do not appear to exist. It is a sad and disturbing fact that today there is almost no agricultural produce springing forth from Samsonvale at this time apart from rather insignificant numbers of beef cattle. I can only wonder at the passage of time when I see tractors grinding away, wastefully slashing long grass in paddocks that once produced thousands of gallons of milk. What is "progress" all about?

I sometimes wonder at the achievements of our pioneers in struggling to settle our valley. I think of the hard manual labour, droughts, floods and bush fires, the set-backs and heartaches, the financial worries and failures, the part that their womenfolk played under unimaginable conditions with no modern conveniences. I feel that we pay them scant regard for what they passed on to us. The least we can do is to honour their spent lives and make sure that we look after what we have left in the best possible way that we are able to devise.

I have been truly blessed throughout my active, eventful life that began at Samsonvale. I feel that most of the good things that happened to me derived from a spirit of optimism and adventure that I appear to have been born with. I wish that same spirit on all my readers and friends as they live their lives into the 21st century. When faced with options in life, interesting possibilities await if we will just "have a go".

So ends a brief account of a boy from Samsonvale, who was born in 1932, who spent his childhood on the family farm, who was schooled at Mt Samson State School and Brisbane Boys' College, who farmed in Samsonvale for 25 years before a dam submerged much of the district, changing it and the lives of its inhabitants for ever. May some knowledge of our past inspire later generations on their personal journeys.

# The Author